100 THINGS
REDSKINS FANS
SHOULD KNOW & DO
BEFORE THEY DIE

100 THINGS REDSKINS FANS SHOULD KNOW & DO BEFORE THEY DIE

Rick Snider

TRIUMPH
BOOKS

Library of Congress Cataloging-in-Publication Data

Snider, Rick.
100 things Redskins fans should know & do before they die / Rick Snider.
    pages cm
    Summary: "100 people, places, and facts every fan of the Washington Redskins football team should know"— Provided by publisher.
    Includes bibliographical references.
    ISBN 978-1-60078-936-6 (paperback)
    1. Washington Redskins (Football team)—History. 2. Washington Redskins (Football team)—Miscellanea. I. Title. II. Title: One hundred things Redskins fans should know and do before they die.
    GV956.W3S6 2014
    796.332'6409753—dc23

                                                                    2014017979

This book is available in quantity at special discounts for your group or organization. For further information, contact:

    Triumph Books LLC
    814 North Franklin Street
    Chicago, Illinois 60610
    (312) 337-0747
    www.triumphbooks.com

Printed in U.S.A.
ISBN: 978-1-60078-936-6
Design by Patricia Frey
Photos courtesy of AP Images unless otherwise indicated

To Lisa, Megan, Katie, Spencer, Eric, and Rudy

Contents

Foreword

Class, Family, and Fans are the Redskins Way

When I think about what it meant to be a Redskin during my 23 years, a number of things come to mind.

To be a Redskin meant class. You were expected to act with class. Owner Jack Kent Cooke was class personified. You were expected to act that way and treat people the same way—with class. This was reinforced by John Kent Cooke, Jack's son and part-owner who ran the day-to-day operations at Redskin Park.

To be a Redskin also meant that we were a family as an organization. Hall of Fame coach George Allen impressed upon me the importance of everyone's role in the organization. We were all meant to contribute to the effort to win.

This was driven into me during my first year, in 1977, as an intern. We had just lost to the New York Giants for the second time that year. We were 3–3. This was a midseason crisis. George Allen called a staff meeting the day after the game.

With the coaches, scouts, trainers, equipment, video, business, and support staffs present, Coach Allen walked into the room. He had not shaven. It looked liked he had not slept all night. He began his talk by saying he wanted to apologize to those who were new to the organization. There were only two new people in the room—myself and a position coach. He said he did not recognize the team out there. They were not the Redskins. He said he had stayed up all night, trying to figure out why we had lost. The reality is we lost the game because of turnovers.

He looked at the switchboard operator and told her the reason we lost to the Giants was because we were not answering the phone as well as the New York Giants! He looked at the maintenance man and said our building was not as clean as the Giants' building.

I thought he had lost his mind, but after a while I realized what he was saying. We are all part of the team, and we must do our jobs. The next time, we won. When Coach Allen was passing the switchboard operator on Monday, she congratulated him on the win. Coach Allen stopped and told the operator, "No, congratulations to you. You are the reason we won."

That philosophy stuck with me on what it meant to be a Redskin. The Cookes believed that, and so did Hall of Fame coach Joe Gibbs. I can't count the number of times Joe Gibbs praised Otis Wonsley and Reggie Branch, a couple of special team players, for making key contributions to our Super Bowl championships.

His point was the same as George Allen's—you need everyone to contribute to win. That is what it meant to be a Redskin. We were all a family. Everyone is needed to win—from the switchboard operator to the backup players and our Hall of Fame players—as part of the family and team concept. "Once a Redskin, always a Redskin" was what we were taught.

What else represented being a Redskin? It was the fans—the best in world! There is a saying in Washington that if the Redskins won on Sunday, the government would run a lot more efficiently on Monday. That statement alone, whether it is true or not, tells you the importance of the Redskins to our nation's capital.

Who can forget RFK, the stands rocking, the deafening noise? The new stadium is not RFK, but the noise is still deafening to opponents.

If one game could define my thoughts on Redskin fans, it would be the NFC Championship after the 1982 season. We had lost five straight games to the Cowboys. We were home. The fans desperately wanted to beat Dallas.

In the first playoff game against Detroit, in the fourth quarter after we had clinched the win, the fans began to chant, "We want

Dallas. We want Dallas." They did it on their own without prompting by anyone.

The next week we took an early lead on Minnesota. Before the first quarter was over, the fans began to chant, "We want Dallas. We want Dallas." It was only the first quarter!

The stage was now set—Dallas for the NFC Championship with a trip to the Super Bowl on the line. On game day, the stadium was half full an hour before the game. This was unheard of. The fans were into it already. The chants of "We want Dallas!" were deafening, and this was during pregame warm-ups. This is what it meant to be a Redskin—the best fans in the world. That year we went on to win the Redskins' first Super Bowl championship.

Class, family, and fans are what it meant to me to be part of the Redskins. Hail to the Redskins!

—Charley Casserly

Charley Casserly spent 23 years with the Washington Redskins, rising from unpaid intern under coach George Allen to general manager. The Redskins reached four Super Bowls and won three championships during his tenure, two as assistant GM and one as GM. Casserly was later the general manager of the Houston Texans and currently works for NFL Network.

Acknowledgments

The author thanks the following people, in no particular order, for their assistance: Charley Casserly, Sam Huff, Sonny Jurgensen, Mark Moseley, Tom McVean, Brett Conway, Mike McCall, Chris Helein, Nick Sundberg, Kirk Cousins, John Keim, Dan Daly, Dennis Tuttle, Steve Guback, Thom Loverro, Joe Horrigan, Mike Jones, John Pappas, Rich Tandler, Grant Paulsen, Kevin Sheehan, Chris Russell, Scott Jackson, Kevin Dunleavy, Gene Wang, Dave Loeb, Johnny Holliday, Morgan Wootten, Terri Crane-Lamb, Tom Benjey, Chris Reames, Gloria Mamaed, Nate Elgin, Jonathan Forsythe, Boone Hosey, Brendan Deegan, Jane Winston, Chad Woodroof, Jim Magill, Jim Assurian, Bryan Manning, Josh Fink, Dave Bradshaw, Levi Swanson, Miguel Mora, Shane Gooseman, Dominic Orsini, Bryan Manning, Fikret Markovic, Shannon Mullins, Neeraj Gupta, Chris Brown, Christie Lopez, Chris Lopez, Adam Bass, Ankit Mittal, Alex Johnson, Matt Cones, and Samu Qureshi.

Introduction

Nobody talked much about the Washington Redskins in the 1960s. Sure Sonny Jurgensen could score points, but the team rarely won. Many Washingtonians preferred the Senators even though they weren't that good, either.

But then came coach Vince Lombardi in 1969. The Redskins won. Everybody started paying attention.

Two years later, my boyhood heroes were coach George Allen and the Over-the-Hill Gang, Sonny and Billy, Chris Hanburger, Pat Fischer, Mark Moseley, Roy Jefferson, and Diron Talbert.

The best part of covering the Redskins for Washington newspapers was getting to know my idols and realizing they're all great guys. They were the sunshine of my youth and now the sustenance of my sports soul.

The one constant question a writer covering any team is asked is, "Are you a fan?" And every reporter will say no. They're impartial because that's what the job requires. For every reader who is a Redskins fan, there are many who aren't, so fairness and impartiality are mandatory.

How did I put away my boyhood allegiance when first covering the team in 1983? It was easy. My real dream was to be a newspaper reporter; everything else was second. My boyhood heroes were retired, and the players and coaches I covered were separate. I split the past from the present.

While writing this book, I felt a real pull to the past and a thought to the future. After my 31 years off and on around the team, there probably won't be too many more seasons around Redskins Park for me. So this book is more of a thank you to readers over the years, telling some fun tales, sharing some insider stories, and spinning yarns from long ago.

I looked for stories that I'd heard of but didn't know what really happened. Was Lone Star Dietz a Native American Indian or not? What happened to coach Ray Flaherty after he quit to serve in World War II? Did Native Americans really play for the team? Who was the Cowboys Chicken Club? Could RFK Stadium have been LBJ Stadium? Did the team once lose 73–0?

Included are a few of my own insider stories, as well. What really happened in that fight between Michael Westbrook and Stephen Davis? How was Spurrier so overmatched in the NFL? Was a rookie quarterback taped to a handcart and driven around campus behind a golf cart? What about this sex in the stands rumor? Did assistant coaches keep Pepper Rodgers from becoming head coach? What was the best prank among players?

The publisher wanted me to include things to do, so I've included special activities beyond visiting this or that, although Jack Kent Cooke's grave is one stop. Moseley reveals how to kick a straight-on field goal. Kirk Cousins explains how to throw a pass. Nick Sundberg discusses the art of deep snapping. These are things you can try in your yard.

Perhaps the most amazing thing I learned while writing this book was how much owner Dan Snyder reminds me of his late predecessor, George Preston Marshall. Marshall's marketing efforts are reminiscent of strategies Snyder employs.

People often ask me about my favorite player, coach, or game over the years. In this book, I finally answer. Also, I give my thoughts on whether the name will ever change and where the next stadium site will be located.

The great part of this book is you can read chapters in any order. They're short but filled with details of subjects you won't often find. Sometimes the book felt like my autobiography, but mostly it's fun stories and not intended as a history lesson.

The stories included in this book are things you'll laugh about with your buddies over a beer. Who knows, maybe I'll join you.

1 From Braves to Redskins

Let's end the myth right away—the Redskins were not named to honor Native American Indians.

The legend has some truths and certain common sense, but a story in the *Boston Herald* on July 6, 1933, explains the name change from Boston Braves to Boston Redskins before later moving to Washington in 1937.

Under the headline, "Braves Pro Gridmen To Be Called Redskins," the story stated, "Along with the change in coaching, the Boston professional football team has undergone another change, this time in name. Hereafter, the erstwhile Braves of pro football will be known as the Boston Redskins. The explanation is that the change was made to avoid confusion with the Braves baseball team and that the team is to be coached by an Indian, Lone Star Dietz, with several Indian players."

Let's go back over that paragraph one point at a time.

No. 1: Owner George Preston Marshall, who started the team in 1932, changed coaches after one year. The team played one year using the same name as the town's baseball team. Football was the new sport, and many football owners deliberately named their teams after baseball teams to piggyback on the latter's name recognition. Eventually, they changed their team's name when they developed their own following.

Marshall was trying to mesh the new name with two other teams. Using Redskins was a reworking of Braves. But it was also an alliteration of the crosstown Red Sox. Red Skins—Red Sox. Get it?

No. 2: Marshall hired Dietz on March 8, so he was in place when the name was changed. Was Marshall really changing the team name to honor his new coach? It's doubtful. But Marshall was a marketing wizard and knew a good opportunity. In one move, he got away from the Braves name, loosely aligned his team with the Red Sox, and found a new marketing niche with Indians, which in those days was common. Marshall even positioned a cigar-store Indian outside his Washington office in later years.

The Redskins name worked several ways for Marshall, so he went with it. But it wasn't designed to honor Native American Indians, nor was it designed to denigrate them. It was just something that worked well.

Marshall was worried more about the color of money than the color of skin. He was the last NFL owner to sign a black player in 1962, and he did so only after being forced by Congress, which owned the new D.C. Stadium where the Redskins were relocating. But part of the reason behind the delay was that Marshall saw black players as bad for business because the Redskins were the NFL's southernmost team with an extensive radio network throughout the South. Marshall thought he would lose business if he had black players.

But Marshall played Native American Indians in 1933, largely as a carryover from Dietz who came from coaching at the Haskell Institute (now the Haskell Indian Nations University) in Kansas. Dietz brought players he personally knew, which wasn't unusual then. Even now, coaches such as Steve Spurrier signed a few of his former Florida players when he came to Washington in 2002.

Marshall made his Indian players pose in full native garb for photographers before the 1933 home opener against the New York Giants. In later years, there were photos of new players being tossed in the air by teammates while wearing headdresses. The team's cheerleaders were dressed as squaws.

The team's fight song included the following lines:
Braves on the warpath!
Fight for Old D.C.!
Scalp 'em, swamp 'um
We will take 'um big score
Read 'um, Weep 'um, touchdown
We want heap more.

One by one, the team stopped using Indian references until they were left solely with the name, which critics now want changed because they say the name is politically incorrect. Marshall died in 1969, but he surely would have loved the publicity about the name.

Marshall would say he was being a pragmatist. Redskins was a good marketing tool in 1933, and that's all that Marshall cared about when he named the team. He made millions as a laundry chain owner, and whitewashing facts was his specialty.

But was the team's name a conscious slur on the Native American Indian? Maybe 81 years later it feels that way, but Marshall was simply a businessman of his time trying to gain spillover recognition from the Braves and Red Sox.

2 Team's First Black Player

Bobby Mitchell is generally regarded as the first black player on the Redskins. But that distinction plays on the type of semantics that lawyers live on.

Was Ernie Davis the first black player when he was drafted by Washington in December 1961? He was soon traded to Cleveland for LeRoy Jackson and Mitchell, so Davis never donned a Redskins uniform. Indeed, Davis never played for Cleveland either, dying of leukemia in 1963.

Still, Davis was technically a Redskin. Then again, playing in the regular season is what truly counts for someone to say they were on a team. Even preseason games don't matter.

Maybe eighth-round fullback Ron Hatcher was the first black player since he was the first to sign.

Mitchell was a star player and future Pro Football Hall of Famer, so many fans remember him as the team's first black player. But Jackson returned the opening kickoff in the season opener, so he was on the field before Mitchell and guard John Nisby, who was acquired by off-season trade.

So is Jackson the first? A good lawyer would argue yes.

Surely Mitchell's greatness and Jackson's short career make who played first a technicality best used for bar bets.

The trio came to the Redskins after a showdown with federal officials over the team ending its whites-only policy. If the team did not accept black players, the Redskins would be barred from using the new D.C. Stadium.

Owner George Preston Marshall was the last NFL owner to sign blacks for fear of harming business. The Redskins were then the southernmost team, and its radio network covered the South. Indeed, there are still many Redskins fans in the South despite franchises now in Atlanta, Charlotte, Nashville, Jacksonville, Tampa Bay, and Miami.

Marshall finally yielded to the constant pressure, which extended all the way from the White House. But the owner called the legendary Jackie Robinson a race-baiter for urging desegregation, and Marshall left his money to the Redskins Foundation to help underprivileged children...with the stipulation that funds never be used for social integration.

"We'll start signing Negroes when the Harlem Globetrotters start signing whites," Marshall once said. "Why Negroes particularly? Why not make us hire a player from any other race? Why not a woman? Of course, we have had players who played like girls, but never an actual girl player."

Mitchell was already an established star in Cleveland after four seasons of hitting 1,000 yards each year in combined receiving and rushing yards over 12 or 14 games. The seventh-round pick in 1958 was paired with legendary running back Jim Brown to form one of the greatest backfields of all time.

In Washington, Mitchell became a flanker with only six rushes in the first four seasons. He caught a career-best 72 passes and 11 touchdowns in 1962 with 1,384 yards—all NFL highs that sent him to the Pro Bowl. The next season, Mitchell caught 69 passes for a career-best 1,436 yards.

With Sonny Jurgensen arriving in 1964, Mitchell was amazingly consistent, catching 60 passes in three of four years (with 58 the other season) and totaling 866 to 905 yards each year. Mitchell caught only 14 passes in 1968 before retiring with 14,078 all-purpose yards, second most in NFL history at the time.

Mitchell remained with the team in front-office roles until retiring in 2003. Rising from a scout under Vince Lombardi in 1969 to assistant general manager, Mitchell was upset about being passed over for general manager three times.

Jackson was a first-round pick by Cleveland, chosen 11th overall out of Western Illinois. He played only 15 games for the Redskins with one touchdown then was cut in 1963. Jackson opted to retire after working out for two Canadian Football teams.

Was racism behind Jackson's release? In a 2013 Yahoo.com story, Jackson said fumbling or barely averaging two yards per carry weren't the only causes—his release was also caused by his affair with a white woman.

"Interracial things and not being able to hold onto the ball," he told Yahoo.com Sports' Les Carpenter.

Nisby was an interesting choice by Marshall given that Nisby was well known in Pittsburgh for working with companies to ensure equal employment opportunities. He also got a beer company that worked with the Steelers to desegregate.

Nisby was a Pro Bowl selection in 1962, his third honor after earlier playing for Pittsburgh from 1957 to 1961. The guard played three seasons for Washington before he was released at age 28. He became a city councilman in Stockton, California, and was later elected to the Stockton Black Sports Hall of Fame.

Hatcher only played three games for Washington in 1962, but he was the first black player under contract with the Redskins. Gee, maybe Hatcher was the pioneer after all.

3 RFK Over LBJ Stadium— A Political Game

Political games can be so much more intriguing than football games.

In January 1969, seven years after forcing the Redskins to sign black players in order to use D.C. Stadium, Secretary of the Interior Stewart Udall pulled the ultimate end-run around President Lyndon B. Johnson.

And before LBJ could pound his famous fist in defiance, the stadium he hoped would bear his name instead honored RFK.

Robert F. Kennedy Memorial Stadium wasn't meant to honor the assassinated U.S. Senator and brother of slain President John F. Kennedy as much as it was to kick the family's chief rival in the rear on his way out of the Oval Office.

An aerial view of the RFK Stadium outside Washington, D.C., original home of the Washington Redskins, in 1999. (AP Photo/Julia Roberton)

Just hours before Johnson exited the presidency inherited upon JFK's 1963 assassination, Udall used his power to rename the stadium, built on federal parkland, after a Kennedy. By the time Johnson learned of the cabinet member's conspiracy, Richard Nixon was hours from becoming the next president.

And there was nothing Johnson could do about the stadium's name.

The double-cross was eight years in the making and went beyond the grave. Johnson was an uncomfortable but political necessity for John Kennedy to choose as his vice presidential running mate to win the 1960 election over Nixon. The two lived on opposite spectrums of the Democratic Party, and Robert Kennedy tried to prevent the partnership at the Democratic National Convention.

Johnson never forgave Robert Kennedy for that, and the two became intense, embittered, and paranoid rivals. When Kennedy was murdered June 6, 1968, Johnson quietly and spitefully tried to prevent RFK from being buried near his brother at Arlington National Cemetery.

"Johnson had been trying to keep Bobby's body out of Arlington," author Jeff Shesol told C-SPAN's *Booknotes* in 1997 as part of his *Mutual Contempt* book on the feud between the two men. "Bobby was neither a president nor a war hero, Johnson reasoned, and there was no reason to give him a hero's burial. But, of course, the country and the family wanted him to be buried there by his brother's side, and there was nothing Johnson could really do politically to stop it."

Instead, Johnson didn't allocate the funds needed to maintain RFK's grave, which Kennedy supporters considered insulting. But Johnson didn't care because it was those former Kennedy aides and appointees that conspired to have the stadium named for RFK, even though it was well known around Washington that LBJ expected it to be named for him following his presidency.

"And so they conspired to do this, and they also conspired to do it on the very last day of the Johnson presidency so that the president could not countermand the order," Shesol said. "So Udall went ahead and did this, and Johnson was, of course, outraged, but there was nothing he could do. It had already been announced and leaked to the press."

Like so many plans in Washington, the idea was formulated not in political chambers but at a dinner party, Shesol wrote. Attorney Bill Geoghegan, who worked under Kennedy at the Justice Department, asked Undersecretary of the Interior David Black to name the stadium after RFK.

Black took the idea to Udall, a JFK appointee who was never a Johnson favorite, and Interior lawyers. The group decided they were empowered to do so but would wait until two days before the January 20, 1969, inauguration to present the idea to the D.C. Armory Board that operated the stadium. The board approved the plan in 10 minutes, and Udall signed it into law within hours.

"Like his brother, Robert Kennedy left a mark on the nation's capital," Udall said. "Bob was Spartan in his adherence to physical fitness, he loved the out-of-doors, he loved people, and he gloried in the competition of sports."

Udall announced the move at a press conference, and Johnson didn't learn of the name change until he was reading a press account.

As in all political stories, there was a payback for the betrayal. Udall wanted Johnson to sign land grants for national parks in the final hours of his presidency. The president signed some, but a request for one million acres in Udall's home state of Arizona was ignored.

Game over.

4 "I Like Big Hairy Men"

Childish pranks are commonplace around sports teams young and old. What else would you expect from oversized men playing a child's game?

There are the classics of putting hot balm in jocks or talcum powder in helmets, raining down buckets of water, stealing gear, hoisting training-camp bikes up the flag pole, jamming dorm doors, and filling cars with popcorn.

But the best was a counterpunch to a prank that turned into a three-pronged attack.

Kicker Brett Conway wondered why the airline attendant was laughing at him when he awakened on a red eye from San Francisco. The Redskins just clinched the 1999 NFC East championship and it was a celebratory flight back, but Conway, who planned to drive to Pittsburgh after landing for a quick post-Christmas trip to see his girlfriend, had taken a sleeping pill.

Bad move. There is a players' rule—no sleeping on team flights—for exactly what happened to Conway.

It seems offensive tackle Jon Jansen, center Cory Raymer, and fullback Mike Sellers drew on Conway's face. They drew a full beard, scars, and even earrings on his lobes…in black Sharpie. It took days of scrubbing to get it off.

"Kickers have a lot of time for retaliation strategies," Conway said.

And teammates soon learned not to mess with Conway. Back then, kickers finished practice earlier than their teammates, heading back to the locker room with plenty of time for mischief.

Jansen lived about 40 minutes from Redskins Park and, like most offensive linemen, drove a Ford F-150 truck. There are at least a dozen of them in the Redskins Park lot every year, making it the most popular vehicle among players.

Jansen gave Raymer a ride home a few days after face-painting Conway. Players in the same unit often hang out together, and Jansen and Raymer had a lot in common, including weighing 300 lbs. They required a truck for comfort.

The two wondered why nearby cars were honking at them regularly. Being Redskins brings attention, but not like that.

Jansen dropped off Raymer and headed home when another driver pulled alongside and said, "Hey, you have a sign on the back of your truck."

The sign said, "I like big hairy men."

Game over—Conway wins!

Conway scored a big win since that sign described Raymer perfectly. Jansen roared with laughter the next day while telling the story. There were no hard feelings.

But Conway wasn't done. With the help of a worker at Redskins Park, Conway stuffed a rat—an 18" rat—in Sellers' locker where the playbooks were kept. Sellers was grabbing his playbook when the rat popped out. Sellers was so scared he fell backward over a bench, and a camera crew hidden nearby caught the whole thing on video. Then 20 mice popped out from the locker's box for shoes, further scaring Sellers.

"He saw the rat and screamed like a little girl," Conway recalled.

The video was shown around Redskins Park for years. However, team officials weren't wild about mice running throughout the building.

Conway still wasn't done. Raymer needed to be taught a lesson, too. Conway used a classic trick often done during training camps in the 1980s. He filled Raymer's truck cab with Styrofoam peanuts all the way to the top by pouring the final ones through a cracked window. There was a trail of white peanuts leaving Redskins Park for days.

Conway's time with the Redskins was unusual. After handling only kickoffs for six games in 1998, Conway enjoyed a career season in 1999 by converting 22-of-32 field goals and 49-of-50 extra points for 115 points. However, he only played two games in Washington the next year before being released, later playing one game each with Oakland and the New York Jets.

Conway returned to Washington in 2001 to convert 26-of-32 field goals and 22 extra points for 100 points. But Conway suffered a torn leg muscle and played only one game in 2002. After playing five games for the New York Giants and three in Cleveland in 2003, Conway was done with the NFL at age 29. He now owns several fitness studios in Chicago.

Bet his locker room and parking lots are safe havens.

5 Real Indians Played in 1933

Yes, the Redskins really used Native American Indian players.

The Boston Redskins, with a new name and a supposed Indian coach, signed four American Indians for the 1933 season.

Seriously.

They were authentic Indians signed from the Haskell Institute (now Haskell Indian Nations University) where Coach William "Lone Star" Dietz spent the previous four seasons before being hired by Boston.

Owner George Preston Marshall, never one to miss a marketing opportunity, photographed Dietz with "Chief" Larry Johnson, Louis "Rabbit" Weller, and John Orien Crow in war paint, feathers, and headdresses before the home opener against the New York Giants. David Ward also played for the Redskins.

Now, 1933 was a time when professional football was way down the pecking list of top sports. Baseball, boxing, and horse racing were bigger Depression-era sports. Even college football was far more popular than the pro game.

Marshall's scouting system was basically magazines. When Dietz wanted to sign some college players he knew, Marshall didn't object.

Haskell had already sent 15 players to the pros, beginning with wingback Chief Mullen who played for the Evansville Crimson Giants in 1921. The Redskins' quartet was the last in the league from the school in Lawrence, Kansas, and Johnson was the only Haskell player to last more than two seasons.

James Lawrence "Waukechon" Johnson was an enormous player for his time at 6'3" and 223 lbs. The defensive end, linebacker, center, and tight end played three seasons for Boston and five for the New York Giants with linebacker considered his best position.

Johnson played 10 games in 1933 and 12 in 1934 before playing just two in 1935. Mostly, he was a part-time player for the Giants, too, playing five or less games in three seasons and 10 in 1938 as an All-Star. Johnson later played five games for the Washington Redskins in 1944.

A member of the Menominee tribe of Wisconsin, Johnson was elected to the American Indian Athletic Hall of Fame in 1997.

Crow was from Salem, Missouri. Eventually he played at Commerce High in Commerce, Oklahoma, the same school attended by New York Yankees legend Mickey Mantle. Crow, who was one-quarter Cherokee, played two seasons for the Redskins, starting 14-of-22 games while catching two passes in 1934.

Named acting director of the Bureau of Indian Affairs in 1961 by President John F. Kennedy, Crow was later mentioned by Secretary of the Interior Stewart Udall during the testy move by federal officials that forced Redskins owner George Preston Marshall into signing black players later that year.

When asked if Indian players would also be on Udall's agenda to join the Redskins, Udall said, "I have news for this person. My Indian Commissioner, John [Orien] Crow, played football—he is a Cherokee—for George Preston Marshall 30 years ago. Apparently, Mr. Marshall pioneered earlier in getting Indians into the game, and all we want him to do is just open his mind a little further."

Weller only played in 1933, at running back, but he scored a 50-yard touchdown on his first carry. Overall, Weller played seven games with 12 carries for 112 yards and two touchdowns.

A full-blooded Caddo Indian, Weller scored 13 touchdowns of 60 or more yards at Haskell. He was a 1930 Knute Rockne All-American and single-handedly beat undefeated Oklahoma A&M 13–12 in 1930 on a 90-yard kickoff return touchdown and a 95-yard punt return score. At the Chilocco Indian Agricultural

School in Oklahoma, Weller scored on seven punt returns in one game. He was a charter inductee of the American Indian Athletic Hall of Fame.

Ward played only one game for the Redskins in the end. The Yakima Indian was born in Wynnewood, Oklahoma, and is a member of the American Indian Athletic Hall of Fame.

6 Gibbs Almost Fired at 0–3

Joe Gibbs' career nearly ended after three games with the Washington Redskins.

That's right—the same coach who led the team to four NFC Championships and three Super Bowl victories in 12 years (in his first stint with the team) almost never won a game for the burgundy and gold.

It seems owner Jack Kent Cooke was insanely mad after the Redskins started 0–3 under his new coach that was some offensive coordinator that general manager Bobby Beathard sold him. Cooke wanted to fire Gibbs and Beathard. The latter calmed the owner only to see two more defeats follow.

Does this sound like Dan Snyder and Marty Schottenheimer? You betcha—the same conversation happened with Snyder and his partners over firing Schottenheimer at 0–3. Both Gibbs and Schottenheimer would later finish 8–8. Gibbs stayed, but Schottenheimer went.

Unlike Schottenheimer, who had a proven resume, Gibbs was a lifelong assistant with 13 years as a position coach before he became the offensive coordinator in Tampa Bay in 1978 and then San Diego in 1979–80.

Washington Redskins owner Jack Kent Cooke (left) running back John Riggins, and head coach Joe Gibbs (right) share the game ball in the locker room after their Super Bowl XVII win in Pasadena, California, on January 30, 1983. The Redskins beat the Miami Dolphins 27–17. Riggins was named Most Valuable Player. (AP Photo)

Gibbs was only 40 years old, but Cooke liked him in the interview. The Squire sensed Gibbs was a leader, and that was paramount to Cooke. After three years and 24–24 under Jack Pardee, Cooke wanted new energy.

But the season started with a 26–10 loss to Dallas, a 17–7 loss to New York, and a 40–30 loss to St. Louis. At least the Redskins showed some offense in the third game. Joe Theismann threw for 388 yards and four touchdowns, Ricky Thompson caught two scores among his seven receptions for 106 yards, and Wilbur Jackson ran for 104 yards. But the offense struggled once more, and the defense was awful in a 36–13 loss to Philadelphia and 30–17 defeat to St. Francisco.

It's hard to believe Cooke would later hug Gibbs so often in coming years. It's even harder to believe Gibbs would finish 124–60 with 16 postseason wins—or a 154–94 total with 17 postseason wins, if you include his second stint in Washington—eventually landing in the Pro Football Hall of Fame.

Cooke wanted to hire George Allen, the architect of the 1970s glory days, before he was talked out of it. Cooke's son, John Kent Cooke, claims to be the one who saved Gibbs, but we're all the hero of our own stories. More likely it was Beathard.

Meanwhile, Theismann met with Gibbs at the latter's home. Among the things decided that day was the plan to use John Riggins more. Riggo sat out the 1980 season in a contract dispute before meeting with Gibbs during the off-season. Riggins was a big-moment guy who rose to greatness in the 1982 playoffs, but so far the future Pro Football Hall of Famer was off to a so-so start.

The Redskins beat Chicago 24–7 with two Riggins touchdown runs among his 23 carries for 126 yards, but then Washington fell to 1–6 in a 13–10 loss at Miami. Nothing resembles a rollercoaster as much as the emotions around Redskins Park following wins or losses. Cooke was not happy, but at this point he didn't have George Allen on speed dial—that is, if they had speed dial back then. More likely Cooke had a telegram ready to send that would have read:

GEORGE, BY GOD ALL IS FORGIVEN. STOP. COME BACK NOW YOU BLOODY IDIOT. STOP. UNLIMITED BUDGET AWAITS. STOP. — JACK KENT COOKE.

But then the Redskins won four straight over New England, St. Louis, Detroit, and New York to reach 5–6.

Nobody was talking about firing Gibbs now...that is, until the Redskins lost two straight, to Dallas and Buffalo. But Gibbs was hired for leadership, and his abilities came through when the team won the final three games of the season, beating Philadelphia, Baltimore, and Los Angeles and scoring 68 points over the last two games, including four Riggins touchdowns. A formula was born.

Gibbs' 1993 retirement was so sudden that even Cooke said, "I hadn't the foggiest notion." Ironically, Snyder could have said the same thing when Gibbs suddenly retired in 2008, watching the news conference on TV from his office instead of venturing across the building. Both occasions left the Redskins so flat-footed that they ended up hiring disastrous successors, with Richie Petitbon lasting one year and Jim Zorn two.

When Gibbs returned in 2004, Cooke was long dead by seven years and Beathard had retired. The magic of the first tenure couldn't be recaptured. Gibbs was just 30–34 in four seasons, which included two losing marks and just one postseason win.

At least Gibbs coached 16 years for a team that nearly fired him after three games. Cooke loved to call people "bloody idiots," but letting Gibbs go so quickly would have made the owner the foolish one.

7 Tailgate With the Best

Now this chapter might start a fight or two. It's about tailgating with the best group at Redskins games.

There is no real answer. Tailgating with your friends makes it the best group. But let's say you're coming to the game by yourself or with just one buddy and you don't want to bother with the setup. Maybe you want to meet fellow Redskins fans.

If you're coming to the game, you need to tailgate and the one group that everyone loves is the ExtremeSkins.

Nestled against the last row by the woods at the bottom of Green lot E-43, ExtremeSkins (ES) sometimes numbers 500 people, ranging from as far away as Tennessee and Missouri, eating 150 lbs. of steaming wings fried on the spot that seem to disappear every time a new batch hits the pan.

ExtremeSkins is a message board started by fans. They're diehards who have sweated through the bad years following three Super Bowl championships, which were won when many of the followers were kids.

Christie and Chris Lopez, alias Huly and Pez, are the hosts. Christie grew up in South Carolina knowing only that the Dallas Cowboys should be hated. That allowed her to fit in well with her husband, Chris, who grew up a Redskins fan.

They're both in the Pro Football Ultimate Fan Association in Canton, Ohio, alongside fellow Hall of Famers who actually played the game. Pez was selected in 2010, and Christie was chosen two years later.

The two arrive outside FedEx Field at 6:00 AM whether the game starts at 1:00 PM or 8:00 PM. That's the early tailgate. When the gates open hours later, the party moves inside for the pregame tailgate. About one hour before kickoff, the party closes so everyone can get through security in time. When the game ends, they re-open the tailgate until traffic is gone. Chris remembers once spending 24 hours in the parking lot during a night game.

A little extreme, huh?

"No one ever really had a real tailgate to go to," Chris explained about starting the event. "There were so many people on the ES board [that] we decided to get them all together."

The event started with 20 people and just kept growing. Everyone contributes food or money, which goes to a designated charity. "You're with friends and family. [We] just hang out and have fun," Christie said. "The wings, the food, the atmosphere. It's like a huge family picnic."

The tailgate comes complete with fun times like cornhole (a Southern version of horseshoes using bean bags), and at any time a handful of footballs fly amid neighboring cars. Sometimes romance is in the air, too.

"We've seen a couple of people meet and get married," Christie said. "There have been engagements. There's not much we haven't seen yet. You never know what you'll find back here."

For example, a scarecrow Tony Romo has been burned in effigy before Dallas games. But don't worry, there's a fire extinguisher nearby. There are also space heaters for those cold late-season games, too.

Christie wears No. 21 after meeting the late Sean Taylor. He called her a sweetheart for asking Taylor to sign a get-well card for ailing Redskins fan Chief Zee.

Chris has worn No. 10 long before it became fashionable upon Robert Griffin III's arrival. It represents the year Chris was elected into Canton. Now friends tease him about jumping on the band-wagon for the quarterback.

Anybody is welcome at the ES tailgate—even opposing fans. Just bring your manners because this is supposed to be fun.

"As long as you're not a jackass, you can come in and have a good time," Chris said. "We've only had one problem in our history, and it was a [St. Louis] Rams fan. He got belligerent after the game."

Ironically, it's not hated rival Dallas whose fans can be testy in the parking lot, according to Chris. It's fellow NFC East member Philadelphia.

"Even though Dallas is our most hated rival, there isn't much there in terms of fights," Chris said. "It's Eagles fans—they're always so angry. They always want to fight when we're trying to have a good time."

A whole pig is roasted before night games, given the eight hours of cooking time needed to fully cook the pig. But it's worth it for 120 lbs. of meat.

Ironically, the best tailgate party of the year isn't before a game but on draft day. The stadium opens for fans on the final afternoon of the three-day draft, and first-rounders come to meet the crowd. ES and several other tailgates converge in one parking lot. Former Redskins such as Mark Moseley and Gary Clark have come by.

The best tailgate ever came in Canton when Darrell Green and Art Monk were inducted in 2008. Redskins fans dominated the town.

"It was ridiculously massive," Chris said. "[Officials] said they'd never seen any team take over the city like that."

What happens if it's not a great year on the field? No matter—there's still the pre- and postgame parties.

"We live to tailgate," Christie said.

Visit Samu's Museum

If the best things in life are free, then the best Redskins memorabilia collection can be seen for free.

Really.

Samu Qureshi is the No. 1 Redskins memorabilia collector, hands down. It's not even a debate. Other collections don't come close to the 2,000-sq.-ft. whirlwind of memorabilia, sometimes reaching 5' high and covering every inch of wall space. A real fan could spend hours and not see one tenth of the items Qureshi loves to show off in the collection. It's a crazy "mishmash" according to Qureshi. That's being kind. More like symbols of a football-crazed fanatic. It's even hard to describe given the sheer volume of game-day programs, football cards, game-worn jerseys, helmets, newspapers, pennants, signed footballs, and bobbleheads.

But that's the easy stuff. What truly separates Qureshi's collection aren't mass-produced items anyone could buy given enough money but the unique and vintage items that draw many former players to his home.

There's the fedora worn by Jack Kent Cooke. Life-sized mannequins don cheerleader outfits that are far more rare than you'd suspect, including the famed Pocahontas uniform from the early 1960s. And Riggins' jockstrap hangs from the wall.

Wait, Riggo's jockstrap? Nobody wants to know the backstory on that.

There's Joe Gibbs' headset and a signed baseball by early Redskins coach Ray Flaherty. Grandstand seats from Griffith Stadium, RFK Memorial Stadium, and FedEx Field are arranged grandstand-style so visitors can watch Redskins games on a large-screen TV.

Don't miss the movie poster of Sammy Baugh starring in *King of the Texas Rangers*. And then there are the 3'-tall bobbleheads of LaVar Arrington and Clinton Portis. A game-day poster of the 2002 Osaka preseason game has been signed by nearly every player. Plus there are two Chris Cooley paintings of his playbook notes.

The largest piece of all is a life-sized huddle of players like Russ Grimm, Doc Walker, and John Riggins in Super Bowl XVII with an opening for you to wear a helmet while listening to a call. This display came from the defunct National Sports Gallery.

Qureshi's favorite item is a 1937 football signed by every player on the championship team. It was kept in a trunk for nearly 70 years and remains in pristine shape.

"The 1937 ball is special to me," Qureshi said. "To put my hand on a favorite piece, there are so many that I really love. When people ask me who my favorite player was, I'm like, 'Let me give you my top 10.'"

Qureshi recently obtained one of his Holy Grail items—a 1936 championship game program.

"I found it on eBay," he said. "It wasn't listed as a championship game program. Most people think December 13 is a late-season game. I knew it was a championship game. The 1940 championship game program is easily $1,750. This one is so much more rare. I've seen the 1940 program 20 times. This one I've only seen once."

The Maryland realtor began collecting in 1968 after receiving a Charley Taylor card. Soon a friend gave him more football cards, and Qureshi's lifelong obsession began.

"I was immediately hooked, and every penny I could get I bought baseball and football cards," Qureshi said. "When I was five years old, Vince Lombardi came. At seven George Allen filled the city with Redskins fever, and at age eight we went to the Super Bowl. It was easy to be a Redskins fan. All my friends were. You became so attached to the players.

"The memorabilia came when Topps lost its monopoly on baseball cards [in 1981], and I started gravitating toward getting practice jerseys from players. I started saving the programs, then I made it my mission to get every program. It just kind of expanded. I started picking up other pieces, and it mushroomed out of control.

"What really attracted me to the memorabilia is that I found it more interesting than the cards. They told stories whether it was a game-used jersey from a certain game or a program that was at the event."

What would Qureshi do if the team ever changes its name?

"I would think the [collection's] value would double," he said. "It might open the door for me to open the Redskins museum without worrying about the NFL if they're prohibited from using it [for] the team name."

The collection isn't expanding as rapidly as past years since Qureshi already has many of the top items. But that doesn't stop him from standing outside the players parking lot before games, seeking autographs while wearing a 1930s uniform complete with leather helmet.

After all, memories, and memorabilia, are made daily.

9 Baugh Almost Chose Baseball

Sammy Baugh was nearly a one-and-done player with the Washington Redskins.

After winning the 1937 NFL championship for the Redskins as a rookie, Baugh played minor league baseball for the St. Louis Cardinals the following spring. Truth be told, he preferred baseball over football. Indeed, even his "Slingin' Sammy" nickname came from his throws as a third baseman at Texas Christian University, not from his football passes.

There was a lot of interest around St. Petersburg, Florida, during spring training in 1938. Across town from Cardinals camp, a young Joe DiMaggio was holding out for a whopping $40,000 a year from the New York Yankees, diverting on-the-field attention toward Baugh. Cards general manager Branch Rickey signed Baugh the previous summer before the passer joined the Redskins, and

Quarterback Sammy Baugh at the Polo Grounds in New York on December 4, 1938. (AP Photo)

with Sammy's sudden national fame, national writers flocked to see "The Slinger" on the diamond.

Baugh was a slick-fielding third baseman supposedly headed for the Cardinals' opening day lineup. "That bird with No. 21 on his back at third base. That's Sammy Baugh," Redbirds manager Frankie Frisch said. "He can field. He's a natural. Good thrower, too. But can he hit? That's what tells the tale in this league. You've gotta get those base hits, or there's no soap."

Unfortunately, Baugh reported to camp with a sternum injury he received in a Redskins exhibition game after the season. He wasn't healed by spring training, and the injury affected his hitting.

But his defense was sparkling. Said star outfielder Ducky Medwick, who was coming off winning the Triple Crown in 1937, "You can't get one [ground ball] by him, even with a .44. And what an arm. No wonder he can whip that football around."

But Baugh could barely get his batting average above .200. Still, it appeared the Cardinals might keep him on the big-league team—until he made three errors in a game near the end of camp. Thinking he needed to work on his offense, Baugh was sent to the minors where he hit .200 in 130 at-bats over 37 games at Triple A Rochester and 16 at Double A Columbus. He managed one home run among his 26 hits.

The paltry hitting helped Marshall get his passer back. Well, that and a rethinking by the Cards, who wanted Baugh to convert to shortstop, a position he had never played. It was a rare miscalculation of talent by Rickey, and Baugh never really adapted. Then Baugh met shortstop Marty Marion at Rochester.

Marion was destined for big things in the big leagues, later winning the 1944 National League Most Valuable Player award and being a big part of four National League titles. Marion played 109 games at Rochester, while Baugh entered just 37 and hit .183. "After I saw Marion playing shortstop, I knew damned well I would never beat him out," Baugh said.

Near the end of the baseball season, while Baugh's Rochester team was playing in Baltimore, Marshall secretly met his quarterback to hammer out a $35,000 deal, plus promotional monies, that would pay him over three years, the richest in the NFL at the time.

And so ended Baugh's baseball career.

Baugh was invaluable to Marshall as his marquee player. After moving the team from Boston in 1936, where it had never gained a following despite playing in the NFL championship that year, Marshall invested heavily in Baugh as a marketing tool that brought excitement with downfield passes previously unseen in the pro game.

The cheap-minded Marshall signed Baugh to only a one-year deal after convincing him to forgo a baseball coaching job once finishing at TCU. Baugh asked for $8,000—twice what Marshall offered and much more than veterans and future Pro Football Hall of Famers Turk Edwards, Cliff Battles, and Wayne Millner earned—and surprisingly received it.

Baugh went on to become the Redskins' best player ever—that's what Sonny Jurgensen says—as a standout quarterback, defensive back, and perhaps the best punter in NFL history. He played 16 years in Washington while setting 13 NFL records and earning All-NFL seven times. Indeed, Baugh still holds records for six NFL passing titles (along with Steve Young) and five for lowest interception percentage.

Baugh was a member of the Hall of Fame's 1963 charter group. He was the last surviving member of that class until his death in 2008.

As it turned out, Baugh was quite a bargain.

10 Visit Cooke's Grave

You'd figure "The Squire" would have a memorial area comparable to Abraham Lincoln's Greek temple on Washington's border, or maybe an obelisk like George Washington or a Pantheon housing Thomas Jefferson.

Jack Kent Cooke once owned Washington sports, and you might think the Redskins owner's grave was configured to be just as memorable.

Instead, it's a plain bronze plaque with his name and the dates 1912–1997.

The simple marker for Jack Kent Cooke's grave. (Photo courtesy of the author)

That's it?

Cooke's funeral at Trinity Episcopal Church in Upperville, Virginia, was the biggest thing the little crossroad, carved by 19th century traders passing from Winchester to Middleburg, ever saw. The town is so small that the stone-housed library seems like it's big enough for only one book.

The media was kept away from the memorial service, which was a who's who of Washington society and the NFL, including Dallas Cowboys owner Jerry Jones. Reporters sat in a parking lot across the street from the church, which was built in 1950 by philanthropist Paul Mellon.

But these days everyone is free to wander into the graveyard to see where Cooke and several other interesting souls now rest. Cooke is the very first grave seen from the path, located under a tree to the right where his cremated ashes are interred.

Next to Cooke is Elizabeth Cronin, a U.S. State department worker who was among the 52 U.S. Embassy hostages seized by Iranian militants in 1979. Cronin spent 444 days in captivity. She was killed in a 2004 horseback riding accident.

Ironically, just a short screen pass away from Cooke lies the Mellon family, including U.S. Ambassador Andrew Mellon, who was also Secretary of the Treasury under three presidents and the founder of the National Gallery of Art in Washington. His son, Paul Mellon, who is buried nearby, was a noted horse breeder whose Sea Hero won the 1993 Kentucky Derby. Paul Mellon donated the land and funds to build several prominent area buildings and parks, including Trinity.

Cooke and Paul Mellon owned adjoining farms but hated each other. Each said they weren't neighbors despite admitting their property lines met (thus the definition of neighbor.) Ironically, they're now neighbors forever.

Trinity Episcopal Church is located about 20 miles from the edge of Washington's sprawling suburbia and an hour's drive from Washington on a weekend. Stone-cut gray buildings and one-lane winding roads with occasional houses and businesses provide a peek into horse country where polo grounds aren't far from Cooke, whose love of the Redskins was rivaled by his love for Tennessee Walking Horses and thoroughbreds. Beating Mellon in the Kentucky Derby would have rivaled a Super Bowl trophy for Cooke.

John Updike wrote "Upon Learning That a Town Exists Called Upperville," which well describes the 600-plus residents who are mostly rich:

In Upperville, the upper crust
Say "Bottoms Up!" from dawn to dusk
And "Ups-a-daisy, dear!" at will
I want to live in Upperville.

Trinity Church is patterned after a medieval French church. It's the third church that has been built on the 172-year-old site, which was originally bought for $100. The current 1951 church was built by locals who even forged their tools on site. Architect H. Page Cross used 12th century French countryside churches as inspiration with a cruciform plan, shallow transepts, and sandstone and limestone from nearby Warrenton. The stones were hand-cut by W.J. Hanback.

The 350-member parish sits in oak pews whose end carvings of local plants were created by Heinz Warneke. The pipe organ is a Boston Aeolian-Skinner with 55 ranks of pipes designed by Joseph Whiteford. Stained-glass windows were made by Joep Nicolas of the Netherlands. The candelabras are 18th century French and 16th century Austrian with candles from Colonial Virginia, Spain, England, and Poland.

The tower bells were made in England, and the largest bell includes this inscription: "Dedicated to the men of this countryside, who by their skill of hands built this church."

Upperville was the site of two Civil War battles, including one just two weeks before Gettysburg that combined for 400 casualties without a clear victor. The Union cavalry tried to break Jeb Stuart's Confederate unit, which was heading for Gettysburg. Famed Confederate Colonel John Mosby's rangers of the Virginia 43rd Battalion also fought in the area.

Cooke left the bulk of his fortune to a foundation for college scholarships. It was a surprisingly low-key gesture for a man who lived so large. It seems only fitting his grave is modest, too.

11 How Snyder Owns the Team

The son was supposed to inherit it. A New York real estate magnate thought he could buy it on credit. Another billionaire misplayed his hand. Ultimately, a minor investor ended up as the next owner.

The 1999 sale of the Redskins is one twisted story. For two years the team was circled by several bidders, trustees, bankers, and more, all screaming that the other was lying and they were the only ones telling the truth. No one could be trusted—absolutely no one.

Dan Snyder was never expected to be the owner. It was supposed to be John Kent Cooke, son of late owner Jack Kent Cooke and a member of the board of trustees charged with overseeing the sale of the team following the owner's death in April 1997.

Why didn't Jack Kent Cooke just leave the team to his son, who was the second of three generations working in the organization? The true reason might never be truly known, but here are a few thoughts.

The elder Cooke worried about inheritance taxes. Better to let John Kent Cooke buy the team instead. At the beginning of the sale, $250 million seemed a logical and doable price.

But three things happened to triple the cost. In 1997, the team left RFK Stadium for FedEx Field (known as Jack Kent Cooke Stadium until 1999), where revenues skyrocketed. The NFL also signed its first megabucks TV deal, which greatly increased team values. And Cleveland's expansion team price was $530 million, creating a new floor for the value of NFL teams.

These changes suddenly priced Cooke out of the market. He was willing to buy the team at the smaller number, but he never considered adding partners for an $800 million bid. Still, Cooke never dropped out officially because more bidders increased the price. Instead, he inherited 10 percent of the proceeds from the sale of the team and started his own vineyard.

Howard Milstein's offer of $803 million with Snyder as a minor partner was accepted by the trustees. However, there were big worries over Milstein's ability to complete the deal because his fortune lacked liquidity. He delivered a non-refundable $30 million deposit and wanted to finance nearly all of the remainder. The NFL has a rule that one person must control 50 percent so minority partners couldn't pull a hostile takeover. The last thing the NFL wanted was a bank owning a team through loan default.

In a meeting with *Washington Times* editors and reporters, Milstein admitted there were a handful of owners opposed to his bid. Milstein claimed they didn't matter, however, because the majority of owners supported his bid.

It felt like Milstein was underselling the opposition, so league owners and officials were immediately polled. Within hours, Denver, Cleveland, Pittsburgh, and New Orleans were the known core of the resistance. Eventually Detroit, Carolina, Cincinnati, and both New York teams were also willing to block the bid. The NFL required approval by 24-of-32 owners, and Milstein didn't have enough votes.

The NFL let Milstein rework his numbers to increase equity, but it didn't happen. Owners didn't like the high debt ratio, and the Finance Committee voted 3–3 (with one abstention) over advancing Milstein's offer for a general owners vote. Finally, Milstein withdrew his offer, knowing it would be rejected. The NFL voted 28–2 (with one abstention) to accept the withdrawal.

Here's where Snyder worked his magic. Rather than allow trustees to accept new bids, knowing FedEx chairman Fred Smith and his partners were readying a bid that might exceed $1 billion, Snyder said he was assuming Milstein's deal. Snyder claimed the trustees' deal was not with Milstein but with the Washington Sports Ventures Inc.

The trustees, weary of reopening bidding after two years of work while also fearing lawsuits, agreed to Snyder's strategy. Otherwise, it's likely Snyder would have been outbid on the open market by Texas billionaire Sam Grossman or Smith. Snyder gained control of the team in June 1999 after gaining New York publishers Fred Drasner and Mort Zuckerman as initial partners before later buying them out. Smith later became a minority partner.

Milstein's subsequent lawsuits against the NFL, Snyder, and Cooke were dismissed in Superior Court and by an arbitrator.

12 Greatest Single Performance?

Naturally, the greatest game ever played by a Redskin would come from its greatest player ever—Sammy Baugh.

Noted NFL historian and former *Washington Times* columnist Dan Daly declared Baugh's 1943 season the best ever by a player in a lengthy story for The MMQB (Monday Morning Quarterback, part of *Sports Illustrated*'s website). Daly also claimed Baugh played the greatest single game ever that year.

There's no disagreement here. Baugh threw four touchdown passes in a 42–20 victory over the Detroit Lions on November 14, 1943. Actually, Baugh threw a fifth touchdown as Detroit's Frankie Sinkwich returned an interception 39 yards for a score.

Overall, Baugh completed 18-of-30 for 180 yards, four touchdowns, and two interceptions. Baugh threw a 10-yard touchdown to Bob Masterson for a 7–0 first-quarter lead, then followed that in the second with a 28-yard strike to Bob Seymour for 14–0. After the Redskins scored on an interception for a 21–0 halftime edge, Baugh threw another 10-yard touchdown to Masterson. Sinkwich

The 400-Yard Passing Club

If 300 yards is considered a standout game, passing for 400 yards equals greatness. Ironically, for a league that favors passing over rushing during the past decade, the Redskins have seen only one passer—Donovan McNabb—surpass 400 yards since 1999. He completed 28-of-38 for 426 yards in a 2010 loss to Houston.

Brad Johnson is the all-time leader with 471 yards against San Francisco in 1999. Johnson completed 32-of-47 with two touchdowns and one interception. That surpassed Sammy Baugh's 446 yards against Boston in 1948 off just 17 completions.

Mark Rypien passed for 442 yards and six touchdowns off 16 completions against Atlanta in 1991. He also gained 401 yards with four scores against Chicago in 1989.

Doug Williams gained 430 yards against Pittsburgh in 1988. Norm Snead passed for 424 versus Pittsburgh in 1963. Jay Schroeder gained 420 against the New York Giants in 1986. Sonny Jurgensen did it twice, gaining 418 against Cleveland in 1967 and 411 versus Dallas in 1965. Joe Theismann gained 417 against the Raiders in 1983.

countered with a 22-yard touchdown pass to Jack Matheson, making the score 28–6. The passing duel was interrupted by Andy Farkas' 41-yard run for a 35–6 lead after the Joe Aguirre kick. Sinkwich then intercepted Baugh and scored on a 39-yard return for 35–13 in the third quarter. After a 40-yard pass from Sinkwich to Bill Callihan and an Augie Lio kick, Baugh sealed the game with a four-yard touchdown pass to Joe Aguirre.

But that's not all. Baugh also intercepted four passes from Sinkwich as a defensive back. It seems World War II drained manpower from the NFL, and more players played both offense and defense given the 28-man road squads. Baugh threw 203 interceptions over 16 years, but he also intercepted 11 in 1943 and 31 over his career.

As if Baugh wasn't tired from playing both ways that day, he also punted. Baugh unleashed an 81-yarder, the longest punt in the NFL in 1943. He led the NFL in punting from 1940 to 1943. Baugh's 45.1-yard average, bolstered by quick kicks, was an NFL record when he retired.

Certainly, the Redskins have seen many other great single-game performances since Baugh's.

Gerald Riggs rushed for 221 yards and one touchdown on 29 carries against Philadelphia in 1989, surpassing Cliff Battles' 215 yards and one touchdown on 16 carries against the New York Giants in 1933. Timmy Smith gained 204 yards and two touchdowns on 22 carries in beating Denver in Super Bowl XXII.

Brad Johnson broke Baugh's 1948 record of 446 yards and four touchdowns against Boston with 471 yards and two touchdowns versus San Francisco in 1999. Johnson threw 47 passes to Baugh's 24, though.

Baugh threw six touchdowns twice, but Mark Rypien tied him in 1991 against Atlanta while falling four yards short of tying Baugh's record (at the time) for yardage.

Anthony Allen's team-record 255 yards receiving against St. Louis comes with an asterisk—it was a 1987 strike game. Still, it's the best game ever, though some would consider Gary Clark's 241 yards versus the Giants in 1986 the real record.

Can a kicker merit mention? Not only did Curt Knight kick five field goals in a game three times, he also converted four in the second quarter against the Giants in 1970.

All of these efforts were major accomplishments, but they were realized on only one side of the ball. Baugh set major marks in all three phases in the same game.

It was that kind of year for Baugh, though not for much longer. Washington was 5–0–1 after beating Detroit and won the following week against Chicago before losing its last three games. Yet Washington beat New York in the eastern division playoffs after losing to the Giants the previous week to reach the championship against Chicago.

The Redskins beat the Bears earlier that season, but Baugh left the title game early with a concussion and Chicago won 41–21. Baugh somehow returned late in the game to throw two touchdowns; these days, he wouldn't have played for a week.

Maybe that was his greatest game—returning to throw two scores after spending much of the afternoon bewildered and wondering why he wasn't allowed to play.

13 Why Fans Hate the Cowboys

This is like answering, "Why is the sky blue?"

Did it start with Cowboys owner Clint Murchison essentially blackmailing Redskins counterpart George Preston Marshall into voting for Dallas' expansion team?

Did Dallas pranksters wanting to unleash chickens at RFK Stadium begin the rivalry?

Does it have something to do with President John F. Kennedy's assassination in Dallas?

Could it be Redskins coach George Allen needing somebody to hate and the Cowboys were on top?

Is it simply that they were two good teams fighting over one bone for so many years?

Did the Cowboys become the easy team to follow for Washingtonians trying to be anti-social?

Has it simply become a historical trend? Your parents hated the Cowboys, so you do, too?

Ultimately, Allen is the biggest reason, but they all contributed. After all, Allen's fury was four decades ago, and you can't remain rivals without something happening at least every few years to keep it going.

The Redskins weren't very good when the Cowboys joined the NFL in 1960. Sure, the story of how Murchison obtained rights to the "Hail to the Redskins" song to gain Marshall's vote for its return irked some people, but that's more of a personal matter for Marshall.

The attempt by Cowboys fans to unleash chickens is funny, but it didn't happen, so there's not much to get upset over.

There are some Washingtonians who have never forgiven the city of Dallas for Kennedy's death and that could have contributed to the rivalry years later, but it's an add-on reason and not a primary. There are people in their 70s and older who resent Dallas for Kennedy's assassination.

The angle of two good teams vying for a playoff spot certainly played into the rivalry during the 1970s and 1980s. Once the Redskins tailed off in the early 1990s, however, the Cowboys seemed more intent on beating Green Bay and San Francisco to reach three Super Bowls than worrying about a divisional game versus Washington. So it's really not the reason.

The anti-social angle? Dallas owner Jerry Jones once said there are more Cowboys fans in the Washington area than in any other major city nationwide outside Texas. But Jones is known to say that everywhere he goes, so who knows if it's true. Certainly there are tons of Cowboys fans in the Washington area. Sometimes they outnumber Redskins fans at FedEx Field.

It just seems like every family has someone who wants to be different and takes the Cowboys out of spite so they can argue with their relatives. This happens all the time, and they often admit doing it just to be contrary.

And the history part? If your parents are Redskins fans, you're probably one, too, and you hate the Cowboys. But there are plenty of married couples where each roots for different team, so the rivalry only goes so far.

So it really comes down to Allen setting the tone. Upon his 1971 arrival in Washington, Allen knew beating Dallas was the key to success. The Cowboys had won five straight division or conference titles, so Allen went all in on Dallas games. He offered to fight Cowboys coach Tom Landry for the victory, made "Beat Dallas" shirts for players and staff, and wouldn't even call Redskins defensive end Dallas Hickman by his first name.

One year later, the Redskins beat the Cowboys 26–3 in the NFC Championship to advance to the Super Bowl where they lost to the undefeated Miami Dolphins. For a team that hadn't done anything in the postseason since 1945, defeating Dallas for the conference title was Super Bowl–worthy. Fans from that generation easily call it the biggest win in the rivalry even when Washington beat Dallas in the 1982 NFC Championship.

Ironically, Allen was 7–8 against Dallas during his Washington tenure, but his legacy lives on. Fans still chant "We want Dallas" at every opportunity.

Somewhere, George Allen still hates Dallas.

14 The Wreath

It was the perfect payback.

Dallas Cowboys defensive end Harvey "Too Mean" Martin threw a funeral wreath into the Redskins locker room after beating Washington in the 1979 finale. The Redskins were so stunned by the last-second loss that no one responded.

"I just snapped," Martin told *America's Rivalry*. "I grabbed the wreath, walked out the door, asked directions to the visitor's locker room—I had never been there. I walked up, opened the door, threw the wreath into the middle of their prayer, and told them, 'Take this damn thing back to Washington with you.'"

Three things led Too Mean to such madness. The first was inspired by the Redskins, the second was caused by a fan, and the third came from the emotional game.

Four weeks earlier, the Redskins called timeout with 14 seconds remaining so kicker Mark Moseley could kick a field goal despite a 31–20 lead. Nothing ticks off a losing team more than being shown up like that. And that's what it was. The NFL doesn't work off style points to impress pollsters like colleges do. It was the rivalry talking, and Washington was rubbing the win in Dallas' face.

It was a stupid move by the Redskins. It let the Cowboys stew for a month, waiting for the season-ending showdown where the winner would be NFC East champion and the loser would also lose a tie-breaker and miss the playoffs.

The second was a funeral wreath sent to Martin at the Cowboys practice facility in days preceding the game, offering condolences for the loss. Martin was sure it was the Redskins taunting him. No matter that reports later tracked the wreath from a Rockville, Maryland, florist who claimed a Cowboys fan had sent it to motivate his favorite team.

No, Martin didn't believe any of that.

"I got to thinking, 'Man, that means I'm dead or something. They sent me a wreath,'" he told the Associated Press. "I just kept looking at it. So on the way to the stadium, I told [the equipment manager to] bring that thing with us."

Hollywood would have Martin playing the game of his life to beat the Redskins, but in reality Dallas won a shootout 35–34 with Roger Staubach throwing the winning score.

While the Cowboys were celebrating in their locker room, someone asked Martin about the wreath. He just grabbed it and started walking.

"That was dumb and something I guess a member of the Dallas Cowboys shouldn't do, throwing that funeral wreath in the locker room at a time when they were down and they'd been defeated and we all knew that," Martin told the Associated Press. "I'm sorry I did it. As a matter of fact, I sent a telegram to [Redskins] Coach [Jack] Pardee and the *Washington Star* and *Post* up there, apologizing for my action."

"I'm happy the Redskins will be home for Christmas. I gave them the wreath back because they needed it."

Moseley wished Martin had done it differently, too. The wreath bounced off the wall and hit Moseley, whose locker was by the door, in the knee. He needed stitches to close the gash caused by the wire stand.

"The door opened, and that wreath came flying in," Moseley said.

How did such an act not cause a fight by Redskins seeking retribution? Moseley said the team had just finished its prayer and was too drained to quickly respond to Martin's move. It was the last ride of the Over-the-Hill Gang, and many of them knew it.

"It took a few minutes to absorb it. Guys were upset for a minute," Moseley said. "At that time, nobody thought that much about it. The fans were more upset about it. We were ready to go home. We were disappointed in ourselves."

Moseley said Martin would later apologize to him twice for throwing the wreath before the latter's 2001 death. He lives on for throwing that wreath, though.

15 The 2:00 AM Revolt

Pepper Rodgers came within a late-night revolt of becoming the Redskins coach.

Seriously. Rodgers would have replaced Norv Turner with three games remaining in 2000 if not for receivers coach Terry Robiskie and defensive coordinator Ray Rhodes refusing to work under Rodgers.

It's not that they didn't like Rodgers. Everybody loves the guy. He's a million laughs and certainly a legendary college player and coach who was even a USFL head coach. But Rodgers was owner Dan Snyder's confidant and not an NFL head coach.

Personally, Rodgers could have written stories as a virtual quote machine. But making Rodgers a coach would have been so wrong.

Here's an inside look at Turner's last day after seven seasons in Washington.

Snyder wanted to fire Turner when he took over the team in June 1999, but his replacement choice of Pittsburgh defensive coordinator Jim Haslett was blocked by the Steelers because teams can prevent any move after June 1.

Snyder instead fired general manager Charley Casserly and figured Turner would go after the season. However, the Redskins won the NFC East title, so Snyder was forced to re-sign the coach for one year. Turner really wanted to leave, but he stayed so his oldest son could finish his senior season as a local high school quarterback.

Turner seemingly didn't care much that season. Oh, he wanted to win, but Turner thought Snyder asking him about offensive plays and wanting to decide personnel was silly for someone with no football experience.

Snyder loaded the 2000 team with a $94 million payroll filled with aging stars like Deion Sanders, Bruce Smith, and Jeff George. What Snyder didn't learn for nearly 10 years was that you can't buy a title, and the Redskins struggled with newcomers whose best days were behind them.

Washington lost to Philadelphia 23–20 to fall to 7–5. Snyder was fuming, and Turner was gassing out under the tension.

When the Redskins lost 9–7 to the New York Giants after Eddie Murray's late 49-yard field goal was far short—a controversial move given Murray had told Turner he couldn't kick past 47 yards—all hell broke loose.

My *Washington Times* partner Jody Foldesy and I decided to play good cop/bad cop at the postgame press conference. Foldesy asked Turner if he thought Snyder would fire him the next day. Turner exploded, as any coach would have, but Jody's question gave me a back way to talk to Norv as the good guy.

Yes, reporters play games, too.

A lot of reporting is just boots on the ground. I was still at the stadium six hours after the game ended when Snyder left his adjacent luxury box. I bolted to the concourse, something even the New York writers noticed and wrote about, to question Snyder. Of course, Snyder said nothing, but he realized people were watching closely.

Shortly after midnight, Turner said he wasn't coming to Redskins Park at 5:00 AM as usual. He was sleeping in and arriving around 9:00. It was his expectation that Snyder would fire him, so why bother arriving early? That was the final update for the last edition.

Meanwhile, Snyder decided to promote his buddy Pepper for the final three games since the season looked lost. Johnson was a backup quarterback and kicker on Georgia Tech's 1952 national championship and coached Kansas, UCLA, and Georgia Tech over 13 years, but the past 15 seasons included only a stint as the USFL's

Memphis Showboats coach in 1984–85 and the CFL's Memphis Mad Dogs in 1995.

Snyder called in Robiskie and Rhodes at 2:00 AM, ordering them to work under Rodgers. Both said no. They would serve as assistant coaches but they would not call plays knowing Rodgers couldn't do it. Both coaches knew they would be fired soon and didn't care to be part of a circus that might harm their reputations.

Exasperated, Snyder agreed Robiskie would be the interim coach as both coaches wanted. The Redskins went 1–2 under "Coach Robinski," as Sanders erroneously called him, and Rhodes and Robiskie were fired after the season.

Rodgers served as the Redskins director of football from 2001 to 2004 before leaving when Joe Gibbs took over the team. But for a few minutes in the middle of the night, Rodgers was the coach.

16 Seat-Cushion Game

It was an endless wave of yellow cascading from the upper deck. It lasted several minutes and was completely fan-generated.

And it was the most surreal experience between players and fans.

NFL teams talk about the 12th man. Washington Redskins supporters proved it, not with some noise meter but an act that essentially said, "[Blank] you!" to the Atlanta Falcons and Coach Jerry Glanville.

Glanville and his players were talking a lot of smack in the days leading up to the January 4, 1992, playoff game at RFK Stadium. They arrived in fatigues for a team photo at the Iwo Jima Memorial across the Potomac River in Arlington, Virginia.

Redskins fans cheer in the rain during NFL Divisional playoff game against the Atlanta Falcons on January 4, 1992, at RFK Stadium in Washington, D.C. The Redskins won 24–7. (AP Photo/Doug Mills)

Rap star M.C. Hammer and heavyweight champion boxer Evander Holyfield were part of Falcons cornerback Deion Sanders' entourage. They kept bragging over how the "Red Gun" run-and-shoot offense would beat the Redskins—big talk for a team that lost to Washington during the season 56–17 and was 0–7 at RFK.

And then it rained…on the night before the game, during the game, and a couple days more. Not that Washington needed a wet field, but it was a power running offense and Atlanta was a speed team. It was a decided advantage for Washington, though the team already had enough incentive when they spied Glanville shaking a Redskins helmet on the sideline before the game.

A team with a number of veterans sporting two Super Bowl rings didn't like being taunted. Neither did fans. RFK was ready for a smackdown—and it came.

Washington led 14–0 in the second quarter and 17–7 in the fourth. Running back Gerald Riggins scored the clincher on a one-yard run with 6:32 left for a 24–7 victory.

Fans erupted. They wanted to throw the final KO. So they grabbed the yellow seat cushions given away by the team before the game.

The foam cushions sported the Redskins name and logo on one side and "Go Skins" and sponsor Mobil's logo on the other. Maybe they were supposed to be gold for the team color, but they came out mustard yellow.

Fans punctuated Riggs' score by throwing cushions onto the field. Thousands rained down from across the upper deck, then the lower deck added theirs.

It was just a delicious moment that only fans following champions enjoy. Washington would later win its third Super Bowl under Coach Joe Gibbs, but in many ways the seat-cushion toss was the era's final defining moment.

Twenty-plus years later, many fans rated the "seat cushion game" as one of the best alongside beating Dallas in the 1972 NFC Championship and the 1996 RFK finale.

"In the cozy confines of RFK," Jane Winston said, "you felt somehow one with the crowd. Fans saw seat cushions begin to fly out of the stands after the Riggs' touchdown that secured the win. Everyone else just let loose; it was totally spontaneous. [I] don't think they ever gave away seat cushions again. Too bad—they were nice."

According to Chad Woodroof, "I saw a few cushions being thrown. The next thing I knew, it was like being involved in a big snowball/food fight. I remember we threw one cushion and kept the other two."

Added Scott Jackson, now a host at ESPN-980, "I did not throw my cushion, but my brother did after the Redskins scored the icing-on-the-cake touchdown."

Jim Assurian was behind the Redskins bench at midfield, so the cushions came past him.

"I think the seat-cushion toss was an organic event," Assurian said. "It just sort of happened. One cushion was launched and then [it was] as if everyone had the same thought at the same time and they came raining down onto the field. As young as I was, I wanted to toss as well, but our location under the overhang made it impractical. But I thoroughly enjoyed watching the spectacle from my seats."

Ten-year-old Brendan Deegan was ready to throw his cushion, too, but the free-for-all already claimed it.

"I kind of looked up to my dad to make sure it was okay to chuck ours, too," Deegan said. "When he gave me the go-ahead to throw them, by the time we reached down to throw ours, they were already gone."

Jim Magill was watching from home but still found a way to join in by throwing his couch cushions.

"Once Riggs punched it in, Dad and I did our usually screaming and high-fiving," Magill said. "I remember seeing something yellow flash across the TV and soon realized it was a seat cushion. I looked to my dad and smacked him with a pillow. He said those people were crazy for throwing away their free cushions, but he had a good laugh about it."

17 Start Your Own Podcast

Everyone thinks they can do a sports talk show. Just blab about the same thing you talk about endlessly with your buddies, right? The Sports Junkies are just four guys who became rich doing it.

John Pappas knows you can because his "Skinscast" has more than 20,000 listeners weekly after starting as water-cooler conversations.

"Starting a podcast is one of the easier things you'll do in life," he said.

To hear Pappas talk, a podcast is as simple as posting an audio file on a website. Publicize free using Twitter and Facebook, and you're in business.

"Social media is basically built-in advertising in Facebook and Twitter," he said. "We have our own Skinscast.com site, but put a link on Facebook that a new show is up and you get a lot of exposure that way. Thousands of people find you through social media."

Now here's the rub—sure, anyone can blabber about the Redskins, but if you want other fans to actually listen, it has to be more than a couple guys yakking.

"The success is based on quality of product at the end of the day," Pappas said. "We are the No. 1 Redskins podcast because we're a genuine show. We say up front we're just fans talking about the team. Some of the best shows are where we have disagreements.

"Brian Reffkin and I work together, and we talked an hour at work about games. I found our conversations to be compelling. All fans enjoy talking about it. Our conversations were as good as what I heard on the radio."

Skinscast has grown from a few hundred listeners per show in 2006 to more than 20,000 these days. The show can be heard on the website, on Facebook, and at iTunes. All it costs Pappas is $20 for the domain name and $7 monthly for website hosting.

"The key to us is the comic relief between the guys," he said. "We have good rapport between the group. If you and your friends are talking football and insulting each other, if you find that to be funny, that will translate to the podcast. You can't be shy. We were at first."

Pappas even learned a trick to handling one hour of nonstop chatter.

"Go in your bedroom, get a hairbrush, and just start talking to it," he said. "If you think 15 minutes is a short time, just try doing a spontaneous monologue and see how you do. The podcast is like radio—there's no audience. You're talking to air."

"The beauty of the internet is we don't have FCC and time constraints. We had one year we were on a network, but that's not us. It's not scripted. It's literally whatever questions that come to mind. We are at times a little salty, but it reflects how friends talk."

Pappas even created a signature opening of his show straight from late night TV.

"Remember the Johnny Carson *Tonight Show*?" he said. "Remember Ed McMahon saying, 'Heeeeere's Johnny!' I wanted something so I started saying, 'Heeeeere we go, Skinscast!' The 'Dammit Reffkin!' became an add-on to that."

Ironically, Pappas says the show gets more listeners after Redskins losses than wins.

"Fans love it when they win, but they want to understand when they lose," he said. "What the hell's going on here?"

Sometimes podcast crews get the golden ticket to cover the team alongside journalist, like Pappas did. He learned there's a fine line of being a fan and working among impartial journalists. For example, there's no cheering in the press box.

"Writers who cover the NFL team tend to be the best writers, and there's only 32 teams so that's a very select group of writers," he said. "A lot of people don't appreciate there's a real craft there. They've paid their dues, and I thought it would be insulting for me to come and try to be their peer.

"Maybe after a few years people will start saying hi to you."

Turns out that last reference was about me. Pappas said I didn't talk to him the first two years. Ha—he's probably right. Beat writers don't trust outsiders for fear that anything said just for the media room will be put on Twitter, so it's better to say nothing to newcomers. That said, I've appeared on Skinscast many times, and Pappas has been on my videos and written for *Warpath* magazine. So outsiders can become insiders eventually.

Of course, technology has made podcasts just the first step for Skinscast. Video may be next.

"There's stuff listeners don't see like facial expressions," Pappas said. "There's a lot of comedic value there potentially."

18 1937 Debut in Frederick

The beginning came not in the welcoming confines of their new home or a hostile road game. Instead, the Washington Redskins debuted in Frederick, Maryland, on September 6, 1937.

A thousand people reportedly saw the Redskins crush the American Legion All-Stars 50–0 at McCurdy Field. That attendance number is a nice round figure surely upsized by owner George Preston Marshall that was still far short of the 2,500 capacity. Still, that didn't stop the bombastic laundry-chain owner from declaring baseball was boring and football was the future despite playing before what would be the smallest crowd ever to see the team play as the Washington franchise. No matter—Marshall was a showman and the Redskins won big. Surely that would increase ticket sales.

The team was relocating from Boston but wouldn't see Griffith Stadium for another 10 days when 24,500 welcomed the newly renamed Redskins. There was supposed to be another exhibition beforehand against the Wilmington Clippers at Pennsylvania Field, but that was canceled. Marshall would use the team's whopping exhibition victory and the signing of a passer to generate fan interest in the newcomers.

The franchise truly began in Frederick, and one day after a downpour the team was unwilling to play on a muddy field. Indeed, it was a lousy day for the Redskins as the team bus was pulled over near Rockville and the driver charged with reckless driving for passing on a double line, according to the *Washington Post*.

The Redskins returned the next day with Cliff Battles scoring two touchdowns on interceptions. It wasn't unusual for pro teams to play local amateurs in exhibitions to raise money for both sides. Washington's defense permitted only 45 yards rushing and 71 yards.

"The Redskins smothered the willing All-Stars beneath an avalanche of touchdowns," wrote the *Frederick News-Post*.

A 2007 *News-Post* article quoted Bob Marendt, once a lad chasing foul balls who later led fundraising for a second McCurdy Field in 1974, who recalled, "I guess they couldn't find any place else to play. They played a team from Frederick, the Frederick Athletic Club…. Football wasn't a big deal at the time."

Washington rushed for 225 yards and gained another 136 yards passing, but famed quarterback Sammy Baugh didn't play after a prolonged contract negotiation. Instead, the debut of his Pro Football Hall of Fame career would wait until the regular season after arriving September 8.

McCurdy Field opened in 1924. It had a dark brick exterior that hid an aluminum shell that cost just $15,000. It would be known

Never On a Tuesday

The Redskins have never played on a Tuesday and are winless on Fridays.

Washington is 529–490–26 on Sundays, 29–38 on Mondays, 1–2 on Wednesdays, 6–9 on Thursdays, 0–3–1 on Fridays, and 23–24 on Saturdays. That's 588–564–27 overall, including 565–546–27 in the regular season and 23–18 in postseason.

Looking for a good month? The Redskins are 1–0 in August, 108–93–4 in September, 174–157–13 in October, 154–182–6 in November, 129–120–4 in December, and 22–12 in January.

The Redskins are 337–246–11 at home, 248–315–16 on the road, and 3–3 on a neutral site.

Washington is 24–14–1 in overtime.

The Redskins are 2–6 on Thanksgiving, 27–36 on Monday nights, and 17–17 at home. Washington is 16–17–1 on Sunday nights and 7–9–1 at home.

as the minor league home of the Frederick Hustlers, Warriors, and Keys, and it was the spring-training home of the Syracuse Chiefs in 1943 and Philadelphia Athletics in 1944–45 during wartime travel restrictions. The park was condemned in 1968 and torn down in 1971. A new park opened in 1974.

Certainly, it was the start of something big for the Redskins. The team would go on that season to win its first World Championship that season and four more in later years. There were three future Hall-of-Famers on the field in Frederick with Baugh coming soon after.

Seventy-seven years later, the Washington Redskins remain— even if they play in Maryland and critics want the name changed. It all dates back to a little field far away.

Meanwhile, the Redskins connection to Frederick isn't completely lost. Certainly the town evenly divided between Baltimore Ravens, Pittsburgh Steelers, and Washington fans appreciated the loyalty to Frederick when Redskins owner Dan Snyder donated

$10,000 in 2011 to replace Little League baseball equipment lost in a fire.

After all, Frederick is the first home of the Washington Redskins.

19 The Dallas Redskins?

Some things just shouldn't be for sale.

The London Bridge should have stayed above the Thames River. The Great Wall shouldn't become a Walmart. Pieces of the Berlin Wall shouldn't be for sale on eBay.

And everyone knows how that Babe Ruth sale went.

But if not for late greed by owner George Preston Marshall, the Washington Redskins would have become the Dallas Redskins.

Pause 10 seconds for that to sink in.

The Dallas Redskins? Oh, the name probably would have been changed to Dallas Cowboys, just like the Washington Senators became the Texas Rangers in 1972 and the Montreal Expos turned into the Washington Nationals in 2005.

But it's mind-boggling for Redskins fans to accept losses to their rival, much less nearly losing the team to Dallas. Selling the Redskins to an out-of-town buyer, much less one in Dallas, seems insane. Why don't they just peddle the Washington Monument to New York to stand beside the Statue of Liberty? Move the White House to St. Louis by the Arch like the federal government nearly did in 1870? Tell Congress to go back to Philadelphia and take the U.S. Capitol with them?

Clint Murchison wanted to buy an NFL team and move it to Dallas. The Texas oilman tried to buy the San Francisco 49ers in

1952 and later on the New York Giants and Chicago Cardinals.

Finally, Murchison made a deal with Marshall to buy the team in 1958 for $600,000. The Redskins were losing money and fans, and the 62-year-old Marshall was tiring of running the team. A cashier's check was readied. But, according to the book *The Murchisons—The Rise and Fall of a Texas Dynasty*, Marshall changed the terms at the 11th hour and 59th minute.

Marshall trying to rework a deal? Imagine that.

Murchison agreed to Marshall's previous demand of continuing to run the team for five years. Suddenly, Marshall wanted 10 years. Murchison wasn't about to let someone whose team was awful on the field for more than a decade and terrible in the stands run the team in a new city for 10 years.

"Tell him to go to hell," Murchison reportedly said.

The non-sale didn't seem a big deal in Dallas. According to Barry Horn of the *Dallas Morning News*, the December 12, 1958, edition of his paper devoted five paragraphs to the non-sale complete with a denial by one unnamed Murchison associate. Naturally, Murchison couldn't be reached for comment.

Clint Murchison's son, Burk, told Horn his father rarely discussed the Redskins deal before dying in 1987.

"Dad was a future-oriented guy," Burk Murchison. "When the Redskins deal died, he never dwelled on it. It was over and done. He was a doer. He moved on."

Murchison did get the last laugh on Marshall, buying rights to the song, "Hail to the Redskins," from the team's disgruntled bandleader who wrote the music for $2,500. Murchison then leveraged the return of the song rights for Marshall's vote to approve a Dallas expansion team in 1959.

Murchison later said, "It was a nice meeting. [I] gave George the song; George gave me his vote for admission into the NFL.... The Little Big Horn wasn't the only Indian victory. Hail to the Redskins!"

The cities have since morphed into perhaps the NFL's biggest rivalry, though teams from around the country claim their regional wars are better. Former Redskins coach Jim Zorn used to claim Seattle-Denver was a war.

Dallas fans don't hate Washington nearly as much as Washington hates the Texan team. "We want Dallas!" is often chanted at FedEx Field the game before playing the Cowboys.

Maybe Dallas fans feel they're already one up on Washington given the Rangers are still in nearby Arlington. A generation of Washingtonians haven't forgotten that. Nor have many in the nation's capital forgotten beloved President John F. Kennedy was assassinated in Dallas.

But if the Redskins had been lost to the Texas town, it wouldn't have been nearly the big deal it would be today when eminent domain or something would have been claimed in Washington courts to prevent relocation.

The Dallas Redskins? How weird.

20 Nine Untouchable Numbers

"We hold these truths to be self-evident, that all men are created equal."

Well, the Declaration of Independence aside, some are a little more equal. That's why the Redskins retired No. 33 for Sammy Baugh and unofficially won't use eight other numbers.

Joe Theismann (7), Sonny Jurgensen (9), Charley Taylor (42), Larry Brown (43), John Riggins (44), Bobby Mitchell (49), Dave Butz (65), and Art Monk (81) are untouchables. Longtime equipment manager Jay Brunetti withheld the numbers from use through his 2000 tenure, and no one has donned them since.

Mark Moseley's No. 3 was also put aside by Brunetti after Moseley became the only NFL kicker to win the league's Most Valuable Player award by converting 20-of-21 field goals in 1982. He remains the team's career scoring leader with 1,206 points.

But then came quarterback Jeff George, owner Dan Snyder, and Coach Marty Schottenheimer to activate Moseley's No. 3. The coach replaced Brunetti, who spent a quarter-century with the team after the teen was repeatedly caught peeking through the fence at the old Redskins Park by a security guard nicknamed "007." Brunetti was old-school Redskins Way and the best equipment man in the game. Schottenheimer just wanted to make the change to have his guys scattered throughout the staff. The coach was fired after one year, which made losing Brunetti to the Houston Texans even more exasperating to Redskins fans.

So the keeper of the numbers was gone, and George wanted No. 3. Snyder didn't respect Redskins traditions back then, so George got the number. When fans balked over Moseley's number being recycled to an unpopular player fired three games into his second season, it was too late.

At least Snyder learned not to touch the rest.

It doesn't help Moseley's legacy, though. Punter Hunter Smith wore No. 3 in 2009, and quarterback John Beck donned it in 2010.

Brunetti's system reflects personal bias. These numbers were all worn by either Brunetti's boyhood heroes or those men with whom he worked. Fortunately, they're all great players. Jurgensen, Taylor, Mitchell, and Monk are Hall-of-Famers. Brown could be a Veterans Committee pick for Canton one day. Many have Super Bowl rings.

Surely there are others who are deserving of a retired number. Cliff Battles (20) was the franchise before Baugh's arrival. Instead,

In this December 12, 1999 file photo, Arizona Cardinals quarterback Jake Plummer (16) tries to tackle cornerback Darrell Green (28) who intercepted Plummer's pass during the fourth quarter at FedEx Field in Landover, Maryland. This was Green's 50th career interception. Green retired after 20 seasons with the Redskins and was elected to the Pro Football Hall of Fame during his first year of eligibility. No one has worn his number since.
(AP Photo/Doug Mills)

30 players have worn that number, ranging from safety Ken Stone to fullback Marc Logan to cornerback Richard Crawford.

Turk Edwards (17) signed with Boston over two other offers for a lofty $1,500 salary in 1932. He made All-NFL four of his first six seasons. Thirteen more players have worn 17, but at least Doug Williams (1986–89) won a Super Bowl and Billy Kilmer (1971–78) reached the championship. It helps compensate for John Friez (1994) and Danny Wuerffel (2002) wearing it.

Nobody has worn No. 28 since Darrell Green retired in 2002. Twenty seasons of donning it and later reaching Canton makes it pretty much impossible to give out No. 28 again. The only other notable player to wear No. 28 for Washington was Herb Mul-Key (1972–74), and he was no D-Green.

Sean Taylor's No. 21 hasn't been worn since his 2007 murder. Most likely it won't be used again.

One Isn't the Loneliest Number

Sorry Three Dog Night, but five Redskins have worn No. 1 while five other numbers have seen only one bearer.

Sammy Baugh (33) is the only Redskin with an officially retired number, but it's doubtful anyone else will ever wear Joe Theismann's No. 7 or Sonny Jurgensen's No. 9. John Olsewski was the only one to wear No. 0 from 1958–60, while Steve Nagarus is the sole No. 00 from 1945–46.

No. 25 is the most used of Redskins numbers with 35 players. (Chase Minnifield wore No. 25 in 2013 but didn't appear in a game. He would be the 36th player.) Perhaps safety Ryan Clark is the most notable. No. 26 has seen 30 users, including running back Clinton Portis. No. 20 has 30 players, including safety Ken Stone. No. 22 had 28 and No. 80 had 27 users. Carlos Rogers wore No. 22, while Roy Jefferson donned No. 80.

Incidentally, No. 1 was worn by five players, including punter Matt Turk.

There are two ways to look at Taylor. He was on his way to a standout career but was really only great for only 1½ seasons. That doesn't make him an immortal. Given the chance, Taylor might have become legendary. We'll never know. Because of the circumstances of his death, fans would probably revolt if someone else wore No. 21.

It's not easy withholding numbers. After all, with 53 active players and eight more on the practice squad, there's not a lot of wiggle room, especially at single digits shared by kickers and passers and Jurgensen and Theismann keeping two numbers away. Should the NFL ever increase the season to 18 games, rosters would probably expand, too. That means even more pressure on the numbering system.

But no matter. Some numbers are untouchables. It would be better if the Redskins would simply officially retire the numbers. It sure would be a grand marketing move, something the team loves to do. It would probably sell a few more jerseys, though Jurgensen's number is probably the most worn at games by men 50 years or older. Riggins and Monk have large followings, too.

For good measure, the Redskins should also bring back Brunetti to run the locker room. He did a great job during four Super Bowl runs, remembering everything down to what types of bubble gum players preferred, whose locker was next to whose, and how coaches' clothes were prepared. Brunetti knows the Redskins Way—which the team likes to mention often—better than any of them who are now saying it.

21 Sex in Stands

Sex by the stadium gates, lust in the stands, and romance around Raljon—Redskins fans keep it interesting.

About one hour after beating the Green Bay Packers in 2010, the FedEx Field crowd was largely gone. Some of the late stragglers milked last call in the luxury boxes and were just trickling out. The parking lots were mostly empty, and it was largely quiet.

I was setting up my tripod to record a video with Skinscast's John Pappas. His back was to the concourse, which prevented him from seeing a young couple stumbling out of the gates only to land on the ground. But it was easy to see the lovers entwined. Celebrating the win took on a whole new meaning.

But it wasn't the first time spirits and success produced sex. In 2000, owner Dan Snyder produced a Disney World of sorts at Redskins Park when he moved training camp to the daily Ashburn, Virginia, facility for the first time. The team charged $10 admission, which was roundly denounced. However, Snyder built the nicest temporary stands ever seen for the crowd and brought the NFL Experience. It was a fair deal for fans versus just standing in the grass, as they did during other years. And who can say how fans will spend their money? If they thought the $10 fee was worthwhile, that's their business.

Anyway, one couple experienced training camp in a very different way. The last ones to leave on camp's opening day, they were spotted by security guards romping on the top row of the bleachers as the sun set behind them. The guards had a heart and let them quickly finish and vanish into the dusk, but it was much discussed for years.

One in 60 Million

The Redskins will see their 60 millionth all-time fan in the third regular-season game in 2014.

Washington has drawn 59,821,265 fans since 1932, sans preseason games. The Redskins have seen 30,631,245 at home. Postseason games have seen 2,396,595 fans.

The team drew 63,500 during its first season at Boston's Braves Field in 1932. The team moved to Fenway Park for 1933–36 with 355,923 attending. The team nearly doubled its Boston home average to 28,409 when playing in Washington's Griffith Stadium with 4,119,319 overall from 1937 to 1960. RFK Stadium drew 14,260,098 from 1961 to 1996. At FedEx Field from 1997 to 2013, the Redskins drew 11,241,165. In 2013, the Redskins drew 617,767 at home and 582,240 away.

Figures are for reported attendance, which quite often reflects the number of tickets sold, not the number actually attending. There's no way to distinguish the difference because the Redskins are a privately owned company and they don't have to reveal numbers.

Things happen when passions ignite. Sometimes they're fueled by alcohol. FedEx Field isn't known for fights, but sometimes things happens. After all, my friends in the stands estimate one-third of the crowd is drunk. That's at least 25,000 people. Something's going to happen.

One fight in 2011 occurred right in front of the press box glass, tucked in the lower end zone corner near the Redskins tunnel. Two Redskins fans fought a bigger Cowboys fan, who frankly whipped them both without breaking a sweat.

The bigger trouble fighting fans have is not with each other but with security. The guards don't mess around. They throw everyone out unless those nearby convince guards that one person was blameless. It does happen, but often it does not. The biggest problem for a fan throwing punches is he (although I've seen women fight, too) doesn't know the guy coming behind him is a cop. He wheels around and hits the officer. That means a trip to jail.

What often amazes me is how drunks drive home after games without accidents clogging Landover. A longtime friend was a Prince George's County policeman who worked one of the exit roads. His car was parked on an elevated median strip, and he still feared for his life.

FedEx fans are more tolerant of visitors than many other places. Wear your Redskins gear to Philadelphia and it's only a matter of when, not if, you'll get into a fight. Baltimore and New York aren't much better, and Oakland scares the hell out of everyone.

But Washington is a town of outsiders. If visiting fans mind their business, FedEx fans don't bother them. But start talking trash, and things will change. The most fights in the stands ever was an Oakland game where the visitors seemed dressed for a fight. They wanted it and often got it.

The Steelers game on *Monday Night Football* in 2008 was insane. The crowd was at least 70 percent Pittsburgh fans who waved their Terrible Towels throughout the Steelers' 23–6 victory. It was embarrassing.

The Redskins later countered by giving fans their own towels, but that's stealing another team's act and looks cheap. Redskins fans didn't cause much chaos that night because they were frankly quite outnumbered.

It's not like RFK Stadium where the same 55,000 fans come to each game. FedEx's one-time 90,000 seats allowed many visiting fans. Reducing seats has helped, but winning regularly is the only thing that stops visitors from crowding the stadium.

And then the celebrating will truly begin.

22 Rookie Hazing

Mark Hartsell knew it was coming. Every rookie does. It's just a matter of how bad it gets. And for the 1996 undrafted quarterback, it was about as bad as it gets.

After taping the arms and legs together of several sons of Darrell Green and Terry Robiskie and even AP writer Joe White's son, Harry, leaving them wiggling on the hall floor of the Frostburg gym, several veterans were now blood-thirsty.

Hartsell made the mistake of coming out of the locker room right then. Soon he was taped to a handcart, like those used by UPS drivers. But it gets worse. The handcart was attached to the back of a golf cart, and Hartsell was soon wheeled around campus, his head whizzing just inches above the pavement.

And it gets even worse.

The team ate dinner in a picnic area, so Hartsell watched the entire meal with the handcart taped to a tree. Naturally, the press interviewed him since he couldn't go anywhere.

It was funny, and Hartsell took it well as the fourth-string passer. He wouldn't be there long. Fringe players know just to laugh along or it gets worse.

Nobody risked Robert Griffin III's health as a rookie. Veterans aren't that crazy. These days, newcomers usually perform in a variety show. Kirk Cousins delivered a killer Mike Shanahan impression in 2012, which is easier to do when you know you're making the team.

Yes, it's a kinder, gentler NFL for rookies these days. No more harsh pranks like saying the Turk needs to talk to them on cutdown day when he doesn't, or jamming a penny in their dorm door so they can't open it.

Resistance is futile. In fact, it only makes things worse.

Any rookie who arrived to camp late following a contract holdout was immediately hazed. Veterans hate sweating out practices while some pretty-boy first-rounder is home, wanting for more money.

Heath Shuler was the third overall pick in 1994, and he was taped to the goal post after missing 13 days. And when someone is taped, the rule is that whoever cuts him loose will receive even worst treatment. Usually a trainer comes out, but not before 30 minutes pass.

LaVar Arrington was rudely welcomed after missing the first week as the second overall pick in 2000. Assistant coaches urged a veteran to push Arrington into a bout on the first practice, just to welcome him to the NFL. Sure enough, Arrington was goaded into it. The vet was just as tough as Arrington, so the fight was a draw. Coaches laughed during it.

Sometimes rookies just sang for veterans during dinner. Maybe it was their school fight song, which would always be shouted down. It could be some pop song that was usually shouted down. Either way, it was nerve-wracking for many players.

Maybe they should just sing the National Anthem. Who's going to shout that down?

Of course, veterans and staff could be hazed, too. Russ Grimm and trainer Bubba Tyer were locked in epic training-camp exchanges involving flagpoles, popcorn-filled vehicles, and nasty liquids. Finally, Tyer grabbed Grimm's clothes during practice, walked onto the field, poured lighter fluid over the pile, and dropped the match while Grimm watched from half a field away. That fiery film was shown around Redskins Park for years.

An injured summer intern was told his arm was broken when it wasn't. After a few days, they removed the cast.

Pranks continue throughout the season. A trainer told a player he made the Pro Bowl. The player howled in victory and ran around the facility telling everyone. He was so happy. The trainer was actually shamed into telling the truth. I'm sure there was payback for that.

It was all good clean fun—not the shameless acts that occurred among the Miami Dolphins.

23 Career Ends on a Coin Toss

Albert Glen "Turk" Edwards was legendary even before an infamous ending.

The All-American tackle from Washington State led the Cougars to the 1931 Rose Bowl. The towering 6'2", 260-pounder was massive for his time, and the Boston Braves won a bidding war over the Portsmouth Spartans and New York Giants by offering $1,500 annually—big money at the start of the Great Depression.

Edwards joined the startup Braves in 1932. A year later, they were the Boston Redskins. Four years later, the team moved to Washington and won a world title.

All in all, Edwards was enjoying a terrific nine-year career that would later lead to his enshrinement in the Pro Football Hall of Fame. Sure, he had some knee problems in an age when football players wore little padding and safety was secondary, but Edwards reported in 1940, saying his body was sound.

And then it ended...on a coin toss.

Wait—what?

On the season's second game, versus New York, team captains met for the coin toss. Washington won when New York incorrectly called heads. Edwards then shook hands with Giants captain and former college teammate Mel Hein.

According to *Football Hall of Shame 2* by Bruce Nash and Allan Zullo, the exchange at midfield went something like this:

Edwards: "Good luck Mel."

Hein: "Take care of yourself, Turk. Don't get hurt."

Redskins tackle Albert Glen "Turk" Edwards. In 1932, Edwards played with the Boston Braves, which became the Boston Redskins until the team's move to Washington in 1937. Edwards was an All-Pro tackle in 1932, 1933, 1936, and 1937. Edwards went on to coach the Redskins from 1946 to 1948. (AP Photo)

Edwards: "Thanks, old buddy. I won't."

When Edwards turned to the Washington bench, his cleats stuck in the turf and his knee was shredded. Edwards needed to be carried from the field. He thought it would require only a couple weeks of rest, but the much-injured knee never mended.

Right there, Turk's career ended. A member of the NFL's 1930s All-Decade Team lasted only three games into the next decade.

It's often considered one of football's more bizarre injuries. Redskins quarterback Gus Frerotte's 1997 concussion came when he headbutted the end zone wall after scoring. Arizona kicker Bill Gramatica tore his ACL in 2001 when he landed awkwardly after jumping in celebration over a first-quarter field goal.

Chicago receiver Wendell Davis tore both his knees when he caught a seam on Philadelphia's notoriously awful field in 1993. He missed nearly two seasons before even trying an unsuccessful comeback. The biggest goof may have been Jacksonville punter Chris Hanson who gashed his leg with an axe when trying to follow the team's "Chop wood" motto in 2003.

So Turk is in good company with obscure injuries. At least his wasn't intentional or stupid—it was just bad luck.

Turk was a memorable player for the Redskins. Perhaps his best game was a late-season 1936 game at the Polo Grounds that would decide the NFL's Eastern Division crown. While known as a dominating blocker for fellow future Hall of Fame running back Cliff Battles, the two-way player also batted down a punt and place kick while recovering two fumbles in Washington's 14–0 victory.

All-NFL during four of his first six seasons, Turk led a mediocre team to perennial contender by 1936 and then a title with quarterback Sammy Baugh a year later. Talk about ironmen—Turk once played all but 10-of-720 minutes during the 1933 season...and this from a guy who drove a bus cross-country so his college teammates could also try out with Boston.

Turk was considered fast, especially for his size, in running down opposing players. He was called the "Bouncing Boulder" and "Rock of Gibraltar" for his girth and speed.

After his injury, Turk spent five years as a Washington assistant coach, twice declining owner George Preston Marshall's offer of becoming head coach before taking the job from 1946 to 1948 when he was 16–18–1. Few Redskins have lasted longer than Turk's 17 years with the organization where he was honored as one of the team's 70 greatest players.

Edwards was inducted into the Pro Football Hall of Fame in 1969. Ironically, his presenter that day was Hein. Turk died four years later at age 65. Following wife Bonnie's 1992 death, their ashes were together poured into a lake in front of their home in Lake Washington, Washington.

24 "I Like Sonny/Billy" Bumper Stickers

Sonny Jurgensen and Billy Kilmer liked to play a game away from the football field. The two would drive around the Washington beltway in 1972, trying to spot "I Like Sonny" or "I Like Billy" bumper stickers that fans placed on their cars to support their favorite passer.

Sonny would see a Billy bumper sticker and shake his fist to taunt the driver. Then they'd find one supporting Sonny so Billy could harass the driver.

It was great fun. Four decades later, the pair still chuckle over those bumper stickers.

So does Ted Schumacher, a retired insurance executive who created the bumper stickers as a University of Maryland student.

"Every time I hear the words *quarterback controversy*," said Schumacher in 2009, "in my mind, Billy-Sonny were the first true quarterback controversy."

The controversy was really among fans, not the quarterbacks. Maybe it was Coach George Allen bringing in a brash young passer from the Canadian Football League who gained Heisman recognition at Notre Dame that bonded Jurgensen and Kilmer. Surely third-stringer Joe Theismann telling the veterans he was going to start over them sealed the elders' kinship.

Jurgensen and Kilmer got along famously despite Kilmer replacing Jurgensen when he arrived in 1971 as part of the new coach's massive lineup changes. Jurgensen was winding down an eventual Pro Football Hall of Fame career. After seven years with Philadelphia, Jurgensen was traded to Washington in 1964 where he would pass for more than 2,900 yards during 14 games in four of six seasons.

Allen loved older players, but Jurgensen was turning 37 years old. Even though Jurgensen was coming off a 23-touchdown season with a 91.1 pass rating, which at the time was a career best, Jurgensen was benched for Kilmer.

Well, sorta. Kilmer was the regular who would get hurt and Jurgensen would rescue the team at times. There were plenty of highlights for both men, prompting fans to debate over which quarterback should play next.

That's what Washingtonians do—fight over who should be the starting quarterback. The job is the second most important around the nation's capital, after the Oval Office resident, and even President Bill Clinton once joked he was glad a slumping Redskins quarterback was distracting the media from the White House.

Billy and Sonny may have been the best combination and hottest debate, but many such comparisons have followed the Redskins over the years. Doug Williams or Jay Schroeder? Heath Shuler or Gus Frerotte? Even Kirk Cousins gets some respect versus

Robert Griffin III, the team's latest legend. And there's nary a pre-season that doesn't produce optimism over a third-stringer shining versus opposing reserves.

Partial to Jurgensen, Schumacher was like other fans who wanted to chime in on who should play. The business major started the Washington Fan Football Club, and the $5 membership fee included a bumper sticker, membership card, and kazoo.

It seems Schumacher's real dream was to have fans play the kazoos during the team's "Hail to the Redskins" song during games.

Rodman's Department Stores bought 3,000 bumper stickers. Schumacher and his partners then sold more stickers outside RFK Stadium for $1 until the team sent a cease-and-desist order. Given the bumper stickers never used the team's name, it's doubtful any legal tactic would have been successful, but the business soon ended over a disagreement between partners. More than 10,000 bumper stickers were sold.

Ironically, Schumaker now lives in Florida near Jurgensen's Naples home, while Kilmer is cross-state in Fort Lauderdale. Schumacher sent some of the final bumper stickers to the passer in 2009 to give to Jurgensen's grandchildren. The two even once met on a flight to Florida when they were randomly seated beside each other.

Schumacher made T-shirts adorned with the bumper stickers for friends. His hope of Sam Huff wearing one to tease broadcast partner Jurgensen never happened, though.

"My fantasy would be to have Sam Huff walk into the booth wearing the shirt and have Sonny see him and break out laughing," Schumacher said. "It's all about having some laughs."

The yellow-and-burgundy stickers are now collector items. One shows up on eBay occasionally, often bringing $100. Schumacher toyed with re-issuing the stickers years later but decided the memorabilia was best left in the past.

After all, Billy and Sonny can't keep driving around the Washington beltway taunting fans forever.

25 Heisman Modeled After Redskin

Washington has drafted numerous Heisman Trophy winners, but who knew the sculptured award was modeled after a Redskins fullback?

Not even Ed Smith himself knew the 1935 modeling session for a high school friend became the famed trophy until told by a documentary crew in 1982.

Smith's pro career wasn't much—eight games in 1936 with the Boston Redskins and two games with Green Bay in 1937 before a recurring ligament injury ended his pro career. His final stats were seven carries for 39 yards. He also completed 11 passes for 120 yards—all with the Redskins in 1936.

But the trophy is for college careers, and while Smith's was solid it certainly wasn't Heisman-worthy. He was a triple threat at New York University. Smith ran, passed, and quick-kicked in the single wing from 1933 to 1935. He suffered a torn ligament in his left leg in 1934 that later shortened his pro days.

The Violets were 7–1 in 1935, and after Smith's last game on Thanksgiving Day—a 21–0 loss at Fordham to mar the season—the Downtown Athletic Club awarded its first trophy to the best player east of the Mississippi River two weeks later. Chicago running back Jay Berwanger won the inaugural Downtown Athletic Club award.

But the trophy will always belong to Smith. The bronze statue shows Smith strong-arming an opponent while sidestepping others. Sculptor Frank Eliscu was a high school classmate of Smith's at

George Washington High in New York City. He was given $500 to create the trophy instead of a traditional loving cup or vase. Eliscu sculpted three wax versions, and Downtown officials chose one of a runner evading tacklers, although they wanted the arm to be sticking out to the side instead of straight ahead.

Eliscu asked the 6'2", 205-lb. Smith to pose in a Greenwich Village studio. Eliscu then reworked the stiff arm after watching several Fordham players pose on a football field.

"I figured he wanted it for himself," Smith recalled to *Sports Illustrated* in 1988. "He never told me what it was for, and I never asked."

Eliscu told *Sports Illustrated* the assignment wasn't that important so he didn't bother to tell Smith. Eliscu would later be best known for his bronze "Cascade of Books" over the doors of the Library of Congress' James Madison Memorial Building in Washington.

As for the Heisman pose, the clay model was then set in plaster and inspected by Notre Dame players who approved its thoroughness. Finally, the statue was turned to bronze. The trophy is 14" long, 13½" tall, 6½" wide, and weighs 45 lbs.

Many think the trophy is patterned after namesake John Heisman, a lineman at Penn and Brown from 1887 to 1891. Heisman was the first director of the Downtown Athletic Club. After dying the following year, Heisman was honored by the club as the trophy's namesake.

Ironically, Smith never knew about his connection to the trophy until 1982 when documentarian Bud Greenspan discovered him through his brother-in-law, Bob Pastor, a heavyweight boxer who fought legendary champion Joe Louis twice. The Downtown Athletic Club gave Smith his own Heisman in 1985.

"At first I thought it was some kind of crank call," Smith said of Greenspan. "Then what he was saying sank in. I couldn't believe it. It almost threw me off my feet."

Meanwhile, Smith went on to become a third-round pick by Boston, although 20th overall these days would be mid-first round. After a brief 10-game career that paid $200 per game, he finished the 1937 season with the semi-pro Newark Bears. He returned four years later to play semi-pro with a Springfield, Massachusetts, team in 1941 as a player/coach with Vince Lombardi also on the roster.

Smith lived the rest of his life in his boyhood Washington Heights neighborhood while working for Otis Elevators. He died in 1998.

Smith attended the 1986 awards dinner and told finalists, "Whoever wins the award, I feel sorry for you, because you're going to be looking at my ugly face for a long time."

Turns out it was one for the ages.

26 Attend All 20 Games

It sounds so great—attend all 20 Redskins games in one season. A vacation every other week to some of America's standout cities.

Well, kinda.

Covering 20 games for a handful of seasons includes many great memories and a free way to see the country. It gets old sometimes, like when you see Christmas trees at airports, knowing your kids are having fun without you. When you know where bathrooms are hidden behind staircases at airports around the country, it's time to come home.

Don't let me be a grinch—there are a lot of wonderful places to see and people to meet on the road, but you'll never again think pro athletes have it easy after traveling this schedule from August to year's end.

"Sometimes I felt, 'Wow, is it already time to go again?'" said Redskins diehard fan Samu Qureshi, who came close by attending 19 games in 2010. "But I was always very excited to go to the games." The preseason games count. Score is kept, so they count. Usually, they're a short flight or even drive away.

The Redskins' 2014 road schedule includes NFC East rivals New York Giants, Philadelphia, and Dallas, plus San Francisco, Arizona, Indianapolis, Houston, and Minnesota. Overall, that's not a bad itinerary for fans.

San Francisco is my favorite place to visit in the world over Venice, Italy. It's so vibrant, historic, and picturesque. Leave Saturday morning so you have the whole day to tour the city, given the three-hour time difference.

Strap roller skates to your feet and head to the water. Fisherman's Wharf is iconic. The seafood literally jumps at you from the sidewalk pots. (Watch out for the Alaskan King Crabs, which are still alive.) Pier 39 has great shopping plus seals on barges. Catch a ferry to Sausalito for lunch and Alcatraz prison for the night tour. Buy Alcatraz tickets a week ahead or risk paying scalper prices or getting shut out.

Rent a car and drive down Lombard Street, the most crooked road in America that unbelievably was once a two-way. Then drive over the Golden Gate Bridge and pull over immediately afterward to a park overlooking the city. Muir Woods and Napa Valley aren't far away.

Sadly, the 49ers leave Candlestick Park in 2014. Yes, it was an old barn just like RFK Stadium, but who wouldn't trade FedEx Field to return to RFK? The new venue is Levi's Stadium in Santa Clara, which looks like another of the new mega-stadiums that have popped up league-wide.

Arizona was a popular trip, especially when the Cardinals were in the NFC East with Washington. Usually, it was a warm respite with breathtaking scenery and an active night life. Fly Southwest

Airlines from Baltimore to Washington International because it has a return layover in Las Vegas. Let's just say quarters were lost before boarding.

Visiting Minnesota can be tricky late in the season, but if it's cold head to the Mall of America. It's three floors of the same stores you see in Washington, but the middle has a theme park and it's cool to say you went.

The Vikings are building the Mall of America Field for 2016, so the next two years mean heading to the University of Minnesota's TCF Bank Stadium in Minneapolis. Beware—the "Gopher Hole" is an open stadium, so a late-season game could be rough. Too bad you missed the Metrodome where the Redskins won the Super Bowl in January 1992…you know, the end of an era.

Indianapolis is an easy city to drive. Stay by the airport because it's cheaper and not far from the stadium, which sits on the edge of town. One amazing thing about Colts games is that everybody sings the National Anthem. It's pretty overwhelming. Go eat at St. Elmo's (start with the shrimp cocktails) or Harry and Izzy's.

Houston is the one place I never went around the NFL. I traveled to Osaka, Japan, but not Houston. Still, it's Texas and the food and people are awesome.

Speaking of Texas, you have to experience the Dallas rivalry from the opposing side. It is surreal. The first time there felt like being dropped behind enemy lines with everyone wearing blue jerseys. It's actually more of a "be seen" crowd like San Francisco.

"Dallas was off the charts," Qureshi said. "As much as I don't like the Cowboys, people were very friendly. They don't spew the kind of hate we spew at Cowboys games."

The old Texas Stadium is gone. It was pretty cool to see after years of the TV show *Dallas*, but it was underwhelming, like, "This is it?" The new stadium is some type of spaceship.

If you're going to Philadelphia, you have to eat a cheese steak. Ben Franklin's boys know how to load up on extras.

As for home games, you know the drill. Overpay for parking, overpay for food, and buy tickets cheaper on StubHub.com. This season, pick 10 different parts of the stadium to get a different feel.

You'll be exhausted when you've finished this marathon, but you'll have the time of your life.

27 Sam Huff—Tough Guy

While walking past the cafeteria following lunch during another endless training camp in Frostburg, there was a figure lying in the grass.

Motionless.

That figure was Sam Huff. Oh no, did Sam have a heart attack or something? After racing to his side and shaking him, readying to perform CPR, call for a medic, or something, Sam just opened his eyes and wondered why everyone was upset.

He was taking a nap. In the grass. In the middle of campus.

A few curse words came out of my mouth despite being grateful Sam was okay. He didn't have anywhere to go between practices and just figured he'd nap on the grass.

That's the Sam Huff those close to him know—a simple man who is tough as nails.

Older fans know Huff as the vicious-hitting linebacker of the New York Giants in the 1950s and 1960s before being traded to Washington in 1964. And those from his boyhood days know Sam as a hardscrabble son of a West Virginia coal miner who was willing to knock down anyone who was bent on preventing his exit from small-town life. And young fans know Sam as Sonny Jurgensen's partner in the radio booth before the former called it quits in 2013.

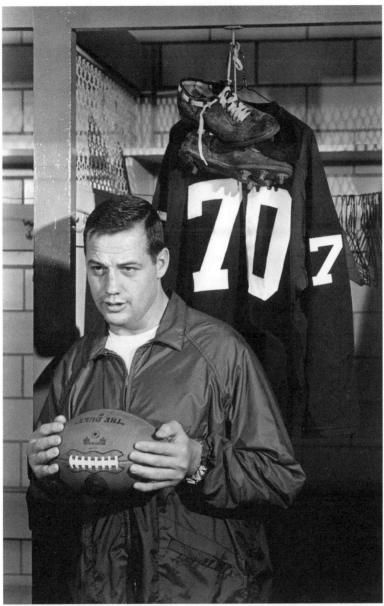

Defensive captain Sam Huff poses in front of his jersey in the locker room in Washington, D.C., on December 12, 1967. Huff had announced his retirement effective December 17, after his team's final game of the year, but he would return in 1969. Huff, 33, spent five years with Washington following an eight year stint with the New York Giants. (AP Photo)

Huff vs. Riggo

Linebacker Sam Huff was known for his violent play. John Riggins was a bruising runner. Who would have won an open-field matchup? Huff retired one year before Riggins started in 1971, but the linebacker once wanted a showdown after practice while Riggins was still playing. Fortunately, cooler heads prevailed and the two became good friends.

"I loved to play against someone like Riggins [or] Jim Brown," Huff said. "They're going to run over you. Come on in here, and we'll see who leaves. That's what goes on on the field. They'd ask, 'Who do you think you are?' and I said, 'Come on and we'll see.' They tried to run over me, and I made up my mind I was going to run over them."

Sam is a warrior, not a bully. He's not just someone looking for a fight. But mess with Sam and you'll see the tip of his sword, just like Jim Brown often did.

Sam lives by the strong values of a generation long gone—when men worked hard, did the right thing, and never surrendered. Value your friends, dominate your enemies.

Sam worked off-seasons despite being one of the NFL's top players. He found himself needing to dial back negotiations after intimidating clients. That glassy-eyed stare chilled them into retreat. Once Sam learned to go easier on folks off the field, he blossomed working for Marriott Hotels.

Sam has always been a player in his mind, even long after his final 1969 season. The goal posts were just extended to everyday life, and a dark charcoal suit replaced his jersey.

Sam viewed himself as a great player who deserved respect. When the Redskins' 1995 top pick Michael Westbrook didn't know who Sam was when they met at practice, it riled the Pro Football Hall of Famer into wishing for one more open-field play to teach the rookie some respect.

Respect is a big thing to Sam. He came out of retirement to play for Coach Vince Lombardi in 1969. It might have been the most fun season of his career. Just working under the NFL's greatest coach ever taught Sam so much about winning in life beyond the end zone. Both Sonny and Sam say Lombardi was the best coach they ever met.

Sam also loves thoroughbreds. He's a long-time breeder with several horses boarded at his Middleburg, Virginia, home. Sam created the West Virginia Breeders Classic card to boost his home state's racing legacy long before the casino arrived at Charles Town. Maybe Sam just admires good athletes in all forms.

Sam's favorite times might have been early Sunday mornings during road games. He would sit in the hotel lobby with Sonny, trainer Bubba Tyer, and other long-time team workers just talking. The conversations would have thrilled any fan overhearing a snippet while walking by. When that gang trickled away, Sam ate with linebacker London Fletcher before games, talking game situations.

When you think of Sam Huff, think of John Wayne in a helmet. Someone who lives by the rules and succeeds no matter the game.

They're both my heroes.

28 Kick Field Goals With Moseley

Nobody kicks straight-on field goals anymore, but Mark Moseley can teach you how.

The former Redskins kicker, now franchising director of Five Guys Burgers and Fries restaurants, still looks like his playing years of 1974–86 when he converted two-thirds of his field goals in Washington. That perfect hair hasn't thinned one follicle, the waistline hasn't expanded one inch, and cowboy boots remain the foundation of the native Texan.

Moseley taught kickers over summer camps for 25 years. There are still private sessions with young prospects. Kicking a field goal, straight-on or soccer-style, requires both mental and physical toughness.

"It's between your ears," he said. "You can't be afraid to fail because you're going to miss some. If you're on the sideline thinking, 'I can't miss this,' you're done. In the last two minutes of the game I was always right by [Coach] Joe Gibbs. He hated that. He wanted to score the touchdown and I'm, 'Let's kick this field goal. Let me be the hero.' There aren't a lot of kickers who want that."

Straight-ahead kickers also need more strength, which was one reason why early NFL kickers were often linemen. Moseley said the straight-on kick requires more leg strength and speed.

"To kick straight-on, you have to be a lot bigger and have the weight and strength behind it," he said. "It's the forward motion. You have to have strength in your legs and speed to get through. It's [about] leverage, like swinging a golf club."

Moseley played soccer in South America before returning to the U.S. in elementary school. He understands the attraction of kicking soccer-style.

"Learning to kick soccer-style is so much easier," he said. "It's more of a natural swing, and once you teach kids how to do that, you can develop pretty easy."

Everybody was kicking straight-on in the 1960s and 1970s until Hungarian brothers Pete and Charlie Gogolak introduced soccer-style. Moseley ignored it and became the last straight-on kicker in the NFL after 1982. Indeed, his helmet, jersey, and cleats are in the Pro Football Hall of Fame as "the last dinosaur," he jokes. Green Bay signed Dirk Borgognone for two games in 1995, but he never attempted a field goal.

"Nobody knows how to do it, so you're not going to see it again," Moseley said. "There's a stigma that kickers aren't football players. They think the kicker position is a sissy position now."

The key is watching your foot make contact with the ball, much like hitting a baseball.

"First thing is lock your ankle and make contact," Moseley said. "Most people try to swing too hard and throw their head and shoulders back and top the ball. You have to have your head over the football looking down and making contact. The most important thing is your plant foot has to be in the right place. Plant your foot straight down rather than on the side like soccer. Bad footing hurts soccer guys more."

The sweet spot is midway from the center to the end, but for straight-on kickers it's half the size for soccer kickers.

"Soccer-style is a lot more accurate because you have a lot more contact surface," Moseley said. "The sweet spot is just below the center of ball. I used white chalk on my foot and looked on the ball to see where he made contact."

You also have to have confidence, said Moseley, who was a clutch kicker as the Redskins career scoring leader with 1,206 points. He made 43-of-44 field goal attempts that would have put the team ahead and 16-of-17 last-second field goals.

"That's why I stayed around so long," he said. "When it came down to that last kick, I was going to make that kick."

Moseley's greatest kick was one he didn't see because of a raging snowstorm, the last time it snowed during a Redskins home game until 2013. The 42-yarder broke the NFL record of 20 consecutive field goals, beat the New York Giants 15–14, and put the Redskins in the 1982 playoffs. He also became the NFL's 1982 Most Valuable Player, the only kicker ever honored.

"You had to strain to see the goal post," he said. "That was the biggest because there was so much riding on it."

So take a breath and kick the ball. No pressure—it's all good.

29 George the Gorgeous

These days, everyone remembers Redskins founding owner George Preston Marshall as a racist who wouldn't sign black players until he was forced to do so by the federal government.

That's true, but Marshall was such an interesting person that it's worth looking beyond his final years and ignorant act. Marshall alone merits a book, so instead here's a series of things you probably don't know about him.

He never drove a car or flew in a plane. Marshall admitted he was too afraid. Instead, he loved trains.

With three partners, Marshall paid $1,500 for the franchise. Two years later, Marshall spent $1,500 to buy out his partners. Dan Snyder paid $800 million for the Redskins in 1999. It's now worth an estimated $1.5 billion.

Marshall sold 25 percent of the Redskins to Jack Kent Cooke for $350,000. The deal also included Marshall's Georgetown home and downtown apartment.

Marshall admired presidents Thomas Jefferson and Calvin Coolidge. Okay, everybody admires Jefferson, but Coolidge? Marshall was a young man during Coolidge's 1923–29 presidency. The owner probably liked "Silent Cal's" *laissez-faire* style of leaving businessmen alone.

After gaining a 30-year lease for D.C. Stadium, Marshall was upset his assistant didn't include a 30-year option afterwards. Marshall said he'd still be alive, but he died eight years later.

Marshall called his halftime shows "Matinee at Midfield," complete with a 225-piece band and chorus.

Marshall cared more about attendance than winning. Said minority Redskins owner Harry Wismer, "He used to tell me,

'Don't worry if you don't win. What the hell, people are coming in and out of here all the time.'"

Marshall returned to Washington in 1918 after his father's death to take over the family laundry business. His slogan: "Long Live Linen."

George Preston Marshall, owner of the Washington Redskins, in an undated image. (Pro Football Hall of Fame via AP Images)

The Redskins weren't Marshall's first sports team. He owned a pro basketball team called the Washington Palace Five after his laundry business. It lasted one season.

Marshall slicked his hair with Savage's Bear Grease.

The owner's pep talk before the 1942 championship against Chicago was writing "73–0" on a chalkboard in reference to Washington's 1940 title loss to the Bears. The Redskins won 14–6.

Coach Lone Star Dietz was ordered by Marshall to kick off if they won the coin toss. By the time Marshall reached his seat, he saw the Redskins were receiving. After yelling on the phone at Dietz for not kicking off, the coach replied, "We did, and the Giants ran it back for a touchdown."

Marshall fired Coach Dud DeGroot after losing the 1945 championship to Cleveland 15–14. Coaches Curly Lambeau and Dick Todd left during training camps.

Marshall sought to become an actor in New York after quitting school at age 17. He didn't last long.

After meeting movie star Corrine Griffith by a hotel, Marshall asked her to lunch and proposed marriage over dessert. She declined but later married Marshall. Her wedding gift from Marshall was a Confederate flag owned by the family since the Civil War.

Marshall's first wife was a former Ziegfeld Follies dancer.

The Redskins might have moved to Washington on Griffith's suggestion that the town's transient citizens had nothing to do on Sundays but feed pigeons and squirrels. She also said D.C. stood for "Displaced Citizen."

The owner bought a $100,000 insurance policy on Sammy Baugh during World War II while the quarterback commuted each week from his Texas home to Washington by airplane. Baugh earned $20,000.

Marshall was never intimidated by the government's demand that he sign black players to play in D.C. Stadium.

"I didn't know the Government had the right to tell a showman how to cast the play," Marshall said. "I would consider it a great honor to meet and discuss this with the President of the United States. Yes, I'd like to debate that kid. I could handle him with words. I used to handle the old man [Joseph P. Kennedy] in Boston."

Marshall wasn't surprised at being called a racist, saying, "I sure have been accused of being anti-everything. Anti-Jewish, anti-Catholic. Oh, I don't know. Maybe I'm just anti-people."

A full-length raccoon coat was Marshall's standard winter garb.

Marshall was publisher of the *Washington Times*—an earlier version, not the current paper.

Enlisting in the army for World War I, Marshall didn't serve overseas.

30 Thomas Almost Wore No. 33

Duane Thomas wanted No. 33 when he arrived in Washington in 1973. That was the number he wore with the Dallas Cowboys and West Texas A&M.

But No. 33 was retired, said the Redskins. It was Sammy Baugh's number, the greatest Redskin ever, excelling at three positions, winning two titles, and becoming a Pro Football Hall of Fame founding member.

"So what?" said Thomas.

Matter closed, said team officials.

Couldn't the team ask Baugh if he would let Thomas wear the number, the running back asked.

Sure, but it would be a waste of time, according to equipment manager Tommy McVean.

And then the story gets really curious. McVean called Baugh, who was already a recluse at his Texas ranch. Baugh didn't have much contact with the team all the way to his 2008 death. The Redskins offered to fly him to games over the years, but Baugh always said no. He preferred life on his remote ranch, which the passer bought with his football earnings.

But to satisfy Thomas, McVean made the call. And Sammy said sure. He didn't care about football. Hadn't played since 1952. If someone else wanted it, Baugh said go ahead and let him have it.

And the team still said no.

Baugh could have made it easier on the Redskins, who wanted to protect team history. Instead, team personnel still decided no one would wear that number again, much less a former Dallas Cowboy.

Instead, Thomas wore No. 47 for his two seasons in Washington.

Thomas was never a beloved figure among Redskins fans. It was the early days of the George Allen era, when the Cowboys were blood enemies. It was a time before free agency and players didn't swap teams nearly as often as they do today.

Thomas' best two seasons came in Dallas. He gained a career-high 803 yards and five touchdowns as a rookie in 1970 after playing alongside Mercury Morris in college. The first-rounder started the season as a backup for five games before ending the year being compared to legendary hard-nosed runner Jim Brown.

And then, to put it mildly, things went to hell.

Thomas wanted a new contract, the after-effect of a divorce and IRS audits. The runner felt he was underpaid for his second season, largely because a rookie signing bonus paid him more overall in the first year than the second.

Thomas wanted the final two years of his contract reworked, but the Cowboys refused. Thomas launched into an epic press conference during the 1971 preseason, denouncing the Cowboys and Coach Tom Landry.

Finally, Dallas traded Thomas, along with Halvor Hagen and Honor Jackson, to New England for its No. 1 pick in 1972 plus Carl Garrett. Thomas immediately clashed with Patriots coaches, and NFL commissioner Pete Rozelle reworked the trade. Thomas and Garrett returned to their teams, while New England sent second- and third-round choices to Dallas for Hagen and Jackson.

Thomas was so incensed over returning to Dallas that he reportedly didn't speak to the media, teammates, or coaches the entire season. He was dubbed "The Sphinx" during this time. Thomas later countered that he obviously spoke to coaches and teammates over plays.

Thomas delivered a great season with 793 yards rushing and 11 touchdowns. Dallas beat Miami in Super Bowl VI, while Thomas ended his media silence before the game by uttering the immortal, "If it's the ultimate game, how come they're playing it again next year?"

But Thomas still wasn't happy, and Dallas traded him to San Diego over the 1972 off-season. Thomas refused to report and was first suspended by the Chargers, then he was placed on the reserve list to miss the season.

San Diego traded Thomas to Washington during the 1973 training camp for a 1975 first-rounder and a 1976 second-rounder. Ironically, Thomas was gone before either draft choice was due, rushing for 442 yards over 1973–74 before the Redskins tired of his antics and cut him.

Thomas later played for the Hawaiians of the World Football League in 1975 where he wore No. 33 before signing with Dallas of all places in 1976. The Cowboys cut him during preseason. Thomas spent a couple weeks with the British Columbia Lions in 1977 before being waived. He tried one last time in 1979 with Green Bay but was released during training camp.

31 RG III—Most Hyped Redskin Ever?

Who was the most hyped player ever to come to the Redskins?

Sammy Baugh was a big deal in 1937, but there was no such thing as social media to create a buzz. There wasn't even TV back then, so how big could his arrival have been? Surely the team's move from Boston that year would have overshadowed Baugh somewhat. Baugh is the team's greatest player ever, but nobody knew that coming in.

Ernie Davis might have been the most hyped since he was a Heisman Trophy winner and would be the team's first black player in 1962. But Davis was traded to Cleveland instead.

There have been dozens of free agents from Deion Sanders to Bruce Smith to Albert Haynesworth over the past two decades, but none created a hurricane of buzz.

And then there's Robert Griffin III, or "RG III" as fans like to scream…as in hysterically, like those crazed women you see in clips of the Beatles' arrival to the U.S.

When teammate Fred Davis dubbed Griffin "Black Jesus," he tapped into something. While not going to that blasphemous extreme, the 2013 training camp practices in Richmond were like revival meetings.

Griffin is the player Washington has waited 20 years to see. He may become the team's best player since Sonny Jurgensen retired in 1974.

Indeed, even Griffin realizes the RG III mania can be divisive in a locker room. When fans don't call any other names from the stands, it wears on teammates after awhile.

"Yeah, it really is a fine line," Griffin said. "Whenever you're out there in team drills and stuff like that, you respect the rest of

Quarterback Robert Griffin III runs the ball against the New York Giants at FedEx Field on Monday, December 3, 2012, in Landover, Maryland. Washington won 17–16. (AP Photo/Aaron M. Sprecher)

the players that are out there. We are all on the same team, so you don't play with the crowd in those moments.

"The only thing I worry about, and I talk to my teammates about it every day, I don't want them to feel bad because the fans are cheering my name and not theirs. As long as they don't mind, then I don't mind, either. But the second that starts getting on their nerves, then we'll curb that real quick and make sure that all these guys get the appreciation and the attention they deserve."

Running back Alfred Morris might normally be the team's centerpiece after a single-season team record 1,613 yards as a rookie in 2012. Yet Morris laughs over kids leaving his autograph line when they see Griffin.

"Robert gets all the attention, but I love it," Morris said. "It's kind of hilarious. I can be in the middle of signing and they go, 'Oh, there's Robert!' and take off running, and I'm like, 'Oh, you're welcome! Okay, bye!' So I don't mind it at all. I'm enjoying it."

So is it really RG III's world and we're all living in it? That was the question Griffin's teammates were asked by *Richmond Times-Dispatch* columnist Paul Woody. After all, a biography and an ESPN documentary followed RG III's rookie year.

"We don't think about it," said linebacker London Fletcher, whose locker adjoined Griffin's before the former retired after 2013. "It's not a situation where we're feeling like, 'It's RG III's world.' He's a dynamic talent. He's a great person, so I think that part of it makes it easy. He gets a lot of attention nationally, and deservedly so. And that's just a part of it. When he came in, he's a Heisman Trophy winner, but he's a charismatic person and a tremendous talent. So you know there is no situation where us as teammates look at him like, 'What about the rest of us?' or anything like that."

Ironically, Griffin was "rested" for the final three weeks of the 2013 season when Coach Mike Shanahan didn't want to risk a serious injury in meaningless games once the team fell to 3–10.

Naturally, backup Kirk Cousins played well the first game, so fans started debating whether to trade Griffin and keep Cousins.

It's all part of the mania. Griffin didn't lose his starting job for 2014. And fans will cheer him once again at training camp. It's all part of the craziness. No one said it was a sane approach.

32 Second Acts

A movie star, U.S. Congressman, and renowned orthopedic surgeon walk into a bar…for a Redskins reunion. Sometimes the NFL is just a stepping stone to bigger things.

Terry Crews was a reserve linebacker in 1995 before he hit in big in Hollywood. Heath Shuler was a failed 1994 first-round quarterback before he represented North Carolina on Capitol Hill. Mark Adickes was a guard in 1990–91 who retired after winning a Super Bowl to become a surgeon who consulted on the knee rehab of fellow Baylor alumnus and Redskins quarterback Robert Griffin III.

Crews plays the funny desk sergeant on Fox sitcom "*Brooklyn Nine-Nine*" after a successful run as the dad in the TV sitcom *Everybody Hates Chris*. His movie credits since 2000 go 40 films deep with *White Chicks* the breakthrough flick followed by *The Expendables, The Longest Yard, Malibu's Most Wanted* and *Cloudy with a Chance of Meatballs 2*.

If a director needs a chiseled actor, they hire Crews, but his comedic chops keep him employed. It's a far world from his days as a journeyman linebacker and defensive end for the Los Angeles Rams (1991), San Diego Chargers (1993), and Redskins.

Crews is an amazing artist, too. Indeed, he created the book cover for *America's Rivalry* by John Keim, Mickey Spagnola, David

Elfin, and myself in 1997. A popular player who was just a step too slow to stay long in the NFL, Crews went to Los Angeles to work as an illustrator for a movie studio. One day the 6'2", 245-lb. Crews was mistaken for an actor while working security part-time around a movie set. Soon actors encouraged Crews to take bit parts, and his career steadily grew. He's even the actor in some of the Old Spice commercials.

"I was never a superstar player," Crews told the *Washington Post* in 2006. "I never made a lot of money. I had enough savings for the first six months out here before it was gone and done. I had to do various odd jobs. It was bad, man. My wife asked how long we were going to give this before deciding it wasn't going to work out. I said, 'We are never leaving. If I'm 90 years old and it hits, it will be worth it.'"

Shuler's Redskins career is still cited as one of the all-time biggest busts. The third pick overall lasted only three seasons with Washington before he was traded to New Orleans in 1997 where a foot injury ended his career that season. Shuler earned $19.25 million from Washington for 13 career starts, none in his third season when he was beaten out by 1994 seventh-rounder Gus Frerotte.

Shuler was unfairly characterized as not smart enough to play pro football. Well, he never did seem to learn where linebackers were when throwing interceptions.

A genuinely nice person, Shuler would discuss making money in the cattle business, factoring costs versus price per pound. He might have been a little naïve, but he was nobody's fool when rattling off the math aloud. It wasn't that Shuler wasn't smart enough to succeed in the NFL—he just wasn't quick enough.

Shuler went on to found the largest real estate company in east Tennessee before selling in 2003. Shuler then moved to his native Waynesville, North Carolina, where he represented the state's southwest corner in the U.S. House of Representatives from 2007 to 2013 as a conservative "Blue Dog" Democratic who espoused "mountain values." Shuler opted not to run for re-election in 2012.

Adickes played for the USFL's Los Angeles Express (1984) before moving to the Kansas City Chiefs (1986–89) and Redskins (1990–91) where his last of 77 NFL career games was Super Bowl XXVI. Like fellow linemate Russ Grimm, Adickes retired after the game.

Adickes studied at George Mason University and Harvard University Medical School before completing an orthopedic residency at the Mayo Clinic. He's now a medical director and surgeon at the Memorial Hermann Hospital Sports Medicine Institute in Houston where he is also the team physician for the Houston Rockets and U.S. ski team. Adickes also hosts *Athlete 360*, featuring those who have undergone orthopedic surgery, such as former Redskins teammate Mark Schlereth.

33 Was Dietz Really an American Indian?

Did a spoonful of sugar expose whether the man who supposedly inspired the Washington Redskins name was really an American Indian?

William Henry "Lone Star" Dietz said he was a Sioux Indian. Others claim he was a white man living as an Indian. The evidence seems pretty overwhelming that Dietz chose to live as an Indian but probably wasn't.

So the man who was partly behind the team's nickname wasn't really an Indian? Oh, the irony.

Not that owner George Preston Marshall switched the Boston Braves name to Redskins in 1933 strictly for his new coach. It was more to play off the name recognition of the Boston Red Sox, which shared Fenway Park with the football team. But Dietz claiming to be an Indian sure helped marketing, and Marshall loved marketing.

Dietz attended the famed Carlisle Indian School in Carlisle, Pennsylvania, just down the road from where the Redskins would later spend training camp. He played with the legendary Jim Thorpe and under Coach Glenn "Pop" Warner.

Dietz even appeared in a cowboy flick *Tom Brown at Harvard* as an Indian extra while in Los Angeles for a college bowl game.

But a chance encounter at a Spokane, Washington, diner where he was coaching Washington State to great success revealed Dietz's heritage.

According to Tom Benjey, author of Dietz's biography *Keep A-Goin': The Life of Lone Star Dietz*, nearby customer J.C. Argell asked Dietz to use less sugar because of World War I rationing. The two argued, and Argell left angry. Turns out Argell became head of the draft board and discovered Dietz claimed "non-citizen Indian," believing his mother was a full-blooded Sioux Indian. At the time, Indians weren't considered U.S. citizens and were thereby exempt from the draft.

Argell used a newspaper report that Dietz wasn't an Indian to indict the latter for draft evasion in 1919. The first trial ended in a hung jury. Among the testimony was Carlisle School officials showing proof Dietz was an Indian.

Dietz was raised by two white parents. Dietz's mother, Leanna Dietz Lewis, testified her child was stillborn and her husband "said that he had a secret and told me of the existence of another child of his, which he asked permission to bring home to replace the one that died." Translation—the man fathered an illegitimate child that was Dietz.

The jury was instructed not to decide whether Dietz was an Indian but whether he believed he was an Indian. The jury couldn't agree.

Dietz was re-tried and, without money for a defense, pleaded *nolo contendere* and was sentenced to 30 days in the local jail. Dietz believed he was a Sioux Indian but had no proof. It was his leap of faith.

Indian Country Media produced a series of reports in 2004 on why Dietz wasn't an Indian. It was pretty damning stuff that showed Dietz "was raised as a typical Euro-American boy who might have been, as a family member confided, teased for 'looking Indian.'"

Indian Country Media wrote that Dietz "created himself from the traces of the missing Oglala man, James One Star. One Star was born about 1872, grew up on the Pine Ridge Reservation in South Dakota, was taken to Carlisle Indian school in 1889 (the year of the Ghost Dance revival), enlisted in the army at Carlisle, Pennsylvania, on August 9, 1892, and disappeared when he was discharged in Alabama on September 15, 1894."

The newspaper further wrote, "Before going to Carlisle, he visited St. Louis at the time of the World's Fair and met an Indian there who told him that he was undoubtedly One Star, his mother being Julia One Star. He got into correspondence with Sally Eagle Horse, who had a brother, One Star, who had left home when 16 years of age and had never been heard from again. So he decided to take the name of Lone Star, it meaning the same as One Star.

"During the trial, the prosecution called the Oglala 'sister' Dietz claimed was his own. Through an interpreter, Sally Eagle Horse confirmed she had not heard from James One Star for nearly 30 years—just before he entered the army after leaving Carlisle in 1892. She further testified that her brother had a scar on his forehead where he was hit with an axe, his ears had been pierced, and he had different features. No, Lone Star Dietz was not her brother."

Dietz's status will never be truly known. Let's give him the last word from the trial: "If they want the truth as to whether I'm an

Indian, they can look me up in the records of Pine Ridge, Dakota Indian reservation, or at Carlisle where I played football."

34 The Intern Who Became a General

Always be nice to interns because you never know who they'll become. One Redskins intern branded a failure by Vince Lombardi ended up running a war.

George W. Casey Jr. was a 21-year-old student and football player at Georgetown University where the Redskins practiced in 1969. Vince Lombardi took an instant liking to the young man whose father was a U.S. Army general serving in Vietnam.

One day, Lombardi told Casey to guard the locker room door from the outside and not let anyone in. The coach planned to chew out players over a poor effort and didn't want to be interrupted.

"Lombardi starts getting on everybody, and the next minute the door flies open and [team president] Edward Bennett Williams flies in with five kids," equipment manager Tommy McVean said.

Lombardi was enraged. According to two people in the room, Lombardi targeted Casey for his ire. While it's hard to believe an intern could stop the Redskins president, the man who hired Lombardi, from entering the locker room, it didn't stop the coach from chewing out the intern.

Lombardi told the youngster he'd never amount to anything. Well, the coach was certainly wrong about that.

The postscript of the episode is indeed quite a story. Less than one year after the encounter, Casey gained his degree in international relations at Georgetown. Two months later, Casey's father—General Edward Casey Sr.—was killed in a helicopter crash in Vietnam. Another two months later, Lombardi died of cancer.

The elder Casey was a West Point graduate who served in World War II and Korea, earning a battlefield commission to captain when leading a platoon at the famed Heartbreak Ridge in Korea. He later commanded the 1st Cavalry Division in South Vietnam. Casey was one of three major generals killed in Vietnam and buried at Arlington National Cemetery near President John F. Kennedy.

The son would do even better, doubling his father's two stars to become a four-star general and U.S. Army Chief of Staff from 2007 to 2011, even though his initial plan was to only fulfill a two-year obligation. Casey entered the army as a Second Lieutenant after finishing Georgetown's Reserve Officer's Training Corps in 1970 with a degree from the Georgetown School of Foreign Service. He would later command the Third Brigade of his father's 1st Cavalry Division. Casey rose as a commander at all levels from platoon to Division while serving in Italy, Egypt, Germany, Southwest Asia, and the U.S.

Casey returned to the Washington area in 2001 as Director of Strategic Plans and Policy at the Pentagon for two years before being promoted to Director of the Joint Staff in 2003 and Vice Chief of Staff of the Army in June 2004.

Casey was the senior coalition commander in Iraq from June 2004 to February 2007. President George W. Bush then nominated Casey to become the 36th Chief of Staff of the Army. He was approved by the U.S. Senate 83–14. Casey was replaced in Iraq by General David Petraeus.

As the army's top official, Casey oversaw 1.1 million people and a $200 billion-plus annual budget. Among his accomplishments were improving care for wounded soldiers and increasing capabilities of the Army National Guard and Army Reserves.

Casey retired on April 11, 2011. At a party shortly before his retirement, Casey invited McVean to attend. McVean was surprised until he learned Casey's true purpose for requesting him—proof of the Lombardi tirade the general wore as much as a badge of honor as the 36 medals, badges, and decorations he earned in the army.

"Casey says, 'Tommy, I want you to meet somebody,'" said McVean, who would hear that opening line another 20 times that evening. "People think [Secretary of Defense Donald] Rumsfeld's tough. Tommy, tell them that story about Lombardi.'"

And the laughter would come of a coach scolding a future general. Imagine telling the army's highest-ranking officer that he'd never amount to anything.

Ironically, that Redskins internship is noted in Casey's Wikipedia bio.

35 "Hail to the Redskins" Lyrics

The Dallas Cowboys might never have existed if not for Washington's fight song "Hail to the Redskins."

The catchy little tune played after Redskins scoring drives these days became the key leverage for obtaining Washington owner George Preston Marshall's expansion approval of Dallas.

The song was written in 1938 for the new marching band formed to play at Redskins events. Marshall felt music would attract more women to games, which would encourage more men to attend. Families would come for the entertainment, too.

Marching bands were big in the early 20th century. After all, Washington was the home of legendary bandleader John Philip Sousa, who now lies in Congressional Cemetery in the shadow of

RFK Stadium. Assembling a 110-person marching band was in keeping with theatrics Marshall used to create interest in the team after moving from Boston to Washington in 1937.

Marshall's wife, Corinne Griffith, an Academy Award–nominated actress but not much of a song writer, came up with the lyrics while Redskins bandleader Barnee Breeskin wrote the music. Only Green Bay's "Go! You Packers! Go!" predates the Redskins as the NFL's oldest fight song.

Now Marshall wasn't the easiest person to get along with and, sure enough, he had a falling out with Breeskin, Texas, oilman Clint Murchison, who twice failed to buy a franchise to move to Dallas. But NFL expansion committee chairman George Halas agreed to put Murchison's bid to a vote among NFL owners.

The key holdout would be Marshall, who didn't want another "southern" team in the league. The Redskins were the league's southernmost club in 1958, and Marshall viewed Dallas as a potential rival for radio-station profits.

But Murchison saw an opening when Breeskin approached the former's attorney over buying rights to "Hail to the Redskins" for $2,500. Murchison knew it would irk Marshall if the latter couldn't play his wife's theme song while Dallas owned it.

Suddenly, Marshall regained the song's rights and Murchison gained the Cowboys.

The lyrics have been sanitized over the years. The original lyrics played off the American Indian angle with such phrases as "scalp 'em" and "heap more" plus "Braves on the warpath." The original words were:

Hail to the Redskins!
Hail Victory!
Braves on the Warpath,
Fight for old D.C.!
Run or pass and score—we want a lot more!

Scalp 'em, swamp 'em—we will take 'em big score!
Read 'em, weep 'em, touchdown—we want heap more!
Fight on, fight on—'til you have won,
Sons of Wash-ing-ton. Rah! Rah! Rah!

Contrary to popular belief, the original score did not say, "Fight for old Dixie," as references to the southern city. The song was changed in 1959–61 to include the phrase before returning to D.C. when the Redskins signed their first black player under orders by Congress if Marshall wanted to use the new D.C. Stadium.

Today's lyrics are a little more politically correct, although the term Redskins continues to draw criticism. Until the team's name is changed, however, the song can't be altered. The current lyrics are:

Hail to the Redskins!
Hail Victory!
Braves on the Warpath,
Fight for old D.C.!
Run or pass and score—we want a lot more!
Beat 'em, swamp 'em,
Touchdown!—Let the points soar!
Fight on, fight on 'til you have won,
Sons of Wash-ing-ton. Rah! Rah! Rah!
Hail to the Redskins!
Hail Victory!
Braves on the Warpath,
Fight for old D.C.!

Ironically, the band only plays along with a taped version of "Hail to the Redskins" after scores. The crowd still sings along while the band is tucked away in the end zone for sporadic songs after a pregame march across the field.

But somehow it doesn't seem right that the band isn't performing the song live after scores. It was part of the fun and the pageantry of the game. Now the song is packaged like every other marketing tool the team employs. The band probably took too long and squeezed out a commercial during the timeout.

At least a sponsor's name hasn't somehow snuck into the lyrics. Fight for old FedEx?

36 Flaherty Says Anchors Away

What does a two-time champion football coach do when he is drafted during World War II? Coach more football, of course.

Ray Flaherty was perhaps the Redskins greatest coach ever with two world titles and four division flags in seven years before he left the team immediately after winning the 1942 championship over Chicago. But his bio always includes just one sentence on serving in the navy during the war before returning to coach the New York Yankees in 1946.

So what did Flaherty do during the war? A *Reading (PA) Eagle* article on December 11, 1942, said Flaherty was sworn in two weeks earlier as a lieutenant senior grade and ordered to report following the championship game. The 39-year-old would have been a lieutenant commander if he had been one year older.

After a few weeks of indoctrination in Hollywood, Florida, Flaherty was made athletic officer, fitness instructor, and coach under commander (and former world heavyweight champion boxer) Gene Tunney at a new naval training center in northern Idaho.

And that's where it gets interesting. According to gnfafootball.org, a site that remembers the Greater Northwest Football Association,

Flaherty ran the Camp Farragut Blue Jackets teams near the Coeur d'Alene Mountains in Idaho. He must have liked the area because that's where he would live after football before dying in 1994.

Camp Farragut—named for the navy admiral who said, "Damn the torpedoes, full speed ahead" during a Civil War battle and who now has two metro stops near the White House named for him—was the world's second largest Navy training center. During its 30 months, 293,381 recruits passed through it.

Flaherty might have won a title of some sort in 1943 with a team supposedly the best in the navy. It seems Flaherty filled his roster with college standouts and pro players from the Brooklyn Dodgers, Philadelphia Eagles, and Detroit Lions plus Washington Redskins Ed Justice and Marv Whited.

The team couldn't arrange a schedule against outside clubs, though. Instead, Flaherty oversaw five camp teams meeting in a seven-game schedule.

In 1944, Camp Farragut formed two leagues that played an exhibition on October 27 (Navy Day) at Gonzaga Stadium, where Flaherty played college ball. It must have been quite a show with a 125-piece Navy band performing. The Signalmen and Quartermasters were both 2–0 that season, while the Radiomen were 1–0–1. And don't dismiss the Hospital Corps, which beat the Dental Corps.

Finally, the camp played in a regional league in 1945, although a "48-hour readiness" order meant only playing locally in case players were forced to ship out quickly. Before the Idaho Day game against the Idaho Vandals, German prisoners of war swept the field of snow.

The Blue Jackets were 5–1 entering the Northwest Service Teams Championship after twice beating Montana University and the University of Idaho plus the Pocatello Marine Devil Dogs. But Fort Lewis won the title 13–7.

The Best Coach Ever?

It's not Joe Gibbs. He's actually fourth.

Ray Flaherty was the most successful Redskins coach ever at 56–23–3 for a winning percentage of .709. George Allen was 69–35–1 for .663. Flaherty's successor, Dutch Bergman, was third at 7–4–1 for .636. Finally, Gibbs was fourth at 171–101.

Gibbs won three championships, Flaherty won two, and Allen lost his only Super Bowl appearance.

So is Gibbs the best coach ever, having won three Lombardi trophies and nearly three times the victories as Flaherty? Then again, Flaherty won two crowns in just 82 games versus Gibbs' 272. Flaherty left for the navy to fulfill draft obligations in World War II—perhaps he would have won more titles than Gibbs.

The war ended after the season, and Flaherty was discharged. The Redskins didn't need him, though. They were now led by Dudley DeGroot and finished 8–2 before losing the championship to the Cleveland Rams 15–14.

Instead, Flaherty coached the Yankees of the All-American Football Conference from 1946 until midway through the 1948 season, then he coached the Chicago Hornets in 1949. His career marks were 80–37–5 with seven division titles and two world crowns.

At age 47, Flaherty was through with football and operated an Idaho beer distributorship for four decades, although Canton came calling in 1976 to induct him into the Pro Football Hall of Fame. It seems Flaherty's creation of the screen pass in 1937, largely meant to protect his rookie quarterback Sammy Baugh from persistent blitzing, was historic. So was his platoon system for either running or passing the ball. And don't forget Flaherty's "Squirrel Cage" kickoff return where eight players gathered at the ball before scattering in all directions to confuse defenses.

Of course, Flaherty was also remembered for his college days when Gonzaga lost only four games. He was a standout end for the

Los Angeles Wildcats (1926), Yankees (1927–28), and New York Giants (1928–35) before leading the Redskins to a championship loss in 1936 as a rookie coach.

Ironically, Flaherty's biggest challenge must have come when everyone wore the same uniform and football being compared to war seemed shallow.

37 Visit Gibbs Racing Fan Fest

Joe Gibbs transferred a lot of his football savvy to the NASCAR world—leading a team, picking personnel, and treating fans right.

So it seems the Redskins Fan Appreciation Day each summer has followed the legendary retired coach to his racing headquarters every fall with Fan Fest.

If you're a Redskins fan, you gotta go.

Fan Fest comes each October when the NASCAR schedules a race at nearby Charlotte, about 15 miles from Gibbs' headquarters at 13415 Reese Blvd. West, Huntersville, North Carolina, 28078. Fan Fest is the Friday before the race and has attracted 3,000 fans in recent years. Call (704) 944-5000 or visit JoeGibbsRacing.com for more information.

It's free just like every other day when touring the facility. Other days, you can take a self-guided tour to see teams working on cars, check out the NASCAR and NFL memorabilia on displayed, such as Gibbs' Super Bowl rings, and visit the gift shop. You may even catch Gibbs or his son, J.D. Gibbs, for a moment. Fans often come weekdays between 8:00 AM and 5:00 PM.

"Fans enjoy the opportunity to see people work on the cars," said Gibbs spokesman Chris Helein, who joined Redskins public relations in 1991. "But one day a year, fans see so much more. Drivers all come. Joe comes."

You might not be a gear head, but who doesn't appreciate great cars? Fan Fest hosts a car show whose winners are decided by fans. Not just Sprint Cup cars, but the same vintage mobiles you see in lots of local shows. You can even enter your own car in the show. Well, not that 1996 Civic Honda with 200,000 miles on it that you drive to games, but if you have a street rod, muscle car, pickup, or even a motorcycle, why not take a shot?

The show cars seen every day by the shop's entrance are displayed for Fan Fest, too. They give you a real sense of what goes on the track. Frankly, it's a little scary to think they're driving so fast with so little metal around them.

Of course, there are bands playing in the background, creating a party atmosphere. Carolina beach music provides a light mood, not some heavy metal racket that Gibbs wouldn't know anyway.

Guided tours of the workshop are available that day (self-guided other days), but don't forget to take your youngsters to the Kids Workshop where they can build their own. That is when they're not climbing over the cool construction and farm vehicles on display. It's hard to hurt those heavy metal monsters. The kids and you will love the racing simulators and remote cars. Hey, let the kids win already. You've probably already eaten the wall anyway.

And maybe you want to say hello to Lugnut, the Charlotte Motor Speedway mascot as well as those M&M's walking around. Red and green came in 2013. I'm partial to yellow and blue.

But here's what you don't want to miss—the morning Question/Answer session with Gibbs' drivers. Last year, Denny Hamlin, Kyle Busch, Matt Kenseth, Elliott Sadler, Brian Vickers, Michael McDowell, Darrell Wallace Jr., and Drew Herring all came. And yes, they signed autographs until the ink ran out. This is like Robert Griffin III, Alfred Morris, Pierre Garcon, and Brian Orakpo coming to chat and sign.

And this is free? Gibbs sure didn't learn anything from Redskins owner Dan Snyder about making money.

Okay, what else is there to do in this little town of 46,000? Well, October weekends usually have a Carolina Renaissance Fair that's one of the largest in the country, and it includes eleven stages, a jousting tournament, and even a circus. That should kill the few hours remaining after attending Fan Fest.

If you come during the summer, Huntersville is also known for two lakes that are great for boating, water skiing, and fishing. Now that sounds fun. Naturally, there are golf courses, too. This is North Carolina after all.

Now be careful—attending Joe Gibbs Racing Fan Fest may turn you into a racing fan. Can you handle two teams? Two seasons?

Just remember to circle Fan Fest in your calendar one fall. It's only seven hours from Washington, and there are plenty of barbecue stands along the way to keep you from starving.

38 The Squire

There are a million stories about Jack Kent Cooke. Some people loved him, even more hated him, and quite a few feared the Washington Redskins owner.

Here are a few of my own interactions with "The Squire."

The phone rings in the Redskins Park press room and someone is just cursing at me nonstop. It takes only a moment to realize it's Cooke and he's mad as hell. That's not good.

As a reporter, people are often mad at you. But nothing was worse than Cooke being mad. Redskins owner Dan Snyder's worst day couldn't come close to Cooke. And unlike Snyder, whom the press calls by his first name, you didn't even think of saying anything other than "Mr. Cooke."

See, Cooke knew how to hurt a reporter by giving stories to your competitor. That means your boss is mad, your credibility is shot, and a lot of hard work is wasted.

This time, Cooke was angry over a story over him losing money when he sold his Lexington, Kentucky, horse farm. Cooke bought at the top of the market and sold at the bottom following the death of his son, Ralph Cooke, who ran the farm. Cooke didn't like people knowing he was on the short end of a deal.

Cooke yelled for about 20 minutes, and reporters always endured these tirades because further enraging him by dismissing him as you would any other irate caller would be the worst move possible. But this time the conclusion went my way.

"Why didn't you get my side of the story?" Cooke yelled.

"I called you, and you didn't call back," I said.

"My sincere apologies," said Cooke before slamming down the phone.

Wait, did I just win? Man, I wish I could have framed that moment.

One time I interrupted Cooke yelling at me to ask if we were somehow related.

"By God, you're a bastard," he said, "but you're not mine."

Then I asked, "Do I work for you?"

"By God," he chuckled, "I'd fire you for sure."

Well, I could only say, "I didn't let my own father yell at me, and since I don't work for you, I don't have to take it."

Cooke often lectured writers over missing commas in stories. Newspaper style is not to use commas on dependent clauses. It probably comes down to using less ink. Cooke then instructed us on the proper use of the English language. After all, Cooke would say, he started out as an encyclopedia salesman.

"Big deal," I'd say. "Back then there were only 12 letters. How hard could it be?"

Wow, that earned a big lecture for being a wise guy, but it was worth it.

Cooke once called to ask about my little vending company. It was just a bunch of gumball machines for a quarter, but we talked for 45 minutes.

I kept thinking there had to be a catch to this conversation before finally asking if he was thinking of buying a vending company. Cooke wasn't. He just enjoyed talking business.

A billionaire talking about two-bit candy machines? At least that day I was smart enough to listen to two things Cooke told me about business that are absolutely right.

His top two tenets were to always use the bank's money instead of your own so the risk is theirs, and never have partners.

Our best talks were over thoroughbreds. He loved horse racing and had several stables of pricey runners in Los Angeles. Cooke didn't see them race often, but he talked to his three trainers every day and knew exactly how each of a couple dozen horses were doing. Cooke loved to buy the offspring of Danzig, a very success stallion in the 1980s.

Cooke always wanted to win a Kentucky Derby, but his one chance was a long shot that finished "up the track" as they say of distant losers. A year later, Flying Continental was the favorite in the Breeders' Cup Classic at Belmont Park before the Redskins played the New York Giants the next day.

I called Cooke to talk about the race and the Giants game, and I said winning bets on each would make me as rich as he was.

Cooke laughed at my boldness and said, "Let me be the first to welcome you to the club."

Click.

39 Visit Canton

The Pro Football Hall of Fame in Canton, Ohio, should be on everyone's bucket list. Somehow it has evaded me.

I visited Cooperstown, New York, for baseball's shrine as a kid, and I've visited the National Thoroughbred Racing Museum in Saratoga, New York, in 2005 as a Hall of Fame voter.

I walked past hockey's Hall of Fame in Toronto in 2003, although I should have gone in.

But Canton somehow has been elusive, and there's an increasing need to travel 350 miles from Washington to see the 18 Redskins players and coaches whose careers in burgundy and gold earned enshrinement. I watched or wrote about 10 of them. Another nine passed through Washington during their careers, including Deion Sanders and Bruce Smith.

"You can appreciate the days gone by to see Washington's heritage," said Joe Horrigan, vice president of communications/exhibits. "Stop by Sammy Baugh's bust to see when he led the league in punting, passing, and interceptions, where Bill Dudley scored nine different ways. You see the bronze busts of Redskins immortals."

More than 10 million fans have visited the hall since its opening in 1963, including 208,191 in 2013. The center finished a two-year renovation in 2013 to provide more interactive exhibits, such as trying on equipment. NFL Films' entire library is also accessible. According to Horrigan, "We've used them anyway you can imagine."

Wow, that sounds intriguing.

The busts of enshrines seem to be a favorite stop. There's just something about them that creates a more personal connection

Men of the Century

Nobody gained 100 yards like John Riggins. The century mark is considered the status of a good game, and the hall-of-famer did it a team-best 25 times.

Larry Brown gained 100 yards or more 21 times as one of the top runners of the early 1970s. Maybe one day Canton voters will remember that.

Stephen Davis surpassed 100 yards 19 times. Clinton Portis did it 16 times. George Rogers, Earnest Byner, and Terry Allen did it 12 times each, and Alfred Morris did it 10 times in just two years.

Overall, 53 Redskins have gained 100 yards or more in 239 total games. The Redskins are 180–54–1 with a 100-yard runner and 4–0 when two different players rush for 100 yards or more.

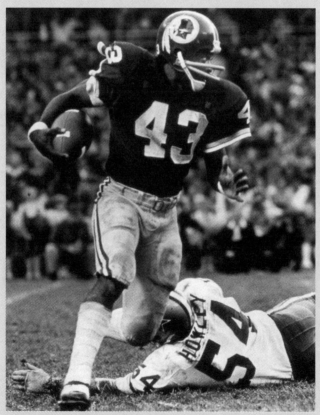

Redskins running back Larry Brown (43) runs upfield avoiding the tackle of Dallas Cowboys linebacker Chuck Howley (54). (AP Photo/NFL Photos)

than a jersey or shoes. Go see what Sammy Baugh, Turk Edwards, and Cliff Battles looked like as young men. Find those guys you watched for years, such as John Riggins, Russ Grimm, Sam Huff, and Sonny Jurgensen. See coaches Ray Flaherty, George Allen, and Joe Gibbs.

Josh Fink traveled from Nebraska to see the 2008 induction of Green and Monk.

"As a lifelong fan of not only the Redskins but also the NFL, it was an experience that I will never forget," he said. "Some of my favorite parts were all of the past history on film and other exhibits, but the part where I spent the most time was the room with all of the Hall of Fame busts. My advice would be to go that particular weekend so you can see the game [and] enshrinement, along with the parade. Canton is all about the Hall of Fame."

Bryan Manning saw Monk and Green's inductions, plus Grimm's, too. The speeches were his favorite part.

"The best part of the day was sitting in the stands and seeing some of the favorite players from my childhood in attendance," Manning said. "Gary Clark, for instance, was my favorite player as a kid. Sitting in the crowd, listening to all of the Hall of Famers, was truly special. Monk and Green were terrific. I had chills listening to them the entire time they spoke. As much as I enjoyed Monk and Green's speeches, every inductee did well.

"If you love football, going to the induction ceremony, especially if it is a player from your favorite team, is something every fan should do. I went to the game, and it was actually my least favorite part of the weekend. The Hall of Fame experience is why you go."

Wander the exhibits. You never know what you'll see.

"Believe it or not, Mark Brunell is in the Hall of Fame," Manning said. "Actually, it was Brunell's uniform. It was in Canton because of his performance against Houston in 2006 when he completed his first 22 passes to start a game."

If you can't make it to Canton, visit their website at profootballhof.com. It has more than enough to satisfy your football fix.

40 Cover the Team

"I wish I had your job" has been said a million times over the years. What could be better than watching your favorite team and getting paid for it?

Explaining that this job is work and how you need to be impartial are never accepted by fans. Nor do they heed my advice when thinking about becoming reporters.

But if your bucket list includes covering the Redskins, WJFK 106.7-FM's Grant Paulsen and Comcast SportsNet Washington's Rich Tandler have shown that former fans can cover the team. They not only took non-traditional paths to the pressroom, their journeys were polar opposites.

Tandler was 55 years old with no journalism experience when he got his break. Paulsen was 10 years old when he first covered the team. Now Paulsen is a veteran of Washington radio at age 26.

"There was an element of luck," Tandler said, "but also the harder you work, the luckier you get. I work hard at it. I had to do a lot for little to nothing [financially] for 10-plus years before I got there. It wasn't easy."

Said Paulsen, "I still don't know how it all played out, but it was awesome. You have to work hard at it. If it's your passion, do it well and put a lot of work in it."

Tandler's *The Redskins From A to Z, Volume 1: The Games*, chronicling every Redskins game until 2002, was his entry into the press corps. He was soon hired by *Warpath* magazine to increase its Redskins coverage, while Tandler also created his RealRedskins.com blog. "The book got me some notoriety around Redskins media and the Internet," he said. "The press knew I wasn't going to be fan boy or embarrass anyone. I was going to be professional. I was setting myself up as a professional."

By January 2011, Comcast offered Tandler a part-time deal that grew to full-time in July 2012. Now he's a staple on CSN's shows and website. Yet Tandler admits it's all a little surprising.

"I didn't really see a path to a job doing that," he said. "It wasn't a master plan, but I was hoping."

Paulsen was 10 when he showed up at the 1999 training camp in Frostburg. At the time, the press corps didn't always welcome outsiders. The Internet was just heating up, and newcomers were treated with suspicion.

But there was something veterans reporters liked about Paulsen. Mainly, he didn't try to tag along with us, and he did his own interviews.

Paulsen was soon picked up by WUSA-9 as a kid reporter and for years he used his age to get interviews with players who didn't want to blow off a youngster.

"It was different," Paulsen said. "People liked seeing a cute kid talking football."

But just like child actors, Paulsen reached a crossroads shortly before attending George Mason University over earning work on merit versus cuteness.

"It did get to a point where the novelty wore off," he said. "I wasn't the kid anymore, and opportunities were few. I was doing shows at XM radio and stringing. There was a time I wasn't sure if I would get a break. I was typecast as a gimmick, like a circus act."

Paulsen was named WJFK 106.7-FM's beat reporter in 2011and quickly established himself as a young veteran on the beat who knew the Xs and Os as well as the personalities. He's now a midday show host.

Did reporting on the Redskins ruin him for covering his childhood team?

"What people don't understand is you see so much stuff out here, the underbelly, that the prism you watch through as a fan isn't available to you," he said. "It doesn't mean you don't want the team to do well, but I was always able to hit a switch."

So what advise would Tandler and Paulsen give to others wanting to cover the team?

"Have a point of view. Don't be a cheerleader for the team," Tandler said. "I usually try to take a middle ground. I don't hammer them a whole lot, but I also don't say they're the greatest thing. I don't get too emotional about games, and I take a long-term view."

Said Paulsen, "Get to know everybody and learn from everybody. While things are changing, some of the people around today will be here 10 to 12 years from now, and in a relationship world, that's important."

41 The Payback

Sam Huff had waited three years for this moment, and cries of unsportsmanlike conduct wouldn't deter him.

The Redskins linebacker swore he'd get even with the New York Giants when the latter traded him in 1964. Huff was a legend in New York. The son of a West Virginia coal miner loved everything about New York from the street cars to his Yankee Stadium locker shared with Mickey Mantle.

Huff would later become a Pro Football Hall of Famer based on his eight years in New York where he graced the cover of *Time* magazine and earned a TV show depicting his brutal hits on the field that laid out Jim Brown and Jim Taylor.

The trade was shocking. Being sent to Washington, which hadn't been to the playoffs since 1945, was like being exiled to the minors. Huff blamed Giants coach Allie Sherman for poisoning owner Wellington Mara's mind over Huff.

"I told Wellington Mara, who was a wonderful guy, that he would be sorry for trading me," Huff said.

A payback was promised. And nearly a half-century later, Huff still wishes Sherman could have suffered more. But this field goal would have to do.

The Redskins regained the ball on the Giants 23-yard line with seven seconds remaining. No problem—just take a knee, run out the clock, and enjoy a 69–41 victory.

Instead, defensive captain Huff signaled the special teams unit onto the field.

"Sonny [Jurgensen] said, 'What the hell are you doing?'" Huff said. "I said, 'We need to practice. This is professional football, and we need to keep our kicker happy.'"

And so the remainder of the 50,439 still at D.C. Stadium on November 27, 1966, saw the highest-scoring NFL game ever finish with Charlie Gogolak kicking a 29-yarder.

Huff knew it was his revenge. So did his teammates and the Giants. But Huff can still say it was for the kicker's sake with a deadpan expression.

"I said, 'We need to kick a field goal,'" said Huff 47 years later. "'You see Allie Sherman? He talked Wellington Mara into trading me, so we have to kick a field goal and kick his ass. Amen.'

"The Giants knew what I was doing. They took it personally. I told them I'm going to get Allie Sherman fired. Allie Sherman never liked me. When we practiced, I knocked the hell out of his offensive players."

Ironically, Huff nearly didn't come to Washington after the trade. Only after the Redskins coach went to New York to fetch Huff was the latter convinced to go.

"Bill McPeak came to New York and told me, 'You come with me and you're going to make a lot of money,'" Huff said. "We'll make this thing work. So Carlisle, Pennsylvania, here we come."

It wasn't easy exacting revenge against the Giants. The NFC East rivals split the annual two meetings in 1964–65.

Huff was looking for a knockout victory, and the Giants were vulnerable at 1–8–1 with the only win against the Redskins 13–10. The Redskins were 5–6 with three straight losses, including a 14–3 loss at Cleveland the previous week.

The Redskins jumped ahead 14–0 in the first quarter on A.D. Whitfield's five-yard touchdown catch and 63-yard scoring run. Ironically, Gogolak missed the first extra point before hitting nine straight.

Rookie safety Brig Owens returned a 62-yard fumble for a 20–0 lead before the Giants finally scored. Whitfield and Joe Don Looney then ran for touchdowns en route to a 34–14 halftime lead.

Jurgensen was only 4-of-9 at halftime but soon threw touchdowns of 74 and 32 yards to Charley Taylor. Bobby Mitchell returned to halfback for the first time since being traded to Washington five years earlier to score on a 45-yarder on his second carry. Owens added a 60-yard interception for a score. Rickie Harris returned a punt 52 yards for a touchdown.

Amazingly, the Redskins were outgained by the Giants 389–341 in overall yards, 278–132 passing yards, and first downs 25–16. It was the Washington defense's five interceptions that led to 28 points.

But the stats didn't matter to Huff. Revenge comes in many forms. His came between the uprights.

42 The Basketball Team

The Redskins wanted a real game, not some All-Star approach where everybody took uncontested shots and the crowd enjoyed high scoring.

No problem, said Johnny Holliday. His Radio Oneders were pretty good, and the Redskins might be overmatched in this charity basketball game, he warned Redskins coach Morgan Wootten.

"Morgan said, 'These guys want to play serious,'" Holliday recalled. "I said, 'Let me tell you now coach, you're not going to win if you play serious. We have a pretty good team.' Morgan said, 'Can we play serious for one quarter?' I think we were up by 20, and after that we had a good time."

Long before NFL contracts limited off-season sports because of potential injury and even the days of off-season camps and conditioning, Redskins players used charity basketball games in the 1970s and 1980s to raise money for local schools and to stay in shape.

Some years the team fielded its own squad coached by Wootten, a legendary DeMatha High coach who would win five national prep titles and was inducted into the Naismith Memorial Basketball Hall of Fame. Other years, players would join Holliday's team, which was filled with various pro and college athletes.

It was all in good fun. School faculties played the Redskins with ticket sales going to the school's athletic fund. Players received $25 per game for gas but usually donated it to Children's Hospital at season's end. It was all about having fun, getting some exercise, and raising money.

And there were plenty of packed houses. More than 5,000 people crammed Walt Whitman High. Overflowing crowds were commonplace.

Holliday first came up with the idea in Cleveland as a young disc jockey. The radio personnel included Cleveland Browns cornerback Bernie Parrish, who was an off-season salesman. In New York, Holliday added singer Tony Orlando (but not Dawn) to the lineup. In San Francisco, Holliday included Oakland A's slugger Sal Bando and Golden State Warrior Rick Barry. They were 59–1 with the only loss when Barry missed the game.

After arriving in Washington in 1969, Holliday created the WWDC Radio Oneders. Washington Senators Dick Bosman and Denny McClain were bigger stars than the Redskins back then. But the football team embraced the game, and Redskins Bill Brundidge, Ray Schoenke, Eddie Brown, Ken Stone, Brig Owens, and Terry Metcalf joined. When Holliday switched to WMAL, Joe Theismann, Art Monk, Mark Murphy, and Mark Moseley played.

"Metcalf, Owens, and Monk were good," said Holliday, "but Theismann was the best because he was an All-American high school player. He scored 71 points one game playing against coaches who were pretty good. Murphy, Eddie Brown, and Ken Stone were terrific.

"Brundidge and Jacoby were rebounders, Moseley was a rebounder. [Senators] Hank Allen and Tommy Brown, who played first base and also was a Green Bay Packers defensive back, played. Brown was ambidextrous and shot fouls with each hand."

Indeed, players enjoyed playing so much there was competition to be on the team.

"There were guys waiting to play," Holliday said. "Theismann was a holder and special teams then and wanted to play. Somebody got traded and Theismann played.

"We'd get together after the game. All the guys would come with their wives. Joe Gibbs saw them play once at Robinson high school. He said, 'You guys have a pretty good team. I can't tell you how nice it is to see you guys in the community raising money. I hope nobody gets hurt.'"

The only injury Holliday remembered was Theismann twisting an ankle at St. Albans School before he became a starting quarterback.

Wootten said there were no strategy sessions and no practices when he coached the team.

"We did say have fun," he said. "They just want to see you run up and down the floor. We had a ball."

Occasionally, some young faculty member wanted to create a reputation before his students and would hard foul a Redskin. It didn't take long before players showed teachers who the athletes were.

"One of the faculty knocked down one of the Redskins," Wootten said. "I told them no bad things."

The Radio Oneders ended in 1987, while the Redskins squad ended years earlier. But Holliday's teams in four cities raised more than $2 million for schools while giving fans much to remember.

43 Lambeau, as in Lambeau Field

Redskins coach Earl "Curly" Lambeau was fired for a beer that wasn't even his. Well, that and shoving the owner against a wall.

That's Lambeau, as in Lambeau Field. The frozen tundra. Yet long before Vince Lombardi followed Lambeau as coach of the Green Bay Packers and Washington Redskins, the latter was finishing his famed career with three teams in five years.

And Lambeau did not go easy into the night.

Lambeau started playing for Notre Dame under legendary Coach Knute Rockne and behind fabled fullback George Gipp, better known as "The Gipper." A tonsillectomy led to Lambeau leaving school and taking a job at a meat packing plant in his hometown of Green Bay, Wisconsin.

In 1919, Lambeau convinced his employer to field a team, calling it the Indian Packers. Three years later, new owners Acme Packing Co. funded the team's entry into the American

Coaching staff for the 1953 Washington Redskins, from left to right: Larry Siemering, line coach, from College of Pacific; Bill Dudley, backfield coach; Earl "Curly" Lambeau, head coach; Herman Ball, assistant coach; and Wayne Millner, assistant coach and scout, looking over the Redskins as they workout on the Occidental College field on July 26, 1953, in preparation for their charity game on August 19 with the Los Angeles Rams. (AP Photo/David F. Smith)

Professional Football Association that later became the National Football League.

Well, you know the rest. Lambeau went on to win six titles and go 209–104–21 over 29 years in Green Bay. But a dispute with the executive committee operating the team since 1923 led to Lambeau resigning after 1949.

Lambeau was looking for a job for the first time in his life and opted to coach the Chicago Cardinals in 1950–51. Things didn't go too well there. Lambeau had trouble adjusting to the new wing T formations. The Cardinals were 5–7 and 2–8 before Lambeau was forced to resign again.

The *Toledo Blade* reported Lambeau was taking "the league's hottest coaching spot—the head man's job with the Washington Redskins" in August 1952. Owner George Preston Marshall had a reputation for firing coaches, having just made Dick Todd the sixth coach in 14 years after Todd lost two straight preseason games.

Marshall didn't pretend to be hard to work for, telling the *Blade*, "I am cold blooded when it comes to the Redskins. I owe it to the Washington fans to give them a winner. It's up to the coach to produce. If he doesn't, I get another."

Boy, does this sound familiar.

Lambeau was set to earn $15,000 per season with a bonus if the team did well. Despite saying Washington was "a very fine ball club" and planning no major changes, Lambeau probably didn't cash that bonus. The Redskins were 4–8 in 1952, during quarterback Sammy Baugh's final season, and 6–5–1 in 1953.

The breaking point came during the 1954 preseason. After losing 30–7 to the 49ers in a preseason game in Sacramento, linebacker Don Paul and receiver Hugh "Bones" Taylor wandered into the Senator Hotel bar with coaches already inside. NFL rules allowed a $100 fine to players found in bars, and Marshall soon heard about the incident. One report said Marshall confronted

Taylor over a brown bag under his arm, which was believed to contain beer.

Marshall ordered Lambeau to fine the players. The coach didn't see the big deal given that some players lost 10 lbs. of fluid during the hot game. In his book, *Hail Victory: An Oral History of the Washington Redskins*, author Thom Loverro quoted Gene Pepper who recalled the incident.

"Curly said, 'George, it's no problem. We lost a lot of weight out there today. It was hot. Let them drink a beer,'" Pepper said. "But George raised hell, and Curly wasn't about to take that."

Sure enough, the argument escalated into Lambeau putting Marshall against the lobby wall saying he wouldn't take any more guff from the owner. Ten minutes later, Marshall fired the coach and hired Joe Kuharich, a former coach of the University of San Francisco and Chicago Cardinals.

Lambeau never coached again, although he later made a failed bid to regain his Green Bay job. Instead it went to Lombardi. Lambeau was a charter member of the Pro Football Hall of Fame's 1963 inaugural class.

After his 1965 death when he suffered a heart attack while showing a neighbor how to do the popular dance "The Twist," Green Bay renamed City Stadium in Lambeau's honor. On one side of the stadium is a statue of Lombardi; on the other side is one of Lambeau.

After all, anyone who put Marshall against the wall and threatened to punch him deserves a statue.

44 Unwanted Marshall Memorial

George Preston Marshall remains an unwelcome guest at his old home.

A 10' Missouri rose marble memorial to the Redskins founder and longtime owner sits by the entrance to RFK Stadium along a popular walkway used by fans arriving by metro. It has sat there since 1969, shortly after the owner's death. Nearby are memorials to the stadium's namesake, Robert F. Kennedy, who forced Marshall to integrate the team, and Senators baseball owner Clark Calvin Griffith.

Stadium leaders wanted the memorial moved in 2001 so a lucrative concessions stand could tempt passing fans. Everything seemed to be worked out. Marshall's hometown of Romney West Virginia, or nearby Grafton agreed to accept the memorial. Everyone was happy.

And then the bill came. It would cost at least $20,000 to relocate the memorial, and nobody wanted to pay it—neither RFK, District leaders, Grafton and Romney politicians, Redskins nor the George Preston Marshall Foundation would put up the necessary funds.

And so it remains on the corner of RFK.

Now, memorials are relocated all the time. Years pass and people forget who was being immortalized. There are more than 3,150 statues, monuments, and memorials in the nation's capital, and markers are occasionally moved.

Why, even the statue of the town's 1870 territorial governor "Boss" Shepherd spent three decades at the city's car impound lot by the Anacostia River before it was returned to City Hall where it quietly stands to the side of the front entrance. And Shepherd kept the federal government from leaving town by upgrading streets, sewers, and street lights even though it meant bankrupting the city and his leaving in disgrace.

Marshall's fate is strange given he brought the town's favorite sports franchise to town from Boston. Yet the Redskins declined RFK's offer to take the memorial to FedEx Field when they moved in 1997. The team never gave an explanation, but owner Dan Snyder even removed Marshall's name on a FedEx concourse after buying the team in 1999.

City leaders don't want Marshall's statue moved downtown because he was a racist. With African Americans serving as mayor since the city was awarded home rule in 1974, the thought of relocating a memorial to someone who refused to sign black players until forced by the federal government in 1961 is unthinkable. City leaders wish the memorial would leave for West Virginia but they suffer leaving it at RFK rather than pay the relocation costs.

Grafton leaders had a place picked out for the memorial, but it was nothing fancy. Romney officials would have placed it in the cemetery when Marshall lies.

It seems the memorial with Marshall's bronze image gazing from the top will probably stay at RFK until the stadium is demolished. And that's no time soon. RFK currently hosts DC United soccer games, college football bowls, and occasional events. It's an aged facility, the first of the cookie-cutter stadiums in the nation when it opened in 1961 at the inflated price of $24 million—triple its budget.

Maybe RFK is nothing special anymore as far as its amenities, but the city is wary of closing it until the Redskins choose their next stadium site for 2027. The biggest hope city leaders have of the team returning from Maryland is the RFK venue, despite the fact that it is too small to handle a larger modern stadium.

Still, officials are willing to wait and see. RFK gives the city options for large events that don't fit into nearby Nationals Park.

If the Redskins don't return, the site will likely be commercially developed. Nearby residents want big-box department stores like Costco or Best Buy on the site plus other retail options. Indeed, the city's eastern edge has been long ignored.

What happens to Marshall's memorial whenever bulldozers claim RFK? The memorial would fall to city leaders and most likely moved to a city storage lot where other monuments have spent decades in obscurity. Politicians will just hope everyone quietly forgets about it. Sadly, that happens.

But then, who knows? Maybe someone with deep pockets will realize a monument to the Redskins owner, despite his flaws, deserves a better fate than mothballs and pays to move it to West Virginia.

It's an interesting remembrance for someone who was once so prominent in Washington.

45 Redskins Cheerleaders

Owner George Preston Marshall knew attracting fans required more than winning games. Indeed, that was a bonus.

No, filling the stands was about putting on a good show. Entertaining the crowd. Giving fans something to cheer between plays.

So Marshall created the Washington Redskins cheerleaders in 1962. The NFL's longest-running cheerleaders have evolved from wearing "squaw" outfits to modeling in calendars, but it has always been about promoting good will no matter how they looked.

"Everything changes," said Terri Crane-Lamb, a Redskins cheerleader from 1979 to 1983 who now serves as president of the

Redskins Cheerleaders Alumni Association. "Just because the girls are dancing differently now doesn't mean the ladies in the past weren't professional. It's just a different style of dancing. It's just a different style, a different era."

Called the Redskinettes until 1998, and still referred to that way by older fans, the First Ladies of Football will welcome their 1,000th member in the coming decade. Hundreds of young women often compete for perhaps 10 openings annually, though technically all members are employed on a year-to-year basis and must reapply.

"It's hard to compare an athlete fairly among different eras. Every year they get bigger, strong, faster," Crane-Lamb said. "It's the same with the cheerleaders. It was very competitive [over the decades]. It still is."

The first squad of 30 wore outfits resembling American Indian women with a headband and feather, a dark wig with braids, and buckskin dresses. One version was dropped in 1968, the second ended four years later after the Super Bowl loss.

The outfits have largely reflected contemporary fashion over the years. The 1970s outfits sported plunging necklines and showed more skin until 1978 when Coach Jack Pardee reportedly ordered that midriffs could no longer be exposed after the season opener.

It was only delaying the inevitable. You can't stop white go-go boots and Farrah Fawcett hairstyles after years of Marsha Brady looks.

The team's 1982–83 suede uniforms, also worn for Super Bowls XVII and XVIII, were designed by Toni Leonard, sister-in-law of boxer Sugar Ray Leonard. One of the favorites over the years, those uniforms have influenced the team's current apparel.

Pop star Madonna influenced the mid-1980s look, which included a one-piece burgundy body suit with the singer's short white boots. After the 1988 Super Bowl, the cheerleaders switched to a tank uniform seen more often by Olympic ice skaters.

The mid-1990s saw those go-go boots traded for dance shoes, leg warmers and a "swashbuckling" look complete with puffy sleeves. By 1998, the bare midriff look returned (nobody tell Pardee) with a two-piece outfit that is the basis for today's uniforms.

Go-go boots were back in 2000 along with halter tops, leather shorts, bolero jackets, and 300 rhinestones per outfit. The current uniforms now include 800 crystals.

Games aren't the only performances by the cheerleaders, which is one reason why the team has expanded to about 40 members annually. The team did USO tours in the early 1980s before switching to Department of Defense tours in 1998. The women now perform around the globe; the name was changed to the Washington Redskins cheerleaders in 1998 to avoid confusion abroad.

Former New York Giants defensive end Michael Strahan once called the Redskin cheerleaders "the hottest in the NFL" among the 28 teams that had cheerleaders. The Giants along with Detroit, Pittsburgh, and Green Bay still don't have cheerleaders, although Pittsburgh was the first to have cheerleaders before disbanding. *Men's Journal* named the 2007 group the NFL's best cheerleaders. Past members include former 2007 Miss Maryland Michaé Holloman and 2012 Miss District of Columbia Monique Thompkins.

But Strahan's revelation was no surprise to Redskins fans. The cheerleaders have been regularly featured in national media ranging from *Newsweek* and *Cosmpolitan* to *Sports Illustrated* and *Maxim*. Even late night TV host David Letterman created a Top 10 list for them.

The cheerleaders have performed in 35 countries from China and Japan to Afghanistan, Turkey, and Spain. They've also performed alongside musicians like James Brown, Jerry Lee Lewis, Ricky Martin, and K.C. and the Sunshine Band.

Tryouts begin each April. Applicants must be at least 18 years old, but there are no upper age limits or height/weight restrictions. However, tattoos and body piercings aren't allowed.

46 The Richard Nixon Play

Nothing is ever simple when analyzing Richard Nixon.

Did the U.S. president really do it? Was there a deception that failed? He was called Tricky Dick, after all. Was Nixon even responsible?

Forget Watergate—I'm talking about the alleged Richard Nixon–designed play that lost 13 yards in a 1971 playoff game against San Francisco.

Some people swear Nixon giving Allen a play is true. Others say it's not. They're all credible people who were close to the situation.

The truth always lies somewhere in between. (Or the truth is always lies.)

Allen's daughter, Jennifer, penned an insightful essay for ESPN on the two men's relationship. Nixon and Allen met in 1951 during an NCAA banquet in New York City where the latter was honored for a championship season at Whittier College and Congressman Nixon was the guest speaker. Given Nixon was a Whittier alum, he also met Allen privately.

In the 1960s Allen coached the Los Angeles Rams, and Nixon, a native Californian, sat on the home side. When Allen took over Washington in 1971, Nixon was seeking his second term as U.S. President. He was a big Redskins fan, even watching blacked-out games by traveling to Camp David.

It's often said that the president and the Redskins quarterback are the two most important people in the nation's capital. It's no surprise Nixon backed his old friend.

"I am betting on the Redskins for the championship in either 1971 or 1972," Nixon said.

After two straight losses during the 1971 midseason, Allen asked Nixon to come to Redskins Park for a pep talk. About 20 miles away in suburban Virginia, Nixon flew on a helicopter to the facility's practice fields where he met the team. Ever the politician, Nixon knew many of the players' names, colleges, and statistical rankings.

During practice, Allen asked Nixon for a play. After all, the two talked many times on the telephone about football. Nixon chose a reverse that succeeded.

This is where things get interesting. While prepping for San Francisco in the team's first playoff game since 1945, Nixon called Allen, who handed the phone to quarterback Billy Kilmer. Nixon suggested another reverse play.

Leading 10–3 and nearing halftime, the Redskins ran a reverse with receiver Roy Jefferson that lost 13 yards. A subsequent field goal was blocked, and the Redskins lost 24–20.

When asked if the play was Nixon's during the postgame press conference, Allen joked that it was. Allen wasn't serious, but some reporters believed him and the legend grew.

Marv Levy, then a special teams coach under Allen in Washington before later leading Buffalo to four straight AFC Championships, told the *Syracuse Post-Standard* in 1994 that the whole thing was a joke. Allen gave the play to Nixon, who then told Kilmer.

"[George] wanted the president to look very sage," Levy told the *Post-Standard*. "Afterward, I remember chuckling among ourselves about it. George gave the play to the president, then it didn't work."

Allen and Nixon were good friends. Nixon even wanted to throw a White House dinner in Allen's honor only to be rejected by the coach because he didn't want to be distracted from trying to win the next week's game. Allen did attend off-season dinners, however.

Allen wanted Nixon to look good. The election was coming up, after all. Allen felt the play would succeed and Nixon would look the genius. Unfortunately, the whole thing went badly.

"If George Allen doesn't accept any more plays from Richard Nixon," columnist Art Buchwald wrote, "he may go down in history as one of pro football's greatest coaches."

But mostly, Nixon's involvement in the Redskins loss was quickly forgotten. Six months later, there was a break-in at the Democratic National Headquarters at the Watergate Hotel. In 1972, Nixon was accused of being involved. Another year passed and he declared, "I'm not a crook." And by 1974, Nixon was forced to resign the presidency.

The Redskins went on to the Super Bowl in January 1973 and had a pretty good run under Allen before he was fired after 1977. Given all the bad things that happened to Nixon and all the good things that happened to Allen, the "Nixon play" was quickly forgotten.

But it's a pretty good story—even if it may not be true.

47 Redskins and World War II

Nearly 1,000 NFL players and personnel fought in World War II. Twenty-three died.

Two were once Washington Redskins.

Major Keith Birlem, a Washington end in 1939, died while attempting to land a bomber in 1943 after taking enemy fire.

Lieutenant Eddie Kahn, a guard in Boston and Washington from 1935 to 1937, died from wounds suffered in the 1944 invasion of Leyte in the Philippines.

The NFL has a long history of players serving during wartime, although few have served since the Korean War ended in 1953. The late Arizona safety Pat Tillman was killed in 2004 in Afghanistan, the first NFL player to die serving since Buffalo offensive lineman Bob Kalsu in 1970.

Birlem and Kahn were part of the American wave of professional athletes that just wanted to do their part to keep the world free. Indeed, the 995 players who served during World War II dwarfs any other military action. More than 200 served in the Korean War, including Pro Football Hall of Famer Dick "Night Train" Lane. Only 28 players served in the Vietnam War, including Hall of Famer Roger Staubach, a U.S. Naval Academy graduate.

But World War II saw six NFL team owners such as George Halas and Wellington Mara serve alongside Hall of Famers Chuck Bednarik and Otto Graham. Future Dallas coach Tom Landry flew B-17 bombers, even surviving a crash. Redskins coach Ray Flaherty left the team to serve in the navy, while his players Cliff Battles and Wayne Milner also joined. Future NFL commissioner Pete Rozelle also served.

Born in San Jose, California, in 1915, Birlem played quarterback for his hometown San Jose State University where he was inducted into their sports hall of fame for football and swimming. Birlem was a blocking halfback for the Chicago Cardinals (six games) before being traded to the Redskins for the final three games in 1939. He caught two passes for 17 yards for Chicago.

Birlem decided to join the military in 1940. He wanted to fly planes but failed several eye tests before learning that the chlorine from swimming pools irritated his eyes.

As brief as his NFL career was, Birlem spent even less time in the war. Indeed, he was killed three days after his first mission.

After nearly three years of training, Birlem's debut came on May 4, 1943, as a co-pilot of the Vicious Virgin in the 427th Bomber Squadron as part of the 303rd Bombardment Group. It was his 28th birthday. A report on Combat Mission 33 stated that 27 crews targeted General Motors and Ford Motor Co. plants in Antwerp, Belgium,which was controlled by Germany.

Bombers dropped 52½ tons of 1,000-lb. general purpose bombs at 23,500' during the 4½-hour mission. Nearly 22,000 rounds were also fired with five enemy planes destroyed. Filming the mission was Hollywood star Clark Gable, who manned the radio room gun while later turning the footage into *Combat America*.

The enemy made eight runs at the bomber group. In the report Birlem said, "I never thought those Germans would come so close. I was riding co-pilot to Captain Eddie Broussard, and one FW-190 came right at us. If Captain Broussard hadn't pulled up the nose, he would have hit us head on."

Unfortunately, there's no detailed report on the mission that killed Birlem. Some reports say he was shot down over Germany, while others that he was trying to land the flying fortress at his base in Polebrook, England.

"King Kong" Kahn played 24 games over three years with the Redskins. The University of North Carolina guard led the Tar Heels to 7–1–1 in 1934 as an All-Southern Conference honorable mention. Kahn was second team All-NFL in 1936 and retired after the Redskins won the 1937 championship.

A First Lieutenant in the Marines, Kahn died on February 17, 1945, from wounds suffered in the invasion of Leyte. Led by General Douglas MacArthur, U.S. forces fought nine weeks in late 1944 to liberate the island after three years of Japanese occupation.

It was a decisive victory for the U.S. despite 15,584 casualties, including 3,504 in action. The Japanese lost 49,000 combat troops, 26 major warships, and 46 large transports.

48 No Return to RFK

Washington Redskins fans weren't too upset when the team left RFK Stadium for suburban Maryland. The team would be back one day, fans figured.

They figured wrong.

When a new stadium is needed in 2027 after 30 seasons in Landover, Maryland, the best guess is that the Redskins will likely slide down the beltway near the Wilson Bridge for a new venue. The team will stay in Prince George's County for another generation.

The National Harbor Redskins?

The city has several obstacles to regaining the team. The biggest is there is no readily available site. When late owner Jack Kent Cooke considered sites over a decade, they were the RFK parking lot, New York Avenue, and South Capitol Street. New York Avenue was developed, while a baseball stadium sits on South Capitol Street. The RFK site proved too politically hot to gain.

Basically, the city has run out of room for another stadium.

So it seems RFK is the only choice. The problems are several fold, however. First, the existing stadium footprint is too small for a modern stadium. The old 55,000-seat RFK couldn't be expanded to at least 75,000 seats without moving two nearby bridges, and that would be too costly.

But even worse are the political games that would need to be played with Capitol Hill lawmakers. The federal lawmakers forced the Redskins to desegregate in 1962 if they wanted to use the stadium, which sits on federal land. If the Redskins are still using their nickname, lawmakers will demand the team change it if they want to use the land again.

Meanwhile, the surrounding neighborhood has long opposed a new Redskins facility. They want big-box stores for daily use, not a venue used 10 times annually. While much can change over the next decade, a new stadium isn't a political slam dunk.

This leaves the Redskins with Virginia and Maryland as options. Snyder did some long-range goodwill grabbing with Virginia lawmakers by moving training camp to Richmond in 2013. It was more to get money to fix up an aging practice facility, but having the team in the state capital for three weeks annually will help should lawmakers need to vote on a billion-dollar facility on its Washington border.

That is, if the Redskins can find land for a stadium. The Potomac Yards site, which once housed a stadium press conference that later failed to gain political support, is now developed. Indeed, it's amid a second wave of development. Maybe Virginia can find an alternate site, but the region's heavy density and traffic make it unlikely.

That leaves Maryland, which has both the land and friendly politicians to keep the team.

The current Landover site reverts to county ownership in 2027 as part of the original stadium deal. Who knows why Cooke did that. He certainly knew it wouldn't be his problem by then. Indeed, he died five months before FedEx Field opened.

The Redskins could stay, but it wouldn't be nearly as lucrative for the team. Snyder will want a new venue with all the perks for rich folks. FedEx was built in an American stadium record 22 months. Cooke even tied up all the local concrete companies to ensure his supply over Verizon Center and the Baltimore Ravens stadium being built concurrently. But it's functional at best and not much to look at, so Snyder will want a smaller, more modern stadium.

The Maryland Stadium Authority will be an eager partner barring a major national economic downturn. State and local leaders aren't calling for a name change, either.

All roads lead to Oxon Hill near the Wilson Bridge and National Harbor complex that borders Washington and Virginia. It's actually closer to the city line than Landover.

The one barrier is no metro station. But subway lanes were built into the Wilson Bridge, so connecting a rail station to nearby Eisenhower Avenue in Alexandria, Virginia, is more than possible. Fans will enjoy this site more than the remote Landover.

Snyder needs five years minimum to create a new stadium, so 13 years away really isn't that far. Certainly there will be headlines of talks by city leaders, but it's really just political posturing. They'll still be the Washington Redskins, but they'll be playing in Maryland.

49 Turk Brothers Were Fun

They were loud and they were pranksters, sometimes disliked by teammates, team officials, and even the owner.

And they didn't care.

The Turk brothers—Dan and Matt—were a lot of fun.

Predecessor Joe Don Looney was legendary for his wild stunts, but there was only one of him. When Dan joined Matt with the Redskins in 1997, they were inseparable and sometimes double trouble.

Dan was a former Oakland Raider and loved the outlaw image. A 1985 fourth-rounder by Pittsburgh, he went to Tampa Bay (1987–88) and Los Angeles/Oakland Raiders (1989–96) before opting for a chance to play with his little brother. Dan was six years older, so the two brothers never played on the same team growing up in Milwaukee, Wisconsin.

Center Dan Turk poses for his 1998 team headshot. (AP Photo/NFL Photos/Ben Liebenberg)

Dan was a deep snapper while Matt punted, so it was a perfect partnership to spending time together. They were also the NFL's first brother punter-snapper combo.

Matt landed with the Redskins in 1995 following off-seasons with Green Bay and St. Louis. After five years in Washington, he would later play with five teams, including Miami and Houston twice, through 2011.

"Danny" and "Matty," as they called each other, were pretty independent of the rest of the locker room. They frankly didn't care if their pranks and boisterous behavior were sometimes unwelcome. They were having fun.

Perhaps the most amazing story was Dan becoming Matt's agent in 1999 after three straight Pro Bowls by the latter. Dan convinced Matt to hold out of training camp while the elder brother practiced. It was just so weird for the "agent" to work out in Frostburg while telling his brother to stay away. Dan even met with reporters after practices to give them updates on negotiations—much to the dismay of general manager Charley Casserly. Matt eventually squeezed out a better deal and reported to camp.

The Redskins once decided to take the train to Philadelphia instead of flying, opting for a nostalgic feel. The Turks rode together to Union Station in Dan's truck, but the oversized vehicle became wedged in the parking garage. Rushing to make the train, the two called a third brother, who was staying with Matt, to get the truck while they headed to Philadelphia.

Dan loved being an entrepreneur and created a "Dog Depot" hot dog stand outside a Lowe's near Redskins Park in 1999. Being from Milwaukee, Dan loved a good sausage on the grill. Soon Tuesdays meant celebrity helpers as diners watched Gus Frerotte clean tables, thinking that guy sure looked like the Redskins quarterback.

Dan's career ended badly on a one-hop snap that holder Brad Johnson couldn't get down for the potential winning 51-yard field

The Old Man

Nobody played Redskins football like cornerback Darrell Green. Nobody has even come close.

Green played 20 seasons and 295 games for the Redskins. That's 80 games more than runner-up linebacker Monte Coleman, who served 16 years and played 215 games. Art Monk ranks third at 205, followed by Len Hauss (196), Don Warren (193), Chris Hanburger (187), Jeff Bostic (184), Mark Moseley (182), Mike Bragg (172), and Joe Jacoby (170).

Hauss played the most consecutive games with 196, followed by Moseley's 170 and Joe Theismann's 163.

Jacoby is the postseason leader with 21 games, followed by Warren's 19 and 18 each by Green and Bostic.

Gibb is the postseason leader among coaches with 24 games.

goal in a playoff game at Tampa Bay in January 2000. Turk left the locker room in a trance, saying only that he couldn't believe it happened.

Dan later told the *Washington Times*, "The ball just squirted out of my hands. No excuses. I get paid to put that ball in Brad Johnson's hands, and I didn't do it.

"I'm human. I have to accept that. Humans make mistakes. I didn't want to make a bad snap, but I did. I had a perfect chance to make a perfect snap, and I didn't.

"If I'm the scapegoat, I accept that. That's kind of the way it's been since I've been here. They always look for someone to blame. You know what? Blame me. I don't care. I just feel bad for the 50 guys I let down."

Dan didn't make it to the team plane. He got off the bus and walked all night through the streets of Tampa. Owner Dan Snyder, already upset with the Turks after once accusing Matt of suffering a finger injury in a pickup basketball game, later declared he cut Dan. In fact, Dan's contract expired and wasn't renewed.

But the story grew more tragic. Weeks after the game, Dan was diagnosed with testicular cancer. During his final months, Dan traveled to Miami to see Matt punt for his new team. Matt has been traded by Washington two months following the playoff loss.

Dan died on December 24, 2000, at age 38, less than one year after his errant snap.

Dan's widow claimed the Redskins didn't care about her husband and that no one ever came to see him during his illness. That's just not true. Two trainers and a team official tried. So did several teammates.

So forgive Dan Turk for his mistake. He was a good guy. Hopefully, Dan rests in peace.

50 George Allen and Jhoon Rhee

George Allen once offered to fight Dallas coach Tom Landry at midfield for the game's outcome, but the only time Allen actually threw a punch came in the Redskins locker room.

Allen was studying karate with Jhoon Rhee, who was well-known for his commercials that starred his own kids saying, "Nobody bothers me…. Nobody bothers me, either (wink)."

Those commercials were classics. They're on YouTube if you want a chuckle. Many older Washingtonians can still sing the jingle: "If you take Jhoon Rhee self-defense then you too can say, 'Nobody bothers me…. Nobody bothers me…. Call USA-1000. Jhoon Rhee means might for right."

Well, Rhee was very successful, running a chain of studios, and Allen studied under the master. After taking lessons, Allen wanted to show his players how tough he was.

Allen assembled his players in the locker room one day before playing St. Louis. Out came Rhee with two boards in his hand, and Allen took aim.

"George reached back and whack—he didn't break the boards. He broke his hand," kicker Mark Moseley said. "But instead of

Redskins head coach George Allen in 1972. (AP Photo)

stopping, he reached back again and broke those boards with a broken hand.

"Some guys thought he was nuts, but most of us understood how emotionally into it he was."

If Lombardi said, "Winning isn't everything—it's the only thing," which was earlier attributed to UCLA coach Red Sanders in 1950, Allen was one step ahead with "The Future is Now."

Equipment manager Tommy McVean, who worked under five coaches before leaving with Allen in 1977, said the latter shared the same intensity as predecessor Vince Lombardi in 1969.

"Allen had the same discipline and mindset as Lombardi," McVean said. "Plan, perfection—don't make mistakes. Players looked forward to games because they were fun and they knew more about the other team than they knew themselves."

Indeed, Allen focused so much on football that he was in several car accidents before team president Edward Bennett Williams hired a driver for his coach.

"They had to take his car away from him because he'd get into so many wrecks," Moseley said. "George would drive to work and try to study defense and figure out what was going on and not pay attention to driving.

"George was a fanatic, but his was true fanaticism. He would be like the greatest fan in Washington. Football was his life, and winning was the only thing. There was no discussion of losing. If you're afraid of failing, you shouldn't be in the ballgame. Allen never ever thought of failing. He was a great motivator. He was like Joe Gibbs—you wanted to die for him because you respected him so much."

Moseley's first encounter with Allen was on the track, ringing the practice field at Carlisle, Pennsylvania, before the 1974 training camp. Allen said he remembered Moseley kicking two field goals against Washington in 1971 for Houston, so the kicker was signed over the off-season.

"George said, 'I'll always have a good defense. All I need is a kicker who can make a field goal at RFK in bad weather. I think you can do it. All you have to do is beat out the other 12 kickers in camp.' [So] I went out and made 16 in a row in preseason."

Allen was superstitious. After a preseason winning streak, Allen told a staffer to bring the bottled water tank from Carlisle to Redskins Park when camp broke. And he wanted it refilled with water from Carlisle regularly.

Allen's house was made of gold-colored bricks with mortar that was mixed with burgundy paint to reflect the team's colors. The problem was that the first time it rained, the mortar's burgundy ran onto the brick and almost ruined his whole house.

I wonder if Allen would have karate-chopped those bricks?

51 Finding the 1937 Trophy

The Redskins have so many championship trophies it seems they can throw one away.

Well, almost.

The 1937 trophy was nearly tossed aside. Headed to the landfill. Scrapyard City.

Unlike the three grand Vince Lombardi Trophies won under Coach Joe Gibbs—trophies that look like a silver football on a pedestal and jointly shown at major press conferences—the 1937 trophy went missing for decades. It was thought to be lost or misplaced after the death of owner George Preston Marshall in 1969.

By pure chance, the trophy was recovered in 1996 and is now kept at Redskins Park in Ashburn, Virginia.

Public relations director Mike McCall remembered seeing a trophy in a storage room filled with junk in 1990, but he didn't give it much thought. But when RFK Stadium needed to be cleared to make room for the D.C. United Major League Soccer team in 1996, Redskins owner Jack Kent Cooke asked McCall to oversee the stadium's clean-up, just in case something needed attending.

McCall went to the storage room in the concourse, which is just steps from the media dining room. Sure enough, workers were filling cans with old typewriters, mimeograph machines, and a trophy.

"It was a junk pile," McCall said. "I pulled the trophy out. I thought, 'This trophy has to mean something to somebody. Then I saw the 1937 on it, so I brought it back to Redskins Park and called Joe Horrigan, who is the curator of the Pro Football Hall of Fame.

"I thought it would be a replica. It can't be the real one."

Since this happened before cell phones or other instant communication were possible, Horrigan asked a few questions. Was it a loving cup? Could the top be opened?

It turns out that McCall found the real team trophy. Indeed, it's the only complete trophy from the 1930s with others supposedly destroyed or lost.

A gold coating was removed along with years of neglect to reveal a tall silver cup consistent with trophies of that era. A miniature player was reconnected to the cup to complete the original trophy.

"They were going to throw the trophy away," said McCall, still astonished many years later about how close the Redskins were to losing an artifact of a defining year.

But there are trophies, and then there are trophies. There was a general league trophy and a team trophy, which is often confused as a replica. There were no replicas, said Horrigan. The Redskins have a team trophy.

The hardware is also known as the Ed Thorp Memorial Trophy, which was given annually to the league champion from 1934 to 1969 when it was lost forever by the Minnesota Vikings. It was named after Ed Thorp, a referee who died in 1934.

The Thorp was supposed to be held for only one year by each champion, much like Lord Stanley's Cup in the NHL. Teams were given a team trophy to keep. By losing the league trophy, the Vikings are supposedly cursed—and they have lost four championship games since.

Anyway, 1937 was a big year in franchise history. The team moved from Boston to Washington in 1937 when it drafted a quarterback who would become their greatest player ever. The Redskins had lost the title the previous year to Green Bay in their final game as Boston, so they were primed for a big season in 1937.

Sammy Baugh arrived from Texas to lead the new Washington team to the title, beating Chicago 28–21. Baugh would also lead the Redskins to the 1942 crown over those Bears 14–6. Too bad Washington lost the 1940 championship to Chicago by, uh, well, 73–0.

The whereabouts of the 1942 trophy are unknown. Maybe it was already trashed from the storage room before McCall arrived. Perhaps it's in some Redskins collector's personal stash.

After losing the 1943 and '45 championships, the Redskins didn't need to worry about storing trophies for awhile. The team didn't make the playoffs again until 1971. Washington lost the 1972 championship 14–7 to the unbeaten Miami Dolphins.

Of course, the Redskins have three Lombardi Trophies from the 1982, '87, and '91 seasons. They're pretty, but they're not from the Great Depression era.

As much money as Washington owner Dan Snyder has spent trying to win a championship, the Redskins' next trophy surely won't be lost to the ages.

52 Throw a Ball Back

You're watching training-camp practice from a great spot in front of the line, minding your own business, when a pass skips past a receiver and into your hands.

What do you do?

Well, you have to throw it back. It's not a foul ball at a baseball game that you can keep. But here's the catch—what happens next will be something you'll remember for the rest of your life.

Throw a perfect frozen rope to the waiting ball boy, and your friends will remember it forever. They'll slap you on the back for years while the story grows to throwing it across the field and hitting Pierre Garcon in stride while Robert Griffin III gives you a thumbs up and GM Bruce Allen runs over with a signed contract for $1 million—no, $2 million—to join the team as the new backup quarterback.

But bounce it off the ground like some sissy from the chess club and your buddies will taunt you for years. They'll laugh over it at every barbecue while calling you "Jane" and asking your dress size. You'll be lucky if it's not in your obituary.

Hey, that's what buddies do.

So just like basketball players offer advice to those trying to hit a midcourt shot for $1 million, I asked Redskins quarterback Kirk Cousins for tips to those throwing one pass for a lifetime of street cred. Once he realized it was a serious question, the advice flowed.

"Grab the laces, and make sure you finish the throw," Cousins said. "Bring your shoulder through the motion, and throw all the force you can from your body instead of your arm."

It turns out the laces are a big deal, especially for those with small hands. Your throw is only as good as your grip on the ball.

"I always throw with the laces," Cousins said. "Ninety-five percent of us throw with the laces."

And then there are the little nuances, like holding a tennis racket slightly downward instead of straight so the ball doesn't fly high, or gripping a baseball bat higher when trying to get around faster on a fastball. And don't even get started on golf club grips, foot placement, and swing.

Cousins said most people don't stand correctly when tossing back the ball. Think of it more like someone playing darts who stands sideways or an outfielder lining up on a catch to cut a half second off the throw.

"A lot of people don't step open to the target," Cousins said. "You don't want to step to your target but to the left of your target. If I step to the left with the throw, then I'm in line. If I step at the target, I'm closed off."

Oddly, Cousins said don't feel bad if you don't fare well. Even some football players aren't great at it. But you can do it.

"Throwing the ball naturally for most people is doable," he said. "I play catch with teammates, and they can get the ball back to you."

Now let's talk pressure. Cousins sympathizes with anyone trying to impress their buddies. It's nerve-wracking. Now maybe you'll understand the type of pressure quarterbacks endure. Maybe you won't yell at the TV next time, wondering how the quarterback could miss such a simple pass to an open receiver.

"There's a big difference between a 20-yard pass in training camp to a guy standing there," he said, "and a 20-yard pass with 80,000 in front of you and millions watching on television and a linebacker coming at you. It all factors in."

Which is why those who succeed will always be remembered well by fans. People love Sonny Jurgensen even 40 years after his retirement because they can still envision those great throws to Charley Taylor. It also explains why people still laugh at the memories of slapstick throwers who couldn't hit the side of FedEx Field.

Maybe you won't get the big money off one throw, but at least you'll receive a lifetime of applause, which is worth more in the end. Money is spent, but great reputations last a lifetime.

53 Duncan's Bar

Shar Pourdanesh was a little concerned about the 10-minute walk from Frostburg's Main Street to the players' dorm.

It might be dangerous, he said. This from someone whose family fled Iran during the 1979 revolution and later endured daily schoolyard fights while growing up in Los Angeles.

"I said, 'Shar, you're 6'6" and 300 lbs. When the locals see you walking by their house, they'll be the ones scared.'"

Duncan's Bar was as far as Redskins players ventured from the Frostburg State campus. It was maybe a half-mile away near the bottom of the hill but a million miles from the practice fields during training camp.

Unlike Carlisle, Pennsylvania, where the team trained for 34 years, Frostburg was beyond small. In fact, it made Carlisle look like Manhattan. The team agreed to move camp to the western Maryland campus about 10 minutes from Pennsylvania and West Virginia in 1995 in exchange for the state spending $70 million on FedEx Field infrastructure.

The Redskins signed a 10-year deal with the small college in a town thrilled to get any money in the summer while students were away. The Redskins were worth maybe $500,000 each summer in economic impact, but that was plenty for the locals.

It took 20 seconds to drive through the business section if you made the one light. Maybe 2,000 people lived there during summer breaks. It took incoming owner Dan Snyder one camp to decide never to return and break the deal midway through the pact in 2000.

In some respects, Frostburg was ideal for training. There was nobody at practices since the locals were mostly Pittsburgh Steelers fans. Washington was a world away from the mountain community where even 20 minutes to Cumberland felt like a burdensome trek.

The weather was cool, and the final days of practice even brought a crispness to morning workouts in mid-August. Unlike steambath summers in Carlisle, Redskins Park, and now Richmond, Frostburg's weather was a delight.

But let's be honest—there was nothing to do in town for the almost six weeks of camp. Someone was building a gigantic Noah's Ark off the highway. There was a golf course, but who had time for that? The one movie theater offered well-worn flicks and the saltiest popcorn imaginable.

It was Snoozeville. Nice people, great weather, and boring beyond tears.

Not that idle time plagued players. They received one hour off nightly after meetings from 10:00 PM to 11:00 PM. Anyone returning late to the dorms was fined, though some players threatened interns guarding the door so no one was ratted out.

For that one hour, the Redskins turned to Duncan's Bar. Coaches took a nicer bar on the hill, while the media and players drank at Duncan's.

This was 1995—before Twitter, cell phones, TMZ, and pretty much the Internet, at least in that area. The only way to get any news was to stop by the one drug store each morning to buy Washington newspapers.

Duncan's was like a lot of small-town bars before TVs turned them into sports bars. There was a foosball table, pool table, pinball machine, and dart board amid a no-frills décor of stools, clapboard booths, and wooden floor. A handful of locals nursed beers at the bar.

At least the draft beer was cheap at 75 cents. You gave the bartender the quarter change, and he sincerely appreciated it. Big Jack Beer, a short-lived brew named for late team owner Jack Kent Cooke, was 50 cents.

Players could unwind at Duncan's without fear. Indeed, there was an unwritten rule between media and players—if the cops weren't called, then drink your beer and mind your own business.

Back then, everyone was cool with that. Not that anything nefarious was going on, but players wanted some privacy and I just wanted to drink a beer in peace, too, after a 15-hour day.

Oh, it would get a little wacky sometimes. After teaming with trainer Dan Riley to beat center Cory Raymer and guard Brian Thure in foosball, Thure literally picked up the table and shook it with anger. Beer went everywhere, and Raymer yelled at the rookie for spilling them.

There was only one near-fight between defensive end Dana Stubblefield and receiver Michael Westbrook, and it never came to blows. And there was one incident between a local woman and a player in the parking lot you can read about in the court docket.

Duncan's is the one place everyone still remembers from that little town. It closed in 2012, which is a real shame. But Duncan's was a fun respite for five summers.

54 Cowboy Chicken Club

Well, maybe Dallas Cowboys fans are part chicken after all.

First there was a failed plan to release chickens onto D.C. Stadium's field before the 1961 Redskins-Cowboys game. Then those same Cowboys supporters pulled a second stunt involving chicken banners and two people in costumes throwing eggs onto the field during the 1962 meeting.

Holy Colonel Sanders.

It was an interesting time in Washington. Former Texas Senator Lyndon B. Johnson became vice president in 1961, and a wave of Texans seemed to flood Washington. (Think of them as predecessors of the Texas wave during the two Bush administrations.)

The Cowboys had just been admitted to the NFL in 1960 despite objections by Washington owner George Preston Marshall, who feared he would lose his southern base of fans to Dallas. Marshall later traded his vote to regain rights to the team's song, "Hail to the Redskins," which were purchased as leverage by prospective Dallas owner Clint Murchison. Murchison was still mad over a deal to buy the Redskins and move them to Dallas years earlier, which had failed years earlier when Marshall changed the terms at the last minute.

Those Texans in town wanted revenge for Marshall's acts, so a number of fans slipped inside the stadium before the December 17, 1961, encounter and seeded the field with 10 lbs. of chicken feed. Hours before the game, well-known Washington construction executive Bob Thompson of Texas and three other men stashed two crates of 76 chickens—75 white and one black to symbolize Marshall's boycott of black players—in a dugout that was used for Washington Senators baseball games.

The plan was to unleash the chickens when sled dogs hauled Santa Claus on his sleigh across the field during the halftime show, which would be televised live nationally by CBS. What a sight it would be to see the dogs chasing the chickens, which would be feasting on the feed across the field.

However, an usher heard the chickens and alerted Redskins general manager Dick McCann. When asked what was in the boxes, the prankster said it was ice cream. The problem is that ice cream doesn't make noise.

The Texans offered a $100 bribe to McCann to leave, not knowing he was the GM. They were arrested, and the chickens were hauled away. They were later given to Redskins running back Dick James for scoring four touchdowns that day.

Marshall was furious over the prank and officially complained to NFL commissioner Pete Rozelle, though no sanctions were ever imposed. Instead, the conspirators promised chickens the following year.

Despite changing his number several times, Marshall received late-night phone calls for months where the only sound was a chicken clucking. Only after complaining to Rozelle did the calls stop, although Cowboys officials swore they had no connection to the pranksters.

The Cowboy Chicken Club—led by Tom Webb, Francis "Reds" Bagnell, Irv Davidson, and Thompson—returned before the 1962 meeting in Washington.

Somebody put a large turkey in the bathroom of Marshall's hotel suite. The owner quickly retreated when seeing the bird, saying a mad turkey was dangerous. (It could have been worse. The same crew allegedly got a bear drunk and pushed it into a Chicago hotel elevator before the Cowboys' first Bears game.)

But Thompson, who once led a Tennessee Walking Horse wearing a Cowboys blanket through Duke Zeibert's Washington restaurant, wasn't done. Promising chickens would reach the game after the failed 1961 attempt, four "CHICKENS" banners were unfurled from the stadium's upper decks by hired University of Maryland students. The banners appeared in each end zone and on the 50-yard line on each side of the field.

Thompson then hired two acrobats to wear chicken costumes and rush the field by climbing over the rails from the stands. One was quickly arrested, but the second ran past the band, which was playing the National Anthem, and released a chicken while throwing colored eggs like he was an Easter bunny.

While guards caught him after he tripped over a bench, the chicken bandit slipped away by running to midfield for a quick cartwheel and belly flop before escaping through the stands. The chicken was caught, but his human counterpart remained at large.

The next day's box score of the Cowboys' 38–10 victory appeared in the Dallas news with one interesting note:

Attendance—49,888 (and one chicken).

55 The Greatest Moment?

"I-left, tight wing, 70 chip."

It was the play that framed the greatest era in Washington Redskins history, jumpstarting the Joe Gibbs dynasty and cementing a legend.

John Riggins' touchdown run to take the lead over Miami in Super Bowl XVII was the greatest moment in Redskins history.

It was bigger than Sammy Baugh's 35-yard touchdown pass to Ed Justice in the fourth quarter to win the 1937 championship in the Redskins first season in Washington. It tops Ken Houston's

Running back John Riggins (44) breaks away from Miami Dolphins cornerback Don McNeal on his way to the game-winning touchdown in the fourth quarter of Super Bowl XVII in Pasadena, California, on January 30, 1983. The Redskins beat the Dolphins 27–17. Riggins rushed for 166 yards, a Super Bowl record, and was named Most Valuable Player of the game. (AP Photo)

goal-line tackle of Walt Garrison to save a 14–7 win over Dallas in 1973.

It was superior to Darryl Grant's high-stepping interception for a touchdown that sealed the 1983 NFC Championship over Dallas. And it was even better than Darrell Green's 52-yard punt return for a touchdown to beat Chicago in the 1987 playoffs.

Riggo's moment was supposed to gain merely one yard for the first down. Instead, Riggins went 43 yards for the touchdown. The Redskins now led 20–17 with 10:01 remaining and would win 27–17 for their first of three Super Bowl wins under Gibbs.

The One and Only Riggins

It's not the 43-yard touchdown that won Super Bowl XVII that made John Riggins memorable. It's his hilarious moves off the field that created a legend.

Riggins likes to have fun and is a pretty unassuming guy. If you ever meet him, Riggins absolutely hates people making a fuss over him. I've met dozens of people who drank a beer with Riggo at a bar and came away saying he was the greatest.

So what happened with Supreme Court justice Sandra Day O'Connor at a 1985 Washington Press Club banquet is understandable. Riggins admits to drinking a couple double scotches and several glasses of wine on an empty stomach. Finally, Riggins said to O'Connor at a table of 12, "Come on, Sandy baby—loosen up. You're too uptight."

Riggins then fell asleep under the table for 45 minutes while Vice President George Bush spoke. Oh well. Riggins isn't the first person to fall asleep listening to a politician.

Picking a favorite Riggins quote is almost impossible, but here's one. After missing 1980 in a contract dispute, Riggins told new coach Joe Gibbs, who traveled to the player's Kansas home, "You need to get me back there, and I'll make you famous."

Weeks later, Riggins came to camp saying, "I'm bored, I'm broke, and I'm back."

The play saw tight end Clint Didier in motion to the right, then back to the left to later take out the defender. Riggins gained a clear path between Didier and fullback Otis Wonsley to get the first down when the only free Dolphins defender left—Don McNeal—hit "The Diesel" high at the 41. Riggins outweighed McNeil by 55 lbs. and quickly shed the safety. The sight of McNeal sliding down Riggins became an iconic photo showcased in many Washington homes for decades.

Riggins is probably second only to Sonny Jurgensen as the most beloved Redskin of the past half century and maybe ever. That touchdown run was so emblematic of the power running game that it was deservingly the reason for the team's first championship since 1942. At age 33, Riggins gained 610 yards and scored four touchdowns during the postseason.

But more importantly, it set the tone for 12 great years under Gibbs. It all traced back to that play.

Still, there are many big moments in franchise history. Maybe Baugh's touchdown is No. 2. The Redskins arrived in Washington that season and fans were still learning about this new team, which hadn't drawn well in Boston. There's nothing like a championship to win over Washingtonians, though.

Baugh broke the 21–21 tie in the fourth quarter by finding Justice in full stride at the 17-yard line. Justice went untouched for the score. Who knows what the fate of the Redskins in the nation's capital would have been if they hadn't played so well those first few years?

Houston's tackle is the most memorable regular-season play. It was *mano-a-mano* against Garrison, or simply "The Tackle," as it's remembered.

Houston was ready for the play, having seen it earlier in the game. He even told defensive signal-caller Chris Hanburger to change coverage on the fourth-down play with 24 seconds left.

Intending to intercept the pass, Houston didn't even pick up open Cowboys tight end Jean Fugett. When Dallas quarterback Craig Morton pump-faked, Houston correctly went after Garrison. The two collided at the 4-yard line, and the bigger running back couldn't gain an inch on Houston.

Grant's play is more memorable for his high-stepping dance into the end zone with the 10-yard scoring interception rather than the play itself because it merely sealed the 31–17 victory. It quickly became a footnote when Riggins' touchdown caused the Super Bowl victory.

Still, Grant was a spectacle, a big lineman strutting like a drum major leading the halftime marching band.

Green's return was even more remarkable given the Hall of Fame cornerback didn't return punts. The NFL's Fastest Man and former track star actually tore rib cartilage on the play when hurdling over a would-be tackler just steps into the return before running 52 yards diagonally across the field to score.

It was Green's 50th career punt return but his first in three years. He had two punt returns in the very next game but he never scored on another return.

56 Possible Hall of Famers

Joe Jacoby just missed becoming a 2014 finalist for the Pro Football Hall of Fame. Maybe next year.

Jacoby is probably the next Washington Redskin who will reach the halls of Canton, but the offensive tackle isn't alone. Returner Brian Mitchell is a no-brainer. So is receiver Gary Clark. And one day the Veterans Committee is going to remember running back Larry Brown and kicker Mark Moseley. But special teams are unfairly snubbed, which might hurt Mitchell's and Moseley's chances.

Maybe you think there are others. Quarterback Joe Theismann won a Super Bowl. Ricky Sanders caught a lot of balls. Charles Mann and Dexter Manley were standout defensive ends.

But it comes down to one question—are they the greatest players at their position during their time, or are they just really good ones?

Hall selections are made by 46 writers, one from each NFL market and 14 at-large members with longtime experience covering the NFL. They are criticized every year over the players they leave off, but there is a maximum of five selections so everyone can't make it.

The thought of expanding the voting pool to NFL personnel is ridiculous. The writers come without personal agendas, no matter how much naysayers claim that a player who isn't nice to the media is penalized. Uh, Lawrence Taylor basically told the media to [blank] themselves before the vote, and they still approved him. NFL personnel will push for the induction of their team's players and are biased. It would be a very bad move to change the current format. Writers take this task very seriously.

The Redskins have been to Canton lately with Darrell Green, Art Monk, and Russ Grimm from the Joe Gibbs era, plus Chris Hanburger from the 1970s. All of these players were very worthy, with Monk's induction being long overdue.

Grimm's induction should help the chances of fellow Hogs lineman Jacoby in coming years. They played on three Super Bowl championships together. Jacoby played 170 games over 13 years and was outstanding at both run and pass blocking. At 6'7" and 295 lbs., he was one of the biggest human beings I ever covered.

Was Jacoby one of the top players of his generation? Yes.

Mitchell never gets the proper respect. He was a warrior from 1990 to 2003. With 53 Brian Mitchells, forget about winning a Super Bowl—you could take over a foreign country. He was one of the toughest and smartest players to ever play the game.

Mitchell was technically a running back and gained 1,967 yards while averaging a healthy 5.1 yards per carry. But Mitchell's total game is what makes him special. His 23,330 overall yards are second only to Jerry Rice, one of the game's greats. Mitchell also retired with an NFL-record 13 return touchdowns among 22 league records.

This from a fifth-round pick as a college quarterback who was forced to become a returner and spot running back.

Quarterback Mark Rypien passes under pressure from Philadelphia Eagle Reggie White during first quarter action in a wildcard playoff game on Saturday, January 5, 1991, at Philadelphia Veterans Stadium. Holding off White is Redskins tackle Joe Jacoby. Rypien threw two touchdown passes to lead the Redskins to a 20–6 upset win. (AP Photo/Amy Sancetta)

What really made Mitchell special was his ability to bait opponents on the field. He could take it right up to the edge and get the opponent to throw a punch for 15 yards. Mitchell would just laugh while heading back to the sideline. He was as savvy as they came.

Moseley also suffers from special teams bias. There's only one kicker in Canton—George Blanda—who played 26 years and was the first "fantasy" player ever chosen. It's like voters decided a token was fulfilled and they don't need another. Well, the Redskins sure know how valuable special teams players are when they don't have them.

Moseley made nearly two-thirds of his field goals over 16 years and 300 overall from 1970 to 1986. The NFL's last straight-ahead field goal kicker won the 1982 strike-shortened league MVP award. Ironically, Moseley never even received a trophy or certificate from the NFL for the honor. Now he has been snubbed by hall voters, too.

Clark was overshadowed by Monk, but some felt he was the better receiver. He caught 699 passes for 10,856 yards and 65 touchdowns in 11 years after playing his first two seasons in the USFL where he caught 66 passes for 821 yards and three touchdowns.

Brown's career wasn't long enough for most voters, but he was the best in the game for a few years. Coach Vince Lombardi noticed Brown was slow off the snap and discovered the latter needed a hearing aid. The only sound opponents then heard was a whoosh as he ran to four straight Pro Bowls and the 1972 NFL MVP. Brown finished with 5,875 yards and 35 touchdowns in eight seasons. Maybe the Veterans Committee will appreciate his greatness.

57 Best Trade Ever

Washington's best swap ever wasn't getting Sonny Jurgensen from Philadelphia or all of New Orleans' 1999 selections. It was gaining two first-rounders for a holdout defensive tackle.

Washington sent defensive tackle Sean Gilbert to the Carolina Panthers in 1998 in return for the latter's first-round picks in 1999 and 2000. Those picks led to the Redskins gaining cornerback Champ Bailey, linebacker LaVar Arrington, and running back Clinton Portis.

Who said Charley Casserly couldn't spin a deal?

Casserly even improved the trade by turning down Carolina's initial offer of its 1998 second-rounder and a 1999 first, feeling two first-rounders was always better. By waiting, the second pick gained Arrington, a three-time Pro Bowler.

Washington traded its sixth overall 1996 pick to St. Louis for Gilbert. St. Louis took Lawrence Phillips, who lasted only three seasons with three teams. Gilbert was a solid run defender for Washington but sat out 1997 in a contract dispute when his agent said God wanted the player to hold out for more money. I asked the agent to say that twice.

Ridding themselves of Gilbert was a steal in itself for Washington. That Carolina was willing to sign the franchise player in return for two firsts was staggering. Gilbert played three full seasons then two half seasons for Carolina before spending six games with Oakland in 2003. Overall, he was just an average player.

The Redskins were lucky again in 1999 when that Carolina pick turned out fifth overall. New Orleans coach Mike Ditka wanted running back Ricky Williams so badly he was willing to trade the team's entire draft plus first- and third-rounders in 2000.

The draft opened with Cleveland, Philadelphia, and Cincinnati taking quarterbacks. The wild card was now Indianapolis, which picked running back Edgerrin James. The Redskins gladly sent the fifth choice to New Orleans, knowing the Saints' seventh overall selection would still get Washington who it wanted—Bailey. Sure enough, St. Louis took Torry Holt with the sixth pick, so Washington gained Bailey, which they would have taken fifth overall.

Washington started dealing those extra picks to move up. Ultimately, the Redskins picked up offensive tackle Derek Smith in 1999 and linebacker Lloyd Harrison in 2000 along with Bailey and Arrington. Smith and Harrison did little in Washington; in fact, Smith never played in an NFL game.

But that wasn't the end. After 18 interceptions in five seasons while playing alongside Darrell Green and Deion Sanders, Bailey threatened to hold out if franchised. Washington traded Bailey and a second-rounder to Denver for Portis.

Portis played seven seasons in Washington as one of its more colorful and productive players with three seasons of more than 1,300 yards, including a team-record 1,516 in 2005. He gained 6,824 yards with 176 receptions and 49 total touchdowns with the Redskins.

Washington chose Arrington second overall in 2000. He played six seasons with three Pro Bowls before signing with the New York Giants as a free agent.

Jurgensen gets the nod for second-best trade ever. The Eagles passer and cornerback Jimmy Carr were sent to Washington in 1964 for Redskins quarterback Norm Snead and cornerback Claude Crabb.

Jurgensen played 11 seasons for the Redskins, leading the NFL in passing once, passing yards three times, and completion percentage twice while making four Pro Bowls and one All-Pro as an eventual Pro Football Hall of Fame inductee. Snead made the 1965 Pro Bowl and threw for 3,399 yards in 1967 but broke his leg during the 1968 preseason and threw 21 interceptions in 11 games. He was traded to Minnesota in 1971.

Head to head, Jurgensen went 9–2–2 against Snead.

The third-best trade was Washington sending rights to the 1962 first overall selection, Ernie Davis, to Cleveland for flanker Bobby Mitchell and first-round receiver Leroy Jackson.

Sadly, Davis never played in the NFL and died in 1963 of leukemia. Meanwhile, Mitchell and Jackson were among the Redskins' first black players to end the federal government's bias charges. Jackson was fumble-prone and didn't last long with the Redskins, but Mitchell became one of their greatest players until he retired before the 1969 season.

Finally, the fourth-best trade was sending quarterback Jay Schroeder to the Los Angeles Raiders one game into the 1988 season for offensive tackle Jim Lachey, who was traded a month earlier from San Diego. The Raiders included fourth- and fifth-rounders that proved inconsequential.

Schroeder was an extra arm for Washington, which badly needed a left tackle. Lachey played eight seasons for Washington before knee and rotator cuff injuries ended his career in 1996. Still, he was a three-time All-Pro and the 1990 NFC Offensive Lineman of the Year. Schroeder played five seasons for the Raiders with just one season's rating more than 71.0 before finishing with Cincinnati in 1993 and Arizona in 1994.

58 Watch Film With Casserly

NFL Game Rewind turns any fan into a pseudo-general manager.

Subscribers can watch Coaches Film, including overhead All-22 and EndZone angles, which converts the game into roughly 30 minutes of pure football, sans announcers, while allowing you to see the whole field filled with individual battles.

It's such a different world from the days of just watching the game once while drinking a beer with your buds.

Watching film should teach you how little most people really know about the game. The replays can show that interception wasn't the fault of the quarterback but a guard who was in the wrong lane or the receiver who cut his route short or the running back who botched the handoff and left the passer to improvise.

Film exposes everybody on the field to the coach's wrath. Players often say after games that they expect a chewing out during

Century Receivers

If 100-yard games are a benchmark of greatness for receivers, why is Gary Clark not in the Hall of Fame?

Art Monk's 36 100-yard outings lead the Redskins, which is followed by Clark with 28, Bobby Mitchell with 23, and Charley Taylor with 22. Monk, Mitchell, and Taylor are Canton enshrines, but Clark rarely gets mentioned come selection time.

Clark sorta had the best outing ever by a Redskins receiver, too. Anthony Allen is the official leader with 255 yards against St. Louis in 1987, but that was a strike game and really shouldn't count. Clark gained 241 yards versus the New York Giants in 1986.

There were nine other 200-yard games by a Redskin. Monk has two—230 versus Cincinnati in 1985 and 200 against San Francisco in 1984. Clark also has two, as well—the aforementioned Giants game and his 203 yards versus Atlanta in 1991.

the review session the next day. Coaches on sidelines often hedge postgame comments, knowing they couldn't see the play at ground level. Then again, it's also an easy excuse to avoid commenting when they say they have to see the film.

To translate, the eye in the sky never blinks.

Now here's the downside—the film also fools those who don't truly know what they're seeing. Just like any profession, it takes training to read film, such as when a doctor views MRI results.

"When Eli Manning throws an interception, is it the receiver breaking off the route or did Manning read it wrong?" said former Washington and Houston general manager Charley Casserly. "You have to ask the coaches. [You might] see a blitz and there was no shot, so Manning slides to his left and throws it off his back foot. Turns out the receiver was a yard off his spot."

Casserly watches at least three games, but sometimes 10, when scouting a college player for drafts.

"As a general rule, if you've watched three games, then 99 percent of the time you have an idea of what they are," he said.

"Don't rush to judgment because the guy makes one bad play or bad game. It doesn't mean he can't play. Younger players get better. Is his technique off? Maybe it's not a good play."

Another good recommendation is to get your eyes away from the ball. There's so much else going on across the field.

"You're aware of where the ball is [to get an] idea of his reaction," Casserly said, "but scouting games means you're always looking at the 'triangle'—the center and two guards—that dictated what the play was."

Does film truly tell team officials whether a college player is ready for the pros? Of course not. That's why there are combines, personal interviews, and background investigations.

"[Film] is not something you can measure," Casserly said. "The biggest mistake you can make is to talk yourself into a player because you need the position. You rationalize. Even the best players aren't complete players. You're projecting their college skills to pro skills. Sometimes you talk yourself into correcting mistakes you can't correct."

That's why war-room boards, which are created weeks before the draft, are so critical. It's why the Redskins chose Kirk Cousins with a 2012 fourth-round pick after earlier selecting Robert Griffin III in the first. Cousins' board value was too hard to pass despite the fact that Washington did not have an immediate need at quarterback. When Cousins won a late-season game to reach the playoffs while Griffin was sidelined, the decision to stay with the board proved correct.

"You keep taking the best player on the board," Casserly said. "Just take him. You never know when you need players. Stay with your board."

So keep watching film. It will tell you whether an expensive free agent is really worth taking. When friends are screaming for the Redskins to pay big money for an offensive tackle, sound like an expert when you rattle off plays when the lineman was beat. Offer reasons why that tight end is worth taking because of his route running. And explain whether a running back could be a third-down contributor for the lateral movement needed to punch in at the goal line by often choosing an open lane.

After all, the film never lies.

59 The Road to Raljon

Jack Kent Cooke spent a decade building a stadium.

Cooke tried relocating from RFK Stadium to its northern parking lot before Washington Mayor Sharon Pratt Kelly called him "The Billionaire Bully." The Redskins owner missed predecessor Marion Barry and never wanted to deal with Kelly. Indeed, Cooke would purposely enrage Kelly during negotiations to the point of profane arguments when staffers were forced to separate them. Cooke also didn't want to deal with Capitol Hill lawmakers over the use of federal land for the stadium.

Then it was on to Alexandria where Potomac Yards was then an empty railroad corridor. At the press conference, Cooke roared with laughter over a question on whether it was really going to happen, basically calling the reporter a bloody idiot.

When Richmond lawmakers balked at paying for a stadium on the Virginia border, Cooke cut a deal with a Laurel, Maryland, racetrack owner for excess land. There were precedents of football stadium/racetrack combinations thanks to the New England Patriots in Foxboro, Massachusetts, and the New York Giants and Jets at The Meadowlands in East Rutherford, New Jersey.

Maryland Governor Parris Glendening didn't like that the stadium was one-tenth of a mile from his precious Prince George's

County border and suggested a new spot one mile away so the Redskins wouldn't be so close to Baltimore, which was in the process of looking for a team. Ironically, Cooke considered building in Baltimore and thought Laurel would give him territorial rights to keep away expansion or relocating teams.

So Laurel didn't work out politically, either. Cooke was forced to a dairy farm just off the beltway and not far from Capital Centre whose Bullets and Capitals teams were ironically moving downtown. Landover was in Glendening's home county and would replace two departing teams.

Cooke's deal was that he'd pay $250 million to build the stadium while the state chipped in $70 million for infrastructure. Cooke would also build a Prince George's County Sports and Learning Complex for local athletes and move training camp to Frostburg, which just happened to be in the district of Maryland House Speaker Cas Taylor. And the land would be leased for 30 years before the county would own it in 2027.

But between talks of Laurel and Landover, Cooke also gave thought to relocating the team to Los Angeles where he built the Forum and owned the Lakers and Kings before taking over the Redskins.

"Cooke said, 'What do you think about moving to Los Angeles?'" said then Redskins general manager Charley Casserly. "I said, 'Mr. Cooke, the fans are too loyal. It would be wrong to move it.' He said he could get the stadium in L.A. In the end, he knew moving would be too much for fans and said, 'I gotta build it here.'"

Los Angeles would have certainly been a major move. The NFL has wanted to return to the vacant market since the Raiders left in 1994. Washington even trained at Occidental College from 1946 to 1962 and played before 100,000 annually during a preseason charity game at the L.A. Coliseum.

But one of Cooke's problems was that the native Canadian, who later became a U.S. citizen by an act of Congress, loved being around political power brokers. To gain an invite into Cooke's box at RFK Stadium was equal to attending a White House dinner—maybe more. Vice Presidents Al Gore and Dan Quayle, retired General Colin Powell, playwright Larry King, Virginia Governor Doug Wilder, and pundits George Will and Carl Rowan were regulars among the box's 50 residents.

So with Los Angeles discarded much like George Preston Marshall's near move to Dallas a generation earlier, Cooke was in a race with the Grim Reaper. His health was poor, and Cooke knew it would take two years to build a stadium. At age 82, Cooke knew he was running out of time.

The Verizon Center was also being erected in downtown Washington, while Baltimore was building a new home to the former Cleveland Browns. Three massive sports venues being built at one time meant they would be competing for several things, including concrete. Cooke cornered the local market, forcing the other two facilities to pay more for suppliers located farther away.

Cooke even tried to rename the stadium site as Raljon, Maryland, instead of Landover. The word was a combination of his sons' names, Ralph and John. The media refused. Cooke countered that it was an official mailing address. The media didn't care, just as it later refused to make FedEx Field one word, which the Redskins saw as a marketing gimmick.

Sadly, Cooke failed to see the new stadium. But the day before his April 6, 1997, death, Cooke sat in his car at midfield, inspecting the ongoing construction. He would die suddenly the next morning, five months before Jack Kent Cooke Stadium opened.

60 Learn to Deep Snap

Everybody who has ever played flag football thinks they can be the center. What's the big deal?

Now think about hiking the ball 25' to a holder or 40' to a punter you can't see while a 300-lb. defensive linemen readies to deliver a blindside hit to your head?

Those stars you're seeing aren't the Milky Way.

Your bucket list should include deep snapping, the most specialized job in football. Indeed, snapping is the reason many guys reached the NFL as undersized linemen. They saw a niche that few do and made a career out of it, such as the Redskins Nick Sundberg.

"[My high school team] needed a guy who could snap. I was absolutely terrible," Sundberg said. "That's the thing you have to get past—everyone sucks in the beginning. I was horrible, horrible. Never thought I could do it in high school, much less at this level."

Sundberg said there's no secret to deep snapping; it just takes plenty of hard work. How do you get to Carnegie Hall? Practice, practice, practice.

"Work—practice is everything," he said. "When you're young, creating the muscle memory is the most important thing. Practice is everything. There's no such thing as snapping too much."

Indeed, Sundberg sometimes snaps 100 to 150 times six days per week. That's nearly 900 snaps in a week.

"The only way to get rid of bad habits is to snap more, so the more snapping the better," he said.

Sundberg, who's so flexible he can do three different types of splits, even has a warm-up drill where he snaps the ball on a straight line overhead to prepare different muscles than the ones used to snap between his legs.

"I warm up both shoulders with overhand snaps," he said. "It's a feel thing. That's just warming up."

Sundberg bristles when others claim he has such an easy job because he only snaps a few times per game. Fans forget to combine the punts, extra points, and field goals.

"It's not three times a game," he said. "I average 10 to 11 snaps a game, not three."

Then there are drills needed to counter pass rushers who think they can take advantage of a snapper who's not as ready as other linemen. Sundberg has a split second where he's more vulnerable to being knocked backward while snapping, which could be the difference in a blocked kick.

Long snapper Nick Sundberg prepares to snap the ball during the second half of a game against the Baltimore Ravens in Landover, Maryland, on Sunday, December 9, 2012. (AP Photo/Patrick Semansky)

"That's something you have to get used to—taking hits at random angles," he said. "Just take hits in practice and figure out how your body works. There's no right or wrong way to snap. It's just whatever it takes."

It's also about trusting your preparation and not overthinking it for a critical kick. Just breathe and let yourself do what you've been training to do. Otherwise, a bad snap is sure to come.

"Work ethic is everything with long snapping," Sundberg said. "You have to trust your body will take over and do what you need to do. Everything is feel. I literally shut my brain off and let my body react."

61 Strike Team

The key to the 1987 championship came down to a strike team.

A cast of castoffs went 3–0 while union players boycotted games. Long before the Redskins survived the Minnesota Vikings in the NFC Champions, and before the Redskins experienced the greatest quarter in Super Bowl history, smashing the Denver Broncos, a ragtag group went unbeaten to set up the postseason run.

The Replacements movie starring Keanu Reaves was loosely based on the Redskins strike team. The NFL refused permission to use the Redskins name, so the movie was free to take more liberties than offered in the Bill of Rights.

The movie's script writer contacted me about the team. He loved all the inside info. General manager Charley Casserly spent hours with the writer. In the end, the only thing the movie had in common with the real strike team was the sport was football. Oh, Hollywood.

Here are a few true stories about that replacement team.

After Darryl Grant broke a window on the bus carrying the strike players into Redskins Park, the team snuck the replacement players through the woods to the back gate each morning while posting guards at the team hotel.

The Redskins front office was smart. Led by general manager Bobby Beathard and Casserly, they spent the preseason scouting a strike team, knowing a work stoppage was possible.

"We did sign some players we had in camp," Casserly said. "Defensively, we signed guys that knew the system. If they had been in the Coryell [offensive] system, then at least they knew the terminology. We got four guys out of a halfway house. [Quarterbacks coach] Dan Henning had a friend coaching in Richmond who recommended Tony Robinson and Joe Cofer. There were a bunch of guys out of Canada. Willard Scissum was a guard at 7-Eleven in Washington when we signed him. He shut out Too Tall Jones in the Dallas game. We had a kicker hit a line drive to break a window [at Redskins Park] that was way out of line.

"We're just trying to find guys. This guy is 6'7", 300 lbs., never signed by anybody. We called his college coach who said he had some toughness. That's great. We agreed to a contract over the phone. He comes up to the office, comes up the stairs, huffing and puffing. I thought he was on the treadmill. He's gasping, 'The steps.' He's our eighth lineman. We needed people to practice. He ends up on the roster and got a half Super Bowl check for being active three games."

The Redskins' 3–0 run was especially amazing given they played against many union players. The first game saw 14 St. Louis Cardinals crossing the picket line as 5-point favorites, but the Redskins won 28–21 at RFK Stadium.

"We thought we were going to get killed," Casserly said. "We had Anthony Allen, who had been in the league. We call a post corner and boom! Allen is wide open—touchdown. We could win this game. It's backyard football. Allen breaks the team receiving record [of 255 yards.] We don't know how long we're going with that guy, but he makes that play and stays in."

Next up is the New York Giants, or at least some semipro team hired to impersonate the hosts at Giants Stadium. Washington was a whopping 10½-point favorite and won 38–12. Allen was held to 51 yards, but the Redskins ran for four touchdowns.

"We beat them bad," Casserly said. "There were 4,000 in the stands. Two guys on the Giants fell asleep on bench."

The strike largely ended before Washington played at Dallas on Monday night. The Cowboys played stars Tony Dorsett, Danny White, Randy White, and Jones. It looked like a big mismatch with Dallas as the eight-point favorites.

"Gibbs gave one of his great speeches in pregame," Casserly said. "[He says,] 'It's the last game. This is exactly why you came here. You came to get a chance to prove you can play in the league. What greater stage than the Dallas Cowboys with their starters on national TV so everybody can see how you are?'"

The defense held Dallas scoreless until the third quarter while managing four sacks and two interceptions. Somehow Washington kicked two field goals and a touchdown run for a 13–7 victory. At least the movie showed the right final locker room scene of players celebrating.

Four strike players remained when union players returned, and they were treated like scabs and cast to the far corner of the locker room. One by one, they were gone and nobody cared.

Still, they had memories for a lifetime.

62 Many Faces of Portis

Most players would rather skip talking to reporters.

Players often confuse the media with public relations people. They don't understand why we ask hard questions. Why don't we love them unconditionally like their family and friends have ever since they showed something special on a ball field?

Once in awhile, a player gets the value of working well with the media. Maybe he wants to raise his overall image, improve the possibility of winning postseason honors, promote a business, or increase the chances of getting his own show one day. Either way, there's often a benefit to dealing with the media.

Clinton Portis took it to another level in 2005. He became Clinton the Entertainer.

Lunchtime became showtime with 10 different personalities on the staircase by the locker room. Four more later emerged on a 2008 NFL Network show.

We're talking multiple personalities with the clothes to match.

Dolemite Jones, Choo Choo, Sheriff Gonna Getcha, Southeast Jerome, Dolla Bill, Coach Janky Spanky, Kid Bro Sweets, Dr. I Don't Know, Inspector Two-Two, and Reverend Gonna Change debuted each week in 2005. Dr. Do Itch Big, Prime Minister Ya Mon, Budd Foxx, and Electra followed in 2008.

My favorite was Southeast Jerome because it showed Portis understood the city has four quadrants—Northeast, Southeast, Northwest, Southwest based on their location respective to the U.S. Capitol dome. Redskins Park is in Ashburn, Virginia, about 20 miles outside town, so Portis knowing Southeast showed he had done some homework.

Southeast Jerome wore a black mask and cape while readying to go dancing when the Redskins played at New York that Sunday. Unfortunately, Washington lost 36–0.

Southeast Jerome was never seen again. Sheriff Gonna Getcha, donning fake glasses, long dark hair, and a tin badge, promised to investigate Southeast Jerome's disappearance while playing at Tampa Bay that weekend, even interviewing Bucs Ronde Barber.

It did no good. The angel of Southeast Jerome came two months later to say he died and was in Heaven.

Not kidding.

Dolemite Jones appeared wearing old glasses, a red wig, and a shirt saying, "Vote for Santana (Moss)." A knockoff of the popular movie *Napoleon Dynamite*, Jenkins wanted to dance. So did Choo Choo, who looked like a samurai with a black top knot, claiming to teach Redskins players how to dance after touchdowns.

Coach Janky Spanky was the most energetic as an old coach complete with headset, whistle, fake gut, and huge white ears, which he credited to being excited. This was a real show stopper with the coaching staff. With the Redskins in the playoffs, Coach diagrammed a play on how opponents could stop Portis, saying 13 defensive players would be needed.

Dolla Bill was a purple raised-hair version of Don King with "C-O-O-L" glasses and green jacket. He liked to say "100 pennies, 4 quarters, 10 dimes, 20 nickels—now that's Dolla Bill."

Kid Bro Sweets sported rotten teeth while offering candy to the crowd. His favorite sweet? PayDay candy bars, of course.

Dr. I Don't Know arrived after Washington lost to New York. He didn't know what happened, but he did know his pink glasses used to be white before they were mixed with blood.

When the Redskins fell to 5–6, it was time for Reverend Gonna Change, who promised a new course that indeed produced five straight wins.

Inspector Two-Two wore a fake nose and glasses under a leather football helmet with blonde pigtails.

Portis did some quick-change acts when showing four personalities just minutes apart on NFL Network with Rich Eisen.

Doctor Do Itch Big was a dentist dedicated to "Cleaning up the NFL, one mouth at a time." His clients were New York Giants defensive end Michael Strahan, known for a gap in his front teeth, and Buffalo running back Marshawn Lynch, who sported braces. The Doctor sported his own oversized teeth, which were only overshadowed by his large purple sunglasses.

Prime Minister Ya Mon was running as an independent presidential candidate against Barack Obama and John McCain. Saying he was born somewhere between the U.S. and Jamaica, Ya Mon wore a pointed wizard cap and promised to lower gas prices by 40 cents per gallon.

Budd Foxx was an Ultimate Fighter who wore a mask like the old Mexican wrestlers. He was 0–17 but promised to keep fighting until he won in the 115-lb. weight class despite weighing 220 lbs. He specialized in cracking fingers.

Electra was an environmentalist with a Masters in Electrical Engineering from MIT. His shirt said, "Off the grid is off the chain," and he lived in a solar-powered house. Electra smoked a pipe because tobacco comes from the earth.

63 The Fight

Football is a blood sport—a modern form of gladiator games. Emotions are raw, and violence isn't unusual. It's called Sunday.

So don't be surprised when players fight even amongst themselves. It means nothing and is quite often forgotten the next day. Mostly the fights happen in practice when one player believes another is blocking or hitting him unfairly.

Often these fights go unreported. Heath Shuler once sported a shiner he said came from running into a door. Turned out a linebacker moonlighted as a doorman when enraged by Shuler's poor play in practice.

Really, fighting is no big deal. It's even encouraged by some coaches to liven up practice.

But one fight happened right in front of the media, and it was ugly. Even worse, it was handled badly. And the final straw was diverting attention from media day at soon-to-be-opened Jack Kent Cooke Stadium (now called FedEx Field) that enraged team officials.

Michael Westbrook sucker-punched Stephen Davis during an August 1997 practice, then jumped atop him and hit Davis several more times before stunned coaches and teammates ended it. Davis wasn't seriously hurt.

The two were at the 30-yard line. Standing on the other 30-yard line watching practice, I didn't see the first punch thrown, but I did see Westbrook atop Davis. So did WUSA cameraman Dave Satchel, who filmed the fight. Despite Redskins officials first demanding the video and then saying it couldn't be used—neither claim is correct under the First Amendment—Satchel held firm and aired it.

As they say these days, that's when things went viral.

The story heard that day was Davis insulted Westbrook while teasing him over having bad hands. Westbrook snapped and hit Davis.

But it has been said that we're all the heroes of our own stories, and Westbrook described the situation to ESPN in 2008 as such:

"He didn't call me a name," Westbrook said. "That's where it gets mixed up. It got reported and it got changed into something monstrous. I was talking to him, Brian Mitchell, and Terry Allen. They were talking about 'letting us handle the team.' I was like, 'You all are a bunch of jealous f----. You all are just jealous of everything I have.'

"Stephen Davis told me I needed to shut up, and all that stuff I was saying sounded like some gay s---, like I'm soft, not like I'm gay. That's all he said. It wasn't like, 'You're gay,' but it got changed to that really quick. So the connotation is Michael Westbrook is gay."

Davis has never confirmed that version. His recollection didn't include the gay reference. It's hard to say who's really telling the truth, but both versions have enough in common to support the idea that Davis ticked off Westbrook, who wasn't well liked by teammates.

Two things happened that were textbook PR 101 mistakes that could have defused everything. First, Westbrook's poor relationship with the press led to two days of no commenting, which allowed the story to grow. Finally, he mumbled some half-hearted apology in 30 seconds and disappeared. All Westbrook needed to say was he was angry over Davis insulting him and punched the latter. Every guy in America would have understood. Then Westbrook could have said he was sorry and would try to act better, and the story would have disappeared. But he mishandled it badly.

Second, the team overreacted. Interim owner John Kent Cooke was angry over losing attention from the stadium opening and fined Westbrook $50,000, suspended him a preseason game (who cares), and ordered Westbrook to meet with a counselor weekly for one year.

Westbrook and several other players separately met with the counselor for a year. Players sat with her at the training camp cafeteria where the media ate. Reporters respected their privacy and never repeated anything. Mostly, it was young men who had no family around and needed someone to talk to about the struggles they faced. She did a good job of helping them. Too bad the team didn't renew her deal when the team was sold to Dan Snyder.

Westbrook told ESPN that he and Davis later made up. Well, if they did it was after both men had left the team. Davis was understandably embarrassed and talked to Westbrook as little as possible.

64 Milkshakes by Marty

Young reporters are told that there's no such thing as a dumb question.

Yes there is, and one gained a surprising answer from Coach Marty Schottenheimer during training camp in 2001.

The Redskins were in the midst of a brutal camp. The new coach imposed a get-tough attitude on players who underperformed in 2000, causing the firing of Coach Norv Turner. Turner knew he was a short-timer during the 2000 camp, even quietly letting veteran players sleep at their homes instead of at the team hotel. The NFL's first near-$100 million roster went 8–8 and was reduced to quarterback Jeff George and interim coach Terry Robiskie screaming at each other in the Redskins Park hallways over who was getting fired.

It was pretty chaotic around the team, so owner Dan Snyder hired a tough guy. Schottenheimer was an old linebacker whose hard-nosed attitude brought previous success coaching in Cleveland and Kansas City plus San Diego after his one year in Washington, though he never reached a Super Bowl.

Schottenheimer was tough, treating players, staff, and media all like dogs. To be honest, his limited information, horrific locker room access to players, and no access to staff made him the least favorite coach I covered in 36 years of newspapering. Indeed,

Green Outfoxed Schottenheimer

The longest-tenured Redskins actually played two more seasons by outmaneuvering the Turk.

Coach Marty Schottenheimer was looking to cut cornerback Darrell Green when the coach arrived in 2001. Schottenheimer openly berated the 18-year veteran's skills. The seven-time Pro Bowler didn't take well to change, and the two clashed.

It looked like Schottenheimer would release Green during the final cutdown. But the four-time NFL's Fastest Man blocked the coach by announcing this would be the corner's final season, creating a farewell tour that would raise money for charity.

There was no way Schottenheimer could take the public relations hit and release Green at that point. Ironically, Schottenheimer was fired after the season and Green followed new coach Steve Spurrier's introductory press conference by saying he was returning for yet one more season.

It was quick thinking once again by the future Pro Football Hall of Famer.

Schottenheimer's "One Voice" policy was later barred by the NFL, which now mandates that coordinators speak at least once weekly.

Schottenheimer was a good coach whose ego caused problems. He gained total control over team operations and wouldn't even meet regularly with Snyder over lunch to update the owner on the team's progress. Say what you want about Snyder's meddling with personnel over the years, the man owns the team and deserves to talk to his coach. Schottenheimer feared Snyder would seek more influence if given an inch, so he locked out the owner. It would lead to his dismissal despite an 8–8 season.

Schottenheimer's training camp was the toughest of 20-plus camps I've covered. Every day brought live hitting in both practices, which the NFL no longer allows. The first practice saw a "bull-in-the-ring" drill where the team encircles a runner and a defender. It's not often seen in NFL camps, and reputations can be earned or destroyed in the ring. Players hate the drill, but Schottenheimer made them do it right away while waving fans onto the field to watch.

Bruce Smith and Schottenheimer clashed the first week of camp when the coach refused to allow the defensive end to attend the Pro Football Hall of Fame induction of his former Buffalo Bills coach Marv Levy when the Redskins were only having a rookie scrimmage that day. Smith and Schottenheiner were seen during stretching before practice in a heated discussion with Smith shaking his head sideways quite often. Soon after, Smith was speared in practice and walked off holding his shoulder. He didn't practice the rest of the preseason before suddenly healing in time for September.

Carlisle, Pennsylvania, might be 113 miles north of Washington, but it's no cooler. Biddle Field was a hot box. Fans could enjoy legendary ice cream at Massey's Custard Stand by the entrance gates, but players needed to wait until passing by on the way to their dorms if they wanted one. Unfortunately, players rarely carry money in their jerseys, although fans were glad to buy the shakes.

But Schottenheimer showed some mercy near camp's end. He passed out 100 milkshakes for players and staff as they stood on the field after practicing 30 minutes longer than usual.

Deciding to be a wise guy and testing Schottenheimer's willingness to answer anything, a reporter asked why there were 100 chocolate shakes? Why not a mix of vanilla and chocolate? And what about strawberry?

It was a dumb question intended to mess with the coach. But damn if he didn't answer it well.

"First, we were going to go with 50 vanilla and 50 chocolate," Schottenheimer said. "Then, it was, 'Well, what if 75 want chocolate and 25 want vanilla?' I decided chocolate. I like chocolate."

Typically, it was Schottenheimer's way even when milkshakes were in question. Snyder would return to an easy coach the following year in Steve Spurrier whose replies didn't always match the media's questions. But Schottenheimer was usually in command down to every detail—including milkshakes.

Visit RFK

Robert F. Kennedy Stadium was an outdated facility when the Washington Redskins left after the 1996 season. Today, it's looking more like the Roman Colosseum than a modern arena.

But it's our old dump where dreams of glory became reality and memories were created for lifetimes.

It's hard to believe 18 years have passed since the Redskins left the city. They haven't been worth beans most seasons out in the suburbs.

Fans relish the giddy times when RFK bleachers bounced during victories, when every one of the 56,454 seats was filled by the same fans each game. RFK was family, and a close one at that, versus its FedEx Field successor whose 91,000 seats were sometimes one-third empty and one-third filled with opposing fans.

But 18 years means many current Redskins fans have never been to RFK. They've only heard the stories from older fans.

And that's a shame. Every Redskins fan should visit RFK where the team managed three Super Bowl championships. It's filled with memories. Riggo bowed at midfield. Sonny threw endless touchdowns. The Fun Bunch celebrated in the end zone after touchdowns. The Hogs owned the dirt. Vince Lombardi, George Allen, and Joe Gibbs walked the sideline.

This really was a field of dreams for Redskins fans.

The good news is that the stadium still stands, hosting DC United pro soccer games and occasional college football bowls.

Either way, you can still see a game there. Find your old seats, or those of your parents, and watch from there. It's not pro football, but it's still sports.

Little has changed since the Redskins left. Well, the parking lots were finally paved years ago, but not before I hit a water-filled pothole that was so deep it knocked the rearview mirror off my windshield.

The concourse still smells like wet dog on a rainy day. The concessions stands and restrooms are dated, and the seats are much the same.

But so what? It's like going back to your childhood home and wondering how you ever lived in such a small place. It's reminiscent of James Earl Jones telling Kevin Costner at the end of *Field of Dreams* that people will pay to revisit their childhood dreams. That's exactly what visiting RFK is all about for fans.

Look up at the curved overhead partial dome, which kept humidity inside on a hot day and absolutely baked the fans. RFK was one of the early cookie-cutter stadiums that filled America in the 1960s and '70s, and it's the last one still standing. Indeed, it will probably stand for many more years before the soccer team finally gains a new home. In fact, some football fans hope RFK is a placeholder for the next Redskins stadium.

When standing outside the Roman Colosseum in 2007, it reminded me of RFK as I thought, "This is where Spartacus bled in the sand."

I often think of RFK in similar nostalgia. This is where my dad took me to see the Washington Senators. (We could never get Redskins tickets.) Dad passed away in 1989, and I still look for him in the upper deck every time I'm in the stadium.

As a kid, we'd park in Lot 8 and walk through the tunnel to reach the stadium. The crowd would thicken, and people would moo like cattle. Dad would always say, "Damn drunks." Years later when I was covering Redskins games, I'd marvel at how much smaller that tunnel was than I remembered. And yes, I still moo when walking through it.

Somehow I don't think fans will have such memories years from now of FedEx Field. "Remember when we'd pay $40 to park miles from the stadium?" doesn't have much sentimentality to it.

It's a shame a generation will pass for Redskins fans stuck in Landover. Winning makes a house a home, and the team has done little of it so far, although there's still time. FedEx was built quickly for a dying owner. Patterned after Giants Stadium, which Jack Kent Cooke thought was the league's best, it's too functional.

Visiting RFK is like reading Hemingway's bullfighting books to remember an age of men draped in glory. A time when the nation feared and admired the Redskins, and no one considered it a racist name.

So go home again and visit RFK Stadium. And call your mama tonight, too.

66 The Art of Gaining Autographs

Sonny Jurgensen signed a jersey for a grateful young fan. One hour later when walking to lunch, he spied that same jersey in a store window for sale.

And that's why athletes are sometimes reluctant to sign autographs.

Why fans want autographs is a little perplexing. Sports writers aren't allowed to get them, and frankly I don't know whose I would get anyway. Oh, meeting non-athlete celebrities is cool, but making them sign a napkin seems weird. Is proof needed when telling the story of meeting them?

These days everything seems to be about money or branding, but many athletes sign regularly. Robert Griffin III often spends 45 minutes signing after practices during training camp. Jurgensen has probably signed a million times over 60 years.

Personally, isn't it better to shake their hand, have a brief moment, and move on? That's real. An autograph means the player is looking down and not at you. Seems impersonal to me.

Okay, that long-desired sermon aside, here are some dos and don'ts when seeking autographs.

Do have a Sharpie ready for the player. It makes reluctant players more willing to sign because it won't take long.

Don't have 10 things for them to sign. They know you're a collector looking to resell.

Do say please and thank you. It goes a long way.

Don't yell the player's first name if you're younger than them. This goes to the longstanding courtesy of calling people Mr. and Mrs. if they're older than you and using their first name if they're younger. Darrell Green really tired of kids calling him by his first name when he was old enough to be their father. Darrell tried to teach kids respect by saying they needed to say Mr. Green. It was a life lesson.

Do position yourself on the way they're headed. Players rarely turn back.

Don't bother a player while he is eating. If you have to wait, you have to wait. Imagine what it's like to be interrupted all the time—it's very frustrating for players.

Do send autograph requests to Redskins Park, 21300 Redskins Park Dr., Ashburn, VA 20147 Here's the key—include a self-addressed, stamped envelope. If the player can just sign it right there, put it in the envelope, and leave it with the receptionist to mail, they'll often do it. Anything that's a hassle has less chance of happening. I've seen many players sign requests at the receptionist's desk.

Don't forget the self-addressed, stamped envelope. I'm telling you, it's the key.

Do know the player's name. I've often seen kids who don't know who they're asking. The player feels disrespected. Seriously, if you don't know who it is, why bother asking for the autograph?

Don't approach a player at a restaurant if he's sitting with his wife, family, or lady friend. (Is that what they call girlfriends now?) Wives get tired of the little free time they get with their husbands being interrupted, and players hate it when their dates are interrupted. This is common sense, but it happens all the time.

Do have a camera and someone who can take the photo quickly if you're asking for the player to pose. They're often on the run. Make it quick.

Don't ask the player to record an answering message for your cell. Really?

Do think of an autograph as a personal moment, not a money-making venture.

Don't jump out of line when someone better comes along. Alfred Morris, who is as nice a person as you'll meet, laughs at the many times kids in his line see Griffin and bolt. He jokes of waving goodbye and thanking them for thinking of him. But really, that's disrespectful.

Do mail away to retired players (everybody's address is on the Internet) by including a self-addressed, stamped envelope just like active players. There's no guarantee, but chances are you'll get it.

Don't pay for autographs at card shows. Don't do it.

Don't ask players to personally inscribe a message. Keep the encounter simple.

Don't ask someone to sign a ball for charity if it's not. And the "Feed Myself" charity doesn't count.

Finally, ask yourself if this autograph will mean something to you five minutes later. If not, don't do it. But if it does, then go for it.

And if you see me, I'll be glad to sign your book. I often joke books are $15 unsigned, $10 signed, and $5 if I use my real name. How many Ms are there in Hemingway again?

67 Lombardi's Look of a Winner

Vince Lombardi knew one thing when taking over a team that hadn't won in 14 years—you have to look like a winner to be a winner.

Lombardi gave the Redskins one of their more iconic looks by putting the letter R on the helmet and using new shades for the burgundy jerseys and mustard (sorry, gold) pants during his 1969–70 tenure. Sadly, he died before the second season started and never saw some of the changes completed.

"If you were color blind, you'd think it was the [Green Bay] Packers uniform," joked then–equipment manager Tommy McVean.

Indeed, Lombardi borrowed the look from five championship seasons (1959–67) of his Green Bay days. The Packers uniform was patterned after the Cleveland Browns' 1950s style. The stripes and block letters were simple elegance to Lombardi.

Washingtonians might not have minded a new uniform. After no playoff trips since 1945, no one seemed especially nostalgic for a losing look.

Some of the changes were intentional, but the jersey color might not have been. Lombardi ended an 11-year relationship with uniform maker Sand Knit to go with Rawlings, whose sales representative just happened to be Lombardi's brother-in-law.

Hall of Fame head coach Vince Lombardi talks to Hall of Fame quarterback Sonny Jurgensen (9) during a game in Washington, D.C., 1969. (AP Photo/NFL Photo/Vernon Biever)

The new threads arrived days before the 1969 opener, and after opening the boxes, the Redskins were left scrambling. The preceding deep burgundy jerseys were now—depending on whom you ask—either cardinal, wine, or cranberry red. No matter how described, they were a shade lighter than before.

There was no time to exchange uniforms, so the Redskins concentrated on the helmets. Lombardi's planned R helmets weren't ready and had to wait until 1970. The old helmets were stripped of the elaborate spear and given a new sleek, multi-toned spear with a lighter reddish border to match the jerseys. The single stripe, reminiscent of the Packers and Browns, was also added.

Lombardi fine-tuned the look for 1970 over the off-season, and the R made it on the helmet. The coach died of cancer during the preseason, and the look only remained one more season.

In 1971, new coach George Allen changed practically everything about the franchise, including the uniforms. The helmets returned to a burgundy shell with an American Indian logo that resembled the team's 1930s look. An American Indian tribe in South Dakota provided input for the image. Allen made minor changes to the stripes on the jersey sleeves, which remained until 1979 when general manager Bobby Beathard kept the helmet but changed the jersey. Allen's son, Bruce, revived Lombardi's mustard pants after becoming the team's general manager in December 2009.

In a 2010 interview with Redskins Nation, Bruce Allen said of the uniforms, "We're gonna stick to our historic base. I loved when the Redskins had those throwback games over the last few years, whether it's the arrow or the feather or the R. Y'know, just watching it on tape from afar, you're like, 'Oh, gosh, I remember.'

"I was there when [the current helmet] was being designed," Bruce added. "There's a lot of pride in the Redskins emblem."

There's nothing wrong with tinkering with uniforms. Certainly teams like to change it up to sell more merchandise. As long as the colors and helmets stay the same, they can find more throwback gear to stock the shelves.

But one caveat—don't turn into the pro version of crosstown neighbor University of Maryland. The Terrapins are essentially owned by Under Armour, which technically is a sponsor but seems to dictate endless uniform changes. Some are fine, some ridiculous. The Terps are football's version of Project Runway. The Washington Wizards seem to flip uniforms regularly, too.

If the Redskins ever change the team name, the colors would probably remain. The burgundy and gold are too beloved to revamp even if the team wasn't called the Redskins anymore.

If anything, one possible change to deflect the name controversy is returning to the spear helmet of the 1960s, which remains popular with fans, versus the American Indian image used since the 1970s. Owner Dan Snyder planned to use that spear helmet for his Washington Warriors team in Arena Football, but the franchise never happened despite a press conference.

68 Attend Welcome Home Luncheon

It's the drums that get your blood pumping.

The Redskins Marching Band drum line starts banging away as players and coaches enter the room. There used to be one long table of 80 players and staff that fans would marvel over. Now the players and staff sit at tables with the fans.

The Welcome Home Luncheon is the closest fans will ever get to the players and staff. If you're a fan, you've gotta go at least once.

"It's all about honoring the Redskins," said Redskins Alumni Association president Mark Moseley, who hasn't missed a luncheon since 1974. "It's always been a big part of the Redskins. Fans get to see the active players up close and personal."

The NFL's first Welcome Home luncheon began in 1962. In good years, crowds surpassed 1,000. In lean times it's sometimes half that. The luncheon has been held at downtown hotels as well as Virginia and Maryland. It's currently held at the Gaylord National Hotel on the doorstep of the Woodrow Wilson Bridge, and it always occurs in late August.

The alumni ran the luncheon for many years until Redskins owner Dan Snyder offered to take it over a decade ago. Ticket prices seem a little steep, but all monies go to the team's charitable foundation so figure you're helping someone while having fun. It's business attire with most men wearing a coat and tie.

Think of it as a friar's roast without salty language, so you can bring the kids.

Local TV sportscasters have often emceed the event. Nobody was better than the late NBC-4's George Michael. He would zing anybody and everybody, even Snyder. And when it came to the auctions, George always seemed to double the expected price by baiting the final bidders. He was a born salesman who really loved being around the team.

The media has always attended since owner Jack Kent Cooke announced plans for a new stadium at the 1987 luncheon. It took 10 years for the new venue to open, but it all started at the luncheon so you never know what might happen. Naturally, nothing newsy has occurred since.

The alumni present the Sam Huff Defensive Player of the Year, Bobby Mitchell Offensive Player of the Year, and Mark Moseley Special Teams Player of the Year awards for the previous season plus a community service award to a player.

Of course, the head coach always gives a rousing speech promising greatness. Well, some coaches are better than others. Joe Gibbs was always terrific. Steve Spurrier and Jim Zorn were fun. Marty Schottenheimer took it seriously. Norv Turner was never a good public speaker.

And in 2013, Mike Shanahan's fourth luncheon appearance heard him saying, "Anything short of a Super Bowl is a failure."

The team finished 3–13 and Shanahan was fired, but mostly nobody remembers promises made at the luncheon.

If a joke ever fails and you hear crickets chirping in the room, just predict victory over the Dallas Cowboys and everybody will cheer. Meanwhile, you're munching away on good food and great dessert with a player at the table. How often does that happen in life? Naturally, the top stars dine with longtime corporate sponsors who have bought a table. The press table usually has some guy destined to make the practice squad or be soon released. It's a pecking order, people, but fans usually get plenty of autographs.

The Hogettes, cheerleaders and other diversions are usually found in the lobby beforehand. It's a mixing pool of fans of all types.

So promise to put the Welcome Home luncheon on your bucket list. Afterward you'll wonder why you waited so long to do it.

69 EBW—The Overlooked Boss

One of the more influential people to run the Washington Redskins was an interim team president who lasted two decades.

Edward Bennett Williams was a renowned Washington trial lawyer who kept teamster boss Jimmy Hoffa out of jail and defended high-profile clients such as entertainer Frank Sinatra, presidential would-be assassin John Hinckley, and gangster Frank Costello.

But Williams loved sports and began advising Redskins owner George Preston Marshall in the 1950s. He bought into the club in the 1960s and took control when Marshall was weakened by strokes in 1963. Marshall was team president and became majority owner by buying shares from Marshall's estate in 1970. He later sold controlling interest to Jack Kent Cooke in 1974 but remained president until he was forced to resign by Major League Baseball after buying the Baltimore Orioles in 1979. Many believed Williams would move the Orioles to Washington. Instead he simply courted Washingtonians to drive to Baltimore to see baseball.

Williams is an overlooked person given Marshall and Cooke's mammoth personalities. But Williams was the one who convinced Marshall to end his stubborn refusal to sign black players. Williams convinced Coach Vince Lombardi to leave retirement and come to Washington. Williams hired (and fired) George Allen and general manager Bobby Beathard, who won two Super Bowls with a roster that later took a third crown.

First and foremost a lawyer whose firm, Williams & Connolly, remains a power in Washington today, Williams loved the competition on the field as much as the courtroom.

"I love contest-living," he told the *Washington Post*. "My life in the law has been contest-living. It's a life in which every effort ends up a victory or a defeat. It's a difficult way to live, but it is a very exciting way."

But Williams' biggest victories came in the courtroom despite the Redskins reaching one Super Bowl during his tenure, losing to the undefeated Miami Dolphins. He was considered the Clarence Darrow of this time.

The *New York Times* branded Williams a "superlawyer" for his headline-grabbing victories. He befriended both Democrats and Republicans, a rare feat in Washington. Then again, everyone loves a winner.

"Anyone who is fortunate enough to get close to Ed Williams is well served," Edmund S. Muskie, the former Democratic Senator from Maine and former Secretary of State, told the *New York Times*. "Ed is not directly or actively involved in politics, but he is a political animal with good political instincts. If he were to speak well of a candidate, or to make himself available for counseling, this becomes known and has a rippling effect among opinion makers, party leaders, and fund raisers."

To which Williams retorted, "I'm not a lobbyist, and I'm not a fixer, so my political connections have never benefitted me. I do most of my work in a goldfish bowl of the courtroom."

Williams defended U.S. Senator Joseph McCarthy, once a power Communist hunter during the Cold War who later fell in disgrace, from tax and libel cases. Hoffa was cleared of racketeering and bribery. Williams kept Mafia kingpin Frank Costello from being deported. Former Treasury Secretary John Connally was cleared of taking illegal money from lobbyists. Former Congressman Adam Clayton Powell was found innocent of tax evasion.

President Richard Nixon shrugged off suggestions of hiring Williams to defend him against charges from the Watergate burglary. He later resigned from office. Nixon later said he wished Williams was his lawyer, while Williams reportedly said he would have told the president to burn the phone recordings so pivotal in Nixon's downfall. Ironically, Williams was considered to become the head of the Central Intelligence Agency shortly before his 11-year battle with cancer proved fatal in 1988.

Williams cited the Constitution's Sixth Amendment right to competent counsel as his reason for defending controversial clients. Yet it made him a rich man with a $50,000 annual retainer by the Teamsters as one of the perks of defending Hoffa.

Well known for his ability to pick a sympathetic jury, Williams asked questions to which he already knew the answers. He became the forerunner of using "character witnesses" like Reverend Billy Graham.

Yes, the Redskins were run by a regular Perry Mason.

70 Attend Training Camp

Every fan should attend training camp once a year.

I never liked training camps in far-flung places, having covered four years in Carlisle, Pennsylvania, and five in Frostburg, Maryland. My own bed is much preferred to endless weeks living in a dorm, which I never did in college.

But the new Bon Secours Washington Redskins Training Center in Richmond, Virginia, is a game-changer. Fans rightfully love this place because it was partly built for them in 2013.

There's a hillside to watch practice, as if you're waiting on the 18th fairway to see the end of a golf tournament. Fans can bring their own chairs, which makes life so much more civilized. Redskins Park is largely flat land, so unless you were on the fence, you couldn't see much. Bon Secours is so much better for the overall crowd.

(By the way, for those of you who get upset with reporters who stand in front by the sideline, we can't take a knee for safety reasons. You have to be able to move quickly if an errant pass comes your way. And we're working. It's nothing personal. We move around, but respect that we're working.)

The first summer in Richmond was like a pep rally. Maybe it was new fans from central and southern Virginia getting their first chance to see camp that excited them, but the place rocked all the time.

The facility is about two hours from Washington, but it's an easy drive. Sometimes it's just nice to get out of town, and it's a day trip. There's plenty of nearby parking for $5. Admission to practice is free.

Home Sweet Home

Be it ever so fumble, the Redskins have summered at 18 different places since 1932.

Carlisle, Pennsylvania, has been the sentimental training-camp site, but its 34 summers are less than half of the team's overall number. The Redskins have worked out anywhere from the current camp in Richmond and Redskins Park to California and Washington state colleges. Here is a complete list of training camp sites:

Site	City, State	Years
Bon Secours Washington Redskins Training Center	Richmond, Virginia	2013
Redskins Park	Ashburn, Virginia	2003–12
Dickinson College	Carlisle, Pennsylvania	2001–02
Redskins Park	Ashburn, Virginia	2000
Frostburg State	Frostburg, Maryland	1995–99
Dickinson College	Carlisle, Pennsylvania	1963–94
Occidental College	Los Angeles, California	1946–62
Georgetown University	Washington, D.C.	1945
Balboa Park	San Diego, California	1943–44
Brown Military Academy	San Diego, California	1941–42
Wandermere Resort	Spokane, Washington	1940
Eastern Washington University	Cheney, Washington	1939
Ballston Stadium	Arlington, Virginia	1938
Anacostia Park	Washington, D.C.	1937
Municipal Field	Framingham, Massachusetts	1936
Country Club	Waltham, Massachusetts	1935
Rosebud Gardens	Wayland, Massachusetts	1934
Northwestern University	Evanston, Illinois	1933
City Stadium	Lynn, Massachusetts	1932

The interesting part is many fans stay the three hours between practices and turn it into a giant picnic. There are several fast-food trucks, so fans eat lunch and hang out with fellow supporters.

Naturally there's a team store by the entrance. The Redskins don't miss a chance to make money, but that's capitalism. Fans like buying the stuff anyway.

As for practice, mornings are for walkthroughs and afternoons are full practices. No more two-a-days in full pads thanks to the 2012 labor deal limiting contact. No matter—fans are really watching skills players more than linemen.

Walkthroughs are basically 11-on-11s to practice plays. Nobody wears helmets, so there's no real hitting. If you like passing plays, this is the time for you. Walkthroughs are about 90 minutes of offense with the secondary the only defensive unit that makes plays. You'll see running plays, too, so look for a back's cutting ability and speed.

The two-hour morning practice has more unit drills, so you could walk to the far field to watch defensive players working out for the first hour. Meanwhile, special teams gets its chance. It's mostly for returners and kickers with blockers getting scant attention.

Special teams also work more in the morning. For some veterans, it's a short break while rookies fill coverage and return teams. Watching sky-high punts are interesting for 90 seconds even if they last 10 minutes. Field goal attempts are pretty interesting if there's a camp competition.

Fans are really waiting for passing drills with live hitting. It's mildly more interesting than the morning work because defenders get an even chance. While watching Robert Griffin III is always intriguing, follow all four passers and see what they do best and worst.

Indeed, if you really want to gain insight while watching practice, don't follow the ball. Pick out a unit for a few minutes. Concentrate just on the players away from the ball. Are they making blocks, running crisp routes, or cutting off receivers? You'll learn so much when you don't watch the ball like 99 percent of the crowd.

When the horn blows, it's autograph time. What's your strategy? It should be more than just yelling a player's name. The word "please" goes a long way to players who are tired and heading to the locker room. Be sure to have a Sharpie pen ready, and always say thanks.

Finally, Richmond traffic is nothing compared to Washington's, so heading home isn't a problem. Still, the Arby's on Broad Street is a great quick stop for dinner.

71 RFK Fades to Black

Think of the last game at RFK Memorial Stadium as a series of snapshots.

Close your eyes. Every few seconds, snatch a different glimpse. Not so much the sounds but the sights. A slide show of memories.

It was a surreal experience.

That the Redskins beat their rival Dallas Cowboys that day was a bonus. Certainly it was better than defeating Arizona or Cleveland before leaving their 35-year home. But really, the game was secondary to the postgame celebration.

Police ringed the field in the final minutes to prevent fans from storming the turf. It didn't matter. In seconds, the crowd was on the field seeking souvenirs. The grass looked like a wildfire had burned large chunks. Actually, fans had snatched handfulsof turf.

Gloria Mamaed still has the grass growing in her yard 18 years later. So does Nate Elgin, whose dad managed field passes for the family after his Mount Vernon High band performed during a midseason game. Nate and his brother, Keith, spent a chilly December 22, 1996, behind the Cowboys bench, yelling at Deion Sanders and Emmitt Smith (the latter didn't play) while their father razzed the refs.

"Amidst the chaos of the final seconds," Nate Elgin said, "I remember dumping out my red paper Coke cup, running onto the field, and filling the cup with some burgundy-colored end zone grass."

But grass was just the start for souvenir hunters. More than one fan talks of bringing a wrench for the loosely-bolted seats that would soon find their way to local basements and in front of a TV. Indeed, ushers checked many seats before the game for bolts loosened by ticket holders the previous contest so the seats could be quickly unhinged after the finale.

Those seats even come on the market these days after their original "owners" pass away. They often go for $350 or so.

Boone Hosey gained one from a widow after he promised to give it a good home.

"It just screamed character," said Hosey of the orange seat.

The problem was RFK wasn't being demolished. Indeed, it's still used for soccer games 18 years later. Maybe if the place was being demolished it would have been different, but any missing seats and turf would be costly to replace.

One pair of fans even ventured onto the high overhang and took the Washington banner. It has been spotted by collectors over the years, although no one wants to admit who has it because the pennant would surely be confiscated by police as stolen property.

Also taken was a football from the team locker room. It was signed by Redskins players beforehand, and its disappearance brought angry exchanges and finger pointing that weren't resolved. There was a lot of chaos in the tunnels, too. Given the team was leaving the city, security didn't worry about much.

"I recall a festive atmosphere—a combination of nostalgia and hatred for the rival Cowboys," said Jonathan Forsythe, whose family sat in Section 527 since the stadium's 1961 opening. "It was more a celebration than a typical rivalry game."

Even the walk from the parking lots was memorable.

"Walking out through the tunnel from Lot 8 toward the stadium," Patrick McVean said, "was like a gladiator coming out of tunnel facing the fight which all but certain was victory."

The metal bleachers at midfield, which were once rolled back for baseball games, still shook, although "maybe not as much as [they] did during the glory years," said Chris Reames, who came home from college to see the game in the lower bowl near the 30-yard line. "But it certainly had at least an echo of the good ol' days.

Halftime saw the team's legends introduced, and it left a more lasting impression on Reames than the game itself.

"I remember vividly when Dexter Manley was introduced," Reames said. "He got the loudest and longest ovation, and he seemed generally moved [and] touched by that. He stood on the field, soaking in the love and adoration of the fans. I know that Dexter struggled mightily with his personal demons, but in that moment I like to think that he found some measure of peace and love from those of us who had cheered him on during his career."

It was a farewell performance for a venue that housed three title teams over the previous 13 years that endeared the aging facility to fans. Winning turns a house into a home, and successor FedEx Field has never been accepted by fans because of the team's persistent losing and largeness, which allows massive amounts of visiting fans.

"FedEx Field is everything that RFK was not," Reames said. "FedEx Field is soulless, dominated by out-of-town fans and, for a building with its capacity, surprisingly quiet. RFK, even when things weren't great, was a madhouse. I have never felt a building of that size shake the way it could. For me, RFK is where my best football memories were born. There was a bond between the fans and the team that RFK represented.

"That final game was the last chance to truly experience that bond in my mind."

72 Pearl Harbor Game

Associated Press reporter Pat O'Brien was told to keep his Redskins-Eagles game story short. Why?

"The Japs have just kicked off. Pearl Harbor bombed. War now," was the reply.

What?

It was December 7, 1941, and America was now at war with the Japanese, who bombed Pearl Harbor one hour before the Redskins kicked off. The only people in Griffith Stadium that knew were O'Brien, *Washington Post* columnist Shirley Povich, and some Redskins officials.

But the crowd of 27,102, which included future President John F. Kennedy, sensed something was wrong, Povich wrote in a 50th anniversary column of the game, when eight minutes into the first quarter the stadium announcer began repeatedly paging military and government officials.

"Admiral W.H.P. Bland is asked to report to his office at once," was the first announcement, seeking the navy's Chief of Ordnance.

Next came, "The resident commissioner of the Philippines, Mr. Joaquin Elizade, is asked to report to his office."

"Mr. J. Edgar Hoover is asked to report to his office," was paged for the head of the Federal Bureau of Investigation.

Soon other admirals, colonels, and cabinet officers were requested. Only two other NFL games, at the Polo Grounds and

Comiskey Park, were underway, and both crowds were advised of the attack.

Redskins owner George Preston Marshall refused to make any announcements, later saying, "I didn't want to divert the fans' attention from the game." Redskins general manager Jack Epsey told Povich that day, "We don't want to contribute to any hysteria."

Because, you know, it's only World War II starting. It was the first attack on U.S. soil by a foreign invader since the War of 1812 when the British burned Washington and later fired upon Baltimore in that whole Star Spangled Banner incident. It certainly wasn't worth keeping the crowd from eating hot dogs and watching the game, figured Marshall.

"We didn't know what the hell was going on," Redskins quarterback Sammy Baugh later told *Sports Illustrated*. "I had never heard that many announcements one right after another. We felt something was up, but we just kept playing."

Washington was 5–5 and needing a win to possibly reach the playoffs, which it didn't anyway. Philadelphia at 2–7–1 wasn't lying down. The Eagles jumped ahead 7–0 early, but Baugh threw two fourth-quarter touchdowns for a 20–14 victory. That only one newspaper photographer of an early horde stayed for the game's end meant something was up.

Several hundred fans rushed the goal posts after game. The crowd then left the stadium around 4:30 PM to find newspaper boys hawking special editions containing the news that the U.S. was at war.

Redskins players soon walked to the Japanese embassy less than two miles away, looking for a fight. But the military had already seized the property. The staff was taken to an internment camp in West Virginia before later being swapped for U.S. embassy staff in Japan.

One of the Eagles players that day was kicker Nick Basca, who scored two points. He enlisted three days later and died on November 11, 1944, in France when his tank hit a mine as a member of General George Patton's famed Fourth Armored Division of the Third Army.

The attack on Pearl Harbor began at 12:58 PM East Coast time. Some 353 Japanese fighters, torpedo plans, and bombers damaged all eight U.S. Navy battleships docked with four sunk. Three cruisers, three destroyers, an anti-aircraft training ship, and one minelayer plus 188 aircraft were damaged or destroyed.

There were 2,402 American casualties and 1,282 wounded. The Japanese saw 65 personnel dead or wounded with 29 planes and five midget submarines destroyed.

On December 8, 2013, the Redskins had an on-field ceremony to honor Chief Petty Officer Howard Snell, who served on the USS *Morrison* at Pearl Harbor on that fateful day. He has been a Redskins season ticket holder since 1973. There was a long standing ovation, which Washington fans always give military members honored during games, but Snell's was one to remember.

As was "December 7, 1941—a date that will live in infamy," as President Franklin D. Roosevelt would later say.

73 Join Redskins Marching Band

They don't have 76 trombones, but the Washington Redskins marching band still makes the crowd tap their feet after 77 years.

And you can try out.

It's a volunteer band started by Redskins owner George Preston Marshall in 1937. Marshall saw the band as a way to attract women to games who would bring men, too. A "Teepee Nest" was erected in the grandstand, and a dance band played during games. The band would perform from the field before games and during halftime.

Marshall was a maverick when it came to NFL bands. While college teams usually have bands, many with elaborate programs, only the Redskins and the old Baltimore Colts (and now Ravens) have them in the pros. Strange how the only NFL marching bands are 40 miles apart.

Washingtonians loved marching bands in some part due to famed native John Philip Sousa, who created many a catchy tune such as "The Stars and Stripes Forever" while serving as a bandleader and conductor of military marches. Indeed, Sousa commanded the U.S. Marine Band until his 1932 death. To fill out his 150-member band in 1938, Marshall recruited members from a local reform school and the Chestnut Farms Chevy Chase Dairy Band.

Dairy Band? Guess the brass band knew how to moooove to the groove.

The band wanted "Onward Christian Soldiers" as its fight song, but Marshall chose bandleader Barnee Breeskin's "Hail to the Redskins." The melody was supposedly similar to "Jesus Loves Me," though the modern version sure doesn't sound like it.

One of the band's more interesting sidebars was the Funky Foursome in the late 1990s, which performed in the end zone during third-quarter breaks. The four band members danced to "Play That Funky Music" by Wild Cherry, and it was a regular sensation for several years.

The Funky Four actually started off as a dare. Thomas Clarke, Harry Jackson III, and Michael Dorsey, former bandmates at Norfolk State University, challenged rookie Kenny Scott to dance with a cheerleader during a timeout. A TV cameraman put them on the Jumbotron, and the fans loved it. A new sensation was born.

The Redskins Marching Band perform prior to the game between the New Orleans Saints against the Washington Redskins at FedEx Field on September 14, 2008, in Landover, Maryland. The Redskins defeated the Saints 29–24. (AP Photo/Scott Boehm)

The group would vary routines each game and also performed at community events. "SuperSkin," a Redskins version of Superman, sometimes danced with the group.

The Redskins band plays anything from 1960s rock to traditional marching tunes to current pop songs, but it is best known for "Hail to the Redskins." Starting in 1938, the song created by Breeskin and Marshall's wife, Corrine Griffith, is typically played at the game's start, when the band is on the field, and after scores. These days, the band is seated in an end zone.

Today the band has 120 musicians plus a support staff. More than 90 percent of members carry over each year and word-of-mouth brings replacements, but occasionally someone just calls to apply. There are a handful of members with 50 years or more of service and a couple dozen with at least 20 years.

If a prospective new member applies, and if there's an opening for the instrument they play, the person usually sits in on a few rehearsals to see if they "fit in" with the band and vice versa. Then they are asked to audition—a few major scales, a prepared piece, and perhaps some sight reading. If they pass the audition, they are then invited to join the band. All members must be at least 21 years old.

Now it's not just about showing up on game days. Members practice on Wednesday nights at FedEx Field from April until the season's end, aside from a break in July.

The group performs at all home games, including preseason and playoffs, plus draft day, fan appreciation day, training camp, and parades around Washington.

After a brief silence after touchdowns when a canned recording is played, the band is back in form after all scores. The band plays along with a recorded version of "Hail to the Redskins" after extra points because it includes the words sang by The Redskins Singers from long ago.

So grab that old trombone, slide some scales, and head to auditions. There's nothing like marching across the field playing "Hail to the Redskins," unless it's singing it from the stands after victories.

74 Win Your Point on Sports Talk

You're thinking the guy on the radio is a moron. Anybody can talk about sports. It would be your dream job.

So try it for one minute.

Make the call to either WJFK 106.7-FM or ESPN 980-AM in Washington to talk Redskins. Add to the conversation. Sound intelligent like you always do in your own mind when listening or talking with your friends during the game.

It's easy, right?

So why do so many callers sound like idiots?

Every Redskins fan should be on the radio once. Give your opinion. Sound like a winner.

But several Washington sports talk hosts say it's harder than many believe. Thom Loverro was a colleague of mine with two newspapers over 20 years. He now hosts ESPN 980's midday show with Kevin Sheehan. Loverro offers some simple advice on winning your point.

"Always listen to the Redskin question being asked on the phone," he said. "Come with a response to the question. Don't tell your personal story about how you once ate in the same restaurant with RG III. And don't go off on your own favorite rant. It's not your show. Stick to the question, have an answer under 90 seconds, and you'll become a regular."

Grant Paulsen started calling radio shows when he was 10 years old. Now he's WJFK's midday host. And one day soon, Paulsen's going to be a national big shot.

Just 26 years old, Paulsen relates well to young callers. But he doesn't tolerate sloppy callers who don't know what they're saying. According to Paulsen, the key is knowing facts versus opinion.

"The main thing I would tell anybody calling into a radio station is to have your facts straight," Paulsen said. "Don't call a player the wrong name or say that a guy plays a position that he doesn't. Having a factoid wrong completely cripples any credibility you have, both with listeners and the host.

"If you want to gain extra bonus points, research the topic. Have some stats or evidence to support your claims. Think like a lawyer or perhaps like a student writing a convincing essay. Don't just have an opinion. Back up your opinion not with thoughts but legitimate evidence."

It's fine to bring passion to the airwaves. Just remember not to come off like some raving lunatic.

"Maybe 90 percent of people are passionate about their team," said Chris Russell, ESPN 980's Redskins reporter and show host, "but base your argument on facts."

Facts? Who needs facts when you can scream and call names? Many hosts only tolerate hateful callers for so long, though.

"I had to grow 8,000 layers of skin working in this market," Russell said.

Of course, there are some tricks to becoming a regular. Other listeners will soon know you as Matt from Waldorf, John from Frederick, or Jake from Annapolis, and soon you'll have street cred at tailgate parties.

"Number one—tell show hosts you love the show," Sheehan said. "Number two—answer the question asked, and do it in 15 seconds or less."

Practice your response once or twice while on hold. So many people fumble coming out of the gate and lose all credibility. Write down key words if it helps organize your thoughts. And be sure to listen so the host doesn't say your name two or three times wondering if you're there, making you sound like some oaf. Most of all, don't use a speakerphone. It makes you sound like a dork. Same goes for poor cell-phone reception.

Have something to contribute to the conversation. It makes you sound knowledgeable.

Don't ask open-ended questions like, "What do you think of the Redskins defense?" Please, could you be any sillier? That question doesn't rate a call; it rates therapy for your attention deficit disorder. What's the matter—didn't Mom love you best?

Arguing with a host is fine. It's what makes sports talk radio so fun. Some hosts are more tolerant than others. Some big egos can't take the bruising. They're in radio just to hear themselves talk, but some hosts welcome the chance to debate.

Occasionally, you're going to win your point. And buddy, there's nothing better than being right on the air.

75 The Bingo Caller

A fresh set of eyes gave the Redskins a shiner and delivered a TKO to vice president Vinny Cerrato and Coach Jim Zorn.

How in the world did Sherman Lewis, a retiree calling bingo and delivering meals on wheels, suddenly start calling offensive plays? Welcome to the wacky world of owner Dan Snyder and Cerrato.

Welcome to the birth of the Burgundy Revolution that nearly turned more than 40 years of unwavering fan support into empty seats, confiscated signs, and bitter feelings.

Zorn was doomed entering the 2009 season. Snyder nearly fired him at the end of 2008 after finishing 2–6, but the 8–8 overall record wasn't horrible and Snyder feared more accusations of meddling so the coach received a second year.

It was the shortest of leashes that turned into a choke chain after a 2–2 start. The offense didn't score more than 17 points while ranking 27th overall. The only first-half touchdown was on a fake field goal.

Snyder once more meddled by hiring a consultant.

Lewis, 67, hadn't coached in five years after 22 seasons in the NFL. He was once mentioned as a possible head coach but was essentially a career assistant. Lewis worked in the West Coast Offense in Green Bay and Seattle under Coach Mike Holmgren. Lewis served as Green Bay's offensive coordinator from 1992 to 1999 with a 1996 championship. He was also an offensive coordinator in Minnesota and Detroit before retiring after 2004.

Lewis' resume was respectable, but it was five years old. And in the NFL, that's a lifetime of change. And to bring him in during the season as a consultant was nothing but trouble for Zorn, who was now publicly neutered.

"It's not a threat at all," Cerrato told reporters. "Nothing changes. Jim's still calling plays. Everybody's still doing what they're doing. It's just another fresh set of eyes."

Lewis seemed a little bewildered when meeting with the press, as would be expected by someone who was calling "B-9" just days earlier. He wasn't sure if this was just a quick paycheck for suggestions, and he was reluctant to step on anyone's toes. Basically, Lewis figured he would watch film and try to find little things that could be corrected. Certainly Lewis wasn't expecting to be more than a brief contributor during Tuesday work sessions when coaches decide the coming game plan.

Thirteen days later, Lewis was named offensive playcaller. Zorn should have quit right then, but with $6 million remaining on his contract, lasting another 12 weeks would mean financial security for life.

What Zorn should have done was refuse to let Lewis call plays and be fired by Snyder. That way the coach would have left with his money and sanity. Instead, he entered another circle of hell.

The move was stunning in that many Redskins players didn't even know who Lewis was after nearly two weeks in the facility. They figured he was another of Snyder's spies since Lewis was never introduced to the team. Now he was calling plays near midseason?

Naturally, the next few weeks were chaos. Lewis opened with four straight losses as Washington scored 17 points in three games and two field goals in a 14–6 loss to Kansas City. The Redskins finally broke loose with a 27–17 victory over Denver but then lost 7–6 to Dallas. Washington would later lose to Dallas 17–0 at FedEx Field, too.

December went a touch better for Washington, though there was a 33–30 loss to New Orleans. That was followed in January by a 23–20 defeat to San Diego in the season-ender. Zorn was fired the next day. Lewis wasn't retained by incoming coach Joe Gibbs and hasn't worked in the NFL since. Cerrato had already been replaced a month earlier after trying to blame Zorn for the woes and has also never worked in the league again. Snyder has never hired another consultant again.

The season statistics are startling. Kicker Shaun Suisham's mere 74 points were 29 less than the first year with Zorn, although Suisham was cut with four games remaining in the season. Fred Davis, who had six touchdowns, was the only player with more than three scores. Quarterback Jason Campbell threw 20 touchdowns and 15 interceptions and was released by incoming coach Mike Shanahan.

If anything good came out of the mess, Lewis served as a prime example of why Snyder needed to hire football people to run the team instead of meddling himself. General manager Bruce Allen and Shanahan allowed the owner to worry about the business side in winning the NFC East in their third year, but 3–13 in 2013 brought Shanahan's dismissal.

Still, letting football people run the team is—bingo—a winning formula.

76 Best FedEx Field Seats

Favorite seats are like romances. Some end up better than others.

And just like some fans prefer blondes over brunettes while others like redheads, so it goes with finding the best place to sit at FedEx Field.

After all, there are 79,000 seats from which to choose.

Unlike the RFK days when the only option was to buy from a scalper outside the stadium for the precious few seats available, today's fans can just click on StubHub.com, which has partnered with the NFL for the secondary market. In lean years, the parking pass was often more expensive than the tickets.

But FedEx Field is massive, at one point reaching 91,000 seats. Tickets often sold for less than face value, especially for preseason games.

But where to sit or, even more importantly, what seats should you avoid? It's not as simple as you think.

Prime example No. 1—dream seats. Owner Dan Snyder added them in front of the former front-row seats after buying the team in 1999. Imagine how mad those fans with the former front seats were.

Ironically, some dream seat residents say they're actually horrible because they are too close. Yes, you can be too close to the

The exterior of FedEx Field in Landover, Maryland, before a game against the Carolina Panthers on November 26, 2006. The Redskins defeated the Panthers 17–13. (AP Photo/Paul Spinelli)

action because you can't see over the players and other sideline workers.

"Dream seats are not the best seats," said Redskins die-hard fan Samu Qureshi, who has sat everywhere from luxury suites to the upper deck over the years. "You're way too close in. First five rows, you're trying to see over the players' heads. You want to be 10 to 15 rows up for a great perspective."

Okay, it doesn't take a rocket scientist to know midfield, 10 rows up in the lower deck is the best place. Actually, almost anywhere in the lower bowl is a good seat. The corners can be tricky, though.

Better to be in the end zone where you can see plays straight on than in the corner. Naturally that's where the press box sits.

"It's great when they're playing on our end," said Joe Ziegengeist, who sits in section 135 of the end zone. "Otherwise we're watching the video boards."

Christie Lopez, one of the more diehard fans who has a rocking tailgate party and organizes welcome-home gatherings for the team after road games, sits in Section 105 by the tunnel where the Redskins enter the field.

"It's hard to see the other end of the field," she said. "Thank God for the new big screens. But we love it because the Redskins come out of the tunnel under us."

Said Qureshi, "The undervalued seats are right in the end zone. Each play you're either looking at the quarterback's perspective or the linebacker's. You can see the line and the way it's moving very clearly, and the seats are a fraction of the price of the 20-yard line. If the play is on the other side of the field, you're pretty much watching it on the jumbo screen."

The only warning on lower bowl seats are ones that have obstructed views.

"The warning when I purchased them from StubHub was that they were partially obstructed, which was an understatement," said Adam Bass, who sat in Section 214, row 23. "You can see only about 80 to 85 percent of the field due to the overhang above you. If the ball is kicked or even thrown higher than a few feet in the air, you cannot see it from the seats [because] the overhang blocks the view. To 'rectify' this issue, the Redskins have TVs installed throughout the area, but it is delayed and you do not see any of the replays.

"About midway through the second quarter, we decided to take our chances that no one would be in the 400 level and went up there and found empty seats. The view from the 400 section is 100 times better than Section 214."

Handful of 200-Yard Rushers

The top five best rushing efforts did not come from those who rank in the team's top five all time rushers.

Gerald Riggs delivered the best day ever by a Redskins running back with 221 yards and one touchdown on 29 carries in a 1989 loss against Philadelphia.

But Cliff Battles' 215 yards and one touchdown is even more impressive given just 16 carries in a 1933 victory over the New York Giants.

George Rogers gained 206 yards and one touchdown on 34 carries in a 1985 victory over St. Louis. Timmy Smith gained 204 yards and two touchdowns on 22 carries in the Super Bowl XXII victory over Denver in January 1988. Alfred Morris rushed for 200 yards and three scores in a 2012 win over Dallas.

What about the fancy yellow club seats that are often unfilled because those paying $250 per ticket are watching from an inside bar?

"I sat in the club for 10 years, and it was like a golf clap for an interception or a touchdown," Qureshi said. "It was just a corporate atmosphere."

Anywhere in the upper deck is like watching from another planet. The top seats are so high that fans can see the crosstown skyscrapers of Tyson's Corner, Virginia, roughly 20 miles away. But Ankit Mittal is a fan of the standing-room passes that are cheaper because there are no actual seats.

"Standing room seats are great," he said. "[It's like the] All-22 view [on film] to see what Robert Griffin III is seeing and what the defense is seeing, as well."

77 Name Controversy

Will the Washington Redskins one day be known as the Washington Warriors or something else? Yes.

Will it be anytime soon? No.

Any questions?

The past year has seen steady conversation devoted to changing the team's name. Some American Indians, especially those from the Oneida Nation, say the name is offensive and should be changed. Many long-time team supporters say it's not meant to be offensive and doesn't need to be changed.

If only it were that simple.

(Full disclosure: I'm part Cherokee Indian, but I wasn't raised in a tribal culture and don't pretend to represent the American Indian view.)

I've talked more about this topic with friends, readers, and those on both sides of the issue over the past two years than I have over the rest of my lifetime. That tells me change is coming, but we're in the beginning stages of a long discussion.

Redskins owner Dan Snyder said he would "never" change the name. Hopefully, he now understands such a statement was not only a mistake but an insult. For Snyder to say he wouldn't even consider other views is offensive to those seeking change. He should at least weigh their opinions. Months later, Snyder released a statement saying no disrespect was intended by the name, and in March 2014, he launched the Washington Redskins Original Americans Foundation to "provide meaningful and mea-surable resources that provide genuine opportunities for Tribal communities."

Predecessor George Preston Marshall dialed back some of the Indian references after meeting with tribal leaders, and the Redskins owner was the one who named the team. Some say Marshall used Redskins as a tribute to Coach Lone Star Dietz, who is largely considered a faux American Indian. Some believe Marshall was playing off the Boston Braves and Boston Red Sox names.

Marshall admired American Indians in a time that was far different from today's politically correct world. He was a marketer above all else and saw it as a way to promote the team. American interest in Indian culture peaked in the 1930s, so Marshall was in keeping with the times.

But after meeting with Indian leaders, Marshall stopped dressing cheerleaders as squaws and changed some of the lyrics to "Hail to the Redskins." If Marshall could change, certainly Snyder can bend a half century later.

Today, the dispute comes down to this—Indians say it's offensive, and fans say it's not. Indian leaders make an excellent point in saying no one should tell them whether they should be offended. If they are, they are.

But tribal leaders should also consider fans believe the name is not intentionally offensive. After talking with American Indians from several states, I think they understand fans aren't intentionally offending them.

After a lot of thought, here's how I see it.

Americans once used negative words to describe people of color, sexual persuasion, nationality, ethnicity, and special needs. One by one, we've stopped saying them in everyday conversation. We've learned why those words are offensive and have largely stopped using them. They're not completely gone from our vocabulary, but they aren't said in normal conversation.

But Redskins has never been a word used in everyday conversation, at least around Washington. I'm 54 and have never heard it referenced outside the team aside from a few old westerns. Those who are older than me say they've never heard it used as a slur.

Washingtonians aren't in regular contact with Indians. There isn't a reservation or a high number of Indians in the region, although there are some tribes. Still, it's not something in daily life, so fans aren't looking to insult those they don't know.

That's why fans don't see the need to change the name. And in a town where political correctness is constantly discussed, locals don't like outsiders saying Washingtonians are ignorant racists. It only makes things worse.

The only things that will force a name change are economics, trademark rulings, and stadium sites. If the NFL's major sponsors decided to side with the anti-name leaders, league owners would pressure Snyder to change the name because it would be money out of their pockets. Can that happen? Anything's possible, but it's not on the current radar.

If a future trademark case rules against the Redskins and the NFL would no longer earn royalties off anything sold using Redskins, the name could change. Again, it's a financial incentive.

If the Redskins want to return to the city limits and a name change would be demanded in exchange of gaining a stadium, much like the team relented to signing black players when moving to D.C. Stadium in 1961, then the name would be changed.

It's all about money. Then again, what isn't in the world anymore? Perhaps with continued lobbying, American Indians will finally sway fans into understanding the problem. And maybe then the name will change.

But it won't happen anytime soon.

78 Visit Carlisle

Time for a road trip. A ghost tour of sorts.

Every Redskins fan should visit Carlisle, Pennsylvania, where the Redskins spent training camp during 1963–94 and 2001–02. It is the fan's mecca from a time when the team was often good and players could be easily approached.

About 100 miles from Washington's outer Maryland suburbs, Carlisle is more like small-town America with a Main Street. Where children play on manicured lawns and an ice cream stand beckons passersby amid plenty of small non-chain restaurants and bars for a local touch.

Carlisle was founded in 1751 and is primarily known for its U.S. Army War College and one-time Indian School. Less than 20,000 people now live in a town that's 5.4 square miles.

Right in the middle of town is Dickinson College, which is perhaps best known for its law school. Created in 1773, the school's 2,300 students made way for the Redskins each summer.

The stone dorms were well located with downtown just a couple blocks away and suburban homes around the football field just a short walk or bike ride for players. Legend says the reason there are no driveways is the city outlawed garages after one of the first cars burned down a home.

The tour begins at Biddle Field on the far edge of campus. It was here that fans could sit in the stands and watch the Redskins practice for free. There were none of the heavy marketing ploys now used by NFL teams. Indeed, you might find water at a concession stand at best. Look to the far right and you'll see a wooden deck protruding from one of the bordering homes. Fans used to watch practices from that deck. Many of the Hogs swore that one day they would return to drink beer and watch from it, too.

It's a typical small college field with an encircling track and modest brick locker rooms on the side not far from the stands. Listen closely and you might hear George Allen blowing his whistle or Joe Gibbs calling for the offense to make the play.

Exiting the field, you'll see Massey's Frozen Custard Stand on 600 W. High Street. It doesn't come much better than this. Allen used to make his unpaid intern, Charley Casserly, get ice cream for the coaches every night. Coach Marty Schottenheimer once ordered milkshakes for the entire team after practice.

Massey's was a cool savior on many a hot day. Carlisle may have been up north, but it seemed every bit as hot and muggy as Washington.

Head toward downtown and the Hamilton Restaurant at 55 W. High Street is a favorite spot among the college kids. The Hamilton offers American-style fare and is known for its hot dogs. John Riggins supposedly once ate 22 hot dogs on a dare there one night. They're thin dogs, so it's possible. Just envision Riggo scarfing them down, money surely on the table for side bets among teammates.

Still hungry? Head to the Gingerbread Man at 5 S. Courthouse Avenue. It's basically a couple blocks east of the college near the town's center of High and Hanover with an adjacent parking garage.

Okay, this is where the beer flows and chicken wings fly. The G-Man was more for drinking than eating, but you can do both. Redskins players were known to drink at the G-Man more in the 1970s, but even during the 2001–02 camps, owner Dan Snyder and Coach Steve Spurrier were seen there. Indeed, Snyder bought the team's beat writers a round one night. If you want to see where the boys drank, this was often it.

If you're in the mood for a fine meal, head over to Rillo's at 60 Pine Street. Its white tablecloths and wine accent standout Italian fare, which often brought big crowds during training camp. But Rillo's wasn't so filled that Redskins coaches and front office personnel couldn't find a table there. Maybe this is where general manager Bobby Beathard and Gibbs created some deals.

The town misses the team, and surely Redskins fans miss the carefree summers and successful teams that were spawned annually by the town. But you can go home again, even if no one you remember remains.

Have a beer at the G-Man for me.

79 133 mph to Jail

It was a story ripped straight from the frames of *Smokey and the Bandit*.

Redskins running back Terry Allen was caught driving 133 mph just days before reporting to training camp in 1997. Even worse, he was also charged with reckless driving, driving under the influence of alcohol, refusing to pull over for police roadblocks, striking a fixed object, and no proof of insurance.

Talk about a bad night.

My editor told me to make damn sure we're talking about the same Terry Allen. Sure enough, double checking the birth date on the police report while talking with the Walton County Sheriff's Department in Monroe, Georgia, showed the Redskins running back was in big trouble.

There's some old advice that if an argument with your spouse becomes too heated, get in the car and drive awhile to cool off.

Running back Terry Allen (21) carries the ball during a game against the Dallas Cowboys at RFK Stadium on October 4,1998, in Washington, D.C. The Cowboys won 31–10. (AP Photo/David Stluka)

That's what Allen was doing...only his car was a new $137,000 F355 Ferrari Spider.

Police initially estimated Allen was traveling 150 mph to 180 mph when he was first spotted at 2:00 AM on a rural road in northern Georgia where he lived in the off-season. When a Georgia state trooper lit up his overhead lights, Allen took off.

And here's where Allen made his critical mistake. If he had just pulled over, the worst penalty probably would have been a whopping four-figure fine that Allen could have easily paid. Maybe Allen would have still been arrested for drunk driving, but often convictions don't include jail time. Either way, Allen made things a whole lot worse for himself by hitting the gas pedal.

Indeed, it turned out Allen was better at eluding tacklers than road blocks. After evading the first road block, Allen took off in another direction only to crash into a road sign and tree while trying to elude the second police blockade. Luckily, he suffered only minor injuries. One report said Allen suffered a concussion.

Police say Allen told them he was a "professional ballplayer for the Washington Redskins," but that didn't change anything. Allen's blood alcohol tested .14, well above the state .10 legal limit. He was freed on a $6,863 bond.

It was the beginning of a bad stretch for Allen. After gaining more than 1,309 yards in 1995 and a team-record 1,353 in '96, he managed only 724 yards in 1997 while missing six games with multiple injuries.

Bubba Head, an Atlanta attorney known as "The Gladiator" whose clientele also included rapper Lil' Wayne, managed to delay the case for nearly one year before Allen was sentenced to 10 days in jail, 40 hours of community service, and a $2,000 fine. Allen served five days as a model prisoner in a hot city jail that lacked air conditioning. Two weeks later, Allen arrived at training camp and spoke once about the affair after the opening practice.

Nobody's Catching Riggo

Every few years, it seems like some Redskins running back has a chance to catch John Riggins as the team's career leading rusher if they can just manage three more good seasons. And like a freight train hitting an oncoming locomotive, their career ends and Riggins remains on top.

Riggins' 7,472 yards during 1976–79 and 1981–85 is especially impressive considering he held out in 1980 in a contract dispute and played in 1971–75 for the New York Jets. Riggins' 11,352 career yards could have been around 13,000 overall. That number would have been hard to surpass if he had spent his entire career with Washington and not skipped a year.

Clinton Portis came closest with 6,824 from 2004 to 2010, but injuries limited his last two seasons. Larry Brown was No. 1 before Riggins with 5,875 from 1969 to 1976. Stephen Davis also seems a real challenger with 5,790 from 1996 to 2002.

Riggins is also the leader in carries with 1,988 over Portis' 1,667. Riggins' 375 carries in 1983 are a team mark over Davis' 356 in 2001.

"On the incident that happened last year, that was a mistake that I made," said Allen when he arrived at camp. "I take full responsibility for what I did. I've done my time for that. I lived up to what I had to do and it's behind me, and I'm looking forward to this year."

Unfortunately, 1998 would be Allen's last in Washington after playing only 10 games for the second straight season while gaining just 700 yards and two touchdowns—19 fewer scores than two years earlier. Allen was then released, losing his job and the team rushing record to Stephen Davis in 1999.

Allen started 13 games for New England in 1999 for 896 yards but started just three games in New Orleans in 2000 and eight games in 2001 for Baltimore. Allen gained 8,614 yards with 55 touchdowns over 11 seasons, but he was never a 1,000-yard runner after the accident.

80 Lombardi and McVean

Vince Lombardi was looking for practice dummies.

The problem was that they were at a New Jersey factory. However, that was now equipment manager Tommy McVean's problem. Lombardi was looking for the dummies as the 1969 season started in Washington, and McVean didn't want the legendary coach's "veins popping out of his head, upset over not getting something in time."

McVean called the factory to prepare the night watchman for a midnight pickup. McVean then drove a truck all night to get them. McVean threw the dummies on the field 10 minutes before the 9:00 AM practice.

Whew—mission accomplished.

Days later, Lombardi told McVean of hearing a crazy story of the latter driving all night to get the dummies.

"Lombardi said, 'Don't take me so seriously,'" McVean said. "He pulled out his money clip, gave me five $100 bills, and said buy everyone a round and send the rest to my wife. It was a great, great experience being around the guy."

McVean was a can-do guy who worked under five coaches from 1963 to 1977 before later reuniting with Allen in 1983 with the USFL's Chicago Blitz. McVean now manages the Colony Golf Club men's lounge in Naples, Florida, where quarterback Sonny Jurgensen is a club member.

McVean was working as a groundskeeper with the Washington Senators when a Redskins employee asked if he could drive the team bus to the practice field. McVean said sure despite not having a driver's license. After one trip, a team official taught McVean how to drive in the parking lot for the ride back. He remarkably joined the team after that day.

According to McVean, working for Lombardi was one continuous life lesson.

"Lombardi said, 'Son, do you know why I won all these championships? I'll tell you the secret. You have to get better, or people pass you by. Learn something every day,'" McVean said. "Everything was so regimented. Players met from 8:00 to 9:00 PM, coaches 9:00 to 10:30, and you had to be in your room by 10:30–10:45. When he would leave the coaches meeting room, he'd pop by your room. You had to be there.

"He'd always push the players to the limit. He'd come up to guys and ask what part of the country would you live in if you didn't live here. The player would [ask] why.... He said if you tell me where you live, that's where I'll try to trade you if you don't start getting off your ass."

In Redskins owner Jack Kent Cooke's final years, his young assistant tired of listening to the Cooke's advice about reading and education. The young man finally bought the CliffsNotes to *The Great Gatsby* and fooled Cooke into thinking he was reading the book.

McVean had done the same thing to Lombardi nearly 30 years earlier.

"Lombardi always talked about [the novel] *War and Peace.* Everyone should read the book," McVean said. "So I go out and buy the book for $38. I hear him coming down the hallway. He wore taps on his shoes. I pull out *War and Peace* and he said, 'What are you reading?' [I said,] '*War and Peace.* It's some serious stuff.' He said, 'Next road trip [Lombardi's wife] Marie's not coming. You sit up with me, and we'll talk about it.'"

Lombardi died the following year. Two days later, when playing Miami in a preseason game, McVean remembered the locker rooms before and during the next game.

"There was a moment of silence before the game. Guys are teary-eyed. We're down 16–0 at half. The offense was on one side of the locker room, the defense on the other. [Coach Bill] Austin walked in and just knocked blackboards over. He said, 'The old man is watching us. You ought to be embarrassed. We're going to the funeral in the morning. Let's take the game ball to the old man.'

"We beat them in the second half [to win 26–21]. They took the game ball and put it in the grave.

"Bill Austin never brought up Lombardi again."

81 Two-Time First-Rounder = 0

Imagine Redskins owner George Preston Marshall's note to running back Cal Rossi: "Fool me once, shame on you. Fool me twice, shame on me."

The shame and blame were really all on Marshall, who drafted Rossi in 1946 with the ninth overall pick when the UCLA star was ineligible as a junior. Just to be stubborn, Marshall again selected Rossi with the 1947 fourth overall choice only to learn the latter didn't want to play pro football. Indeed, Rossi never did.

Two first-round picks for someone who never played? Makes Robert Griffin III's three firsts and a second look like a bargain.

Marshall's problem was essentially eliminating a scouting system and drafting based on what he read in magazines and newspapers. Funny, wasn't a later owner accused of doing the same thing?

It's not like the 1946 draft was star-studded. Notre Dame offensive tackle George Connor was the only eventual Pro Football

Hall of Famer, taken fifth overall by the New York Giants. In 1947, Ohio State end Dante Lavelli was chosen 103rd overall by the Los Angeles Rams. Boston College defensive tackle Art Donovan was taken 204th overall by the Giants, though he didn't play until 1950 for Baltimore.

Marshall wasn't the only owner who wasted a draft pick. In 1947, Pittsburgh chose Texas receiver Hub Bechtol, who was selected after Rossi. Bechtol never played for the Steelers, either.

In 1946, Marshall drafted so daftly that only 2-of-30 draftees signed with the Redskins.

Rossi was a halfback and defensive back for the Bruins. He gained 1,490 yards on 255 carries, which was at the time third most in school history in 1947, and the 5.85 yards per carry was the highest average ever. His 169 yards against Oregon in 1945 was a Bruins record until 1960. He was inducted into the Bruins Hall of Fame in 1997.

Rossi was the nation's second-leading rusher in 1947 before his military commitment required his transfer to the Naval Corps Supply School at Harvard University.

Defensively, Rossi made seven interceptions, including three his senior year.

Rossi was also a UCLA baseball first baseman, hitting .456 in 1945.

With all this natural talent, Rossi seemed a natural to help the Redskins. If Marshall knew anything, he would have quickly learned what the rest of the NFL knew—Rossi wanted to become an educator.

Rossi started teaching high school business classes and coached outside Los Angeles. He later became an advocate for teachers before retiring in 1984. He died in 2013.

Ironically, Rossi wasn't the only 1947 pick that rebuffed the Redskins. Fifth-rounder Hank Foldberg, who was the 28th overall pick back then, decided to spend another year at West Point before playing in the AAFC for the Brooklyn Dodgers in 1948 and Chicago Hornets in 1949. He caught 31 passes in two years.

You'd think Marshall would have learned from his 1939 first-round selection of Texas Christian offensive tackle I.B. Hale, who rejected the team.

The Redskins aren't alone with busts like Rossi. The very first pick in NFL history was Philadelphia taking Heisman Trophy winner Jay Berwanger in 1936. But the running back wanted $1,000 so Philadelphia traded him to Chicago, which also couldn't sign Berwanger. Meanwhile, the Redskins used the second pick to take Alabama linebacker Riley Smith, who at least lasted three seasons before suffering a career-ending injury.

82 Coach Out of His League

There was Steve Spurrier, standing on a chair, singing "Hail to the Redskins" in a bar the night before the 2002 training camp opened in Carlisle.

And all he drew were blank stares and silence.

Right there, the media knew that this coach wasn't going to work.

Spurrier was expecting a Gingerbread Man crowd filled with backers even if it was mostly the media grabbing a late supper and drinks. After all, the press always supported Spurrier at the University of Florida. National championships have a way of drawing unbridled support.

But this was Washington, and Spurrier was the fourth Redskins coach in 13 months. Plus the press corps was still stinging from predecessor Marty Schottenheimer's oppressive rules. Spurrier was gaining a fresh start and a whole lot of cash to come to Washington, but he wasn't getting a free pass from the press.

Spurrier was shocked by the cold reaction. It was just the start. His experience at his first Draft Day exposed Spurrier's shortcomings. Spurrier had such little involvement in picking players that the coach was once in the media room when the Redskins were on the clock for a mid-round selection. When later challenged to discuss a draft pick beyond height and weight, Spurrier stormed from the podium in a huff.

Spurrier was a likable person but prickly when reporters asked even simple questions over personnel moves. "Because I'm the ball-coach," he would testily reply without giving any reason.

College coaches have different strengths than NFL counterparts. They have to schmooze alumni and donors and recruit players. Like politicians, college coaches make strangers feel like close friends in 30 seconds. Spurrier could slap you on the back, tell a quick joke, give you a nickname, and move on with your support.

It's a gift, but one not that's needed to be successful in the pros. NFL coaches need to concentrate on the game, and that was Spurrier's weakness. He didn't like the long hours cutting into his golf game. A businessman's eight-hour day was long enough for him; many coaches work 14 hours or more each day.

The problem was Spurrier's obsession with his passing offense, even when it didn't work after he obtained his college passers Danny Wuerffel and Shane Matthews. Every time the offense faltered during a 7–9 season and a 5–11 season, Spurrier would balk, "You don't think my offense can work in the pros?"

Spurrier was woefully lacking as a pro coach, but that was partially hidden during his first year by defensive coordinator Marvin Lewis. When Spurrier asked Lewis which field the defense needed for practice, Lewis explained that the offense and defense share one field in the pros.

Special teams practice was free time for Spurrier. He'd practice his golf swing on the sideline with his quarterbacks. Many defensive players complained that Spurrier didn't even know their names. Even reserve receiver Darnerien McCants was called everything short of "d'Artagnan" by Spurrier.

NFL coaches disliked Spurrier's bravado, although they should thank him for their own pay raises. When Spurrier gained $5 million annually from Snyder, fellow NFL owners were upset over increased staff costs.

But Spurrier rubbed San Francisco coach Steve Mariucci the wrong way after Washington won the preseason opener in Osaka 38–7. It was supposed to be a friendly game since the preseason is meaningless, but Spurrier poured on 14 fourth-quarter points.

When the Washington media talked to Mariucci after the game, Spurrier came into the room and loudly said, "Hey, my guys. My guys over here," which clearly annoyed the 49ers coach. Spurrier whooped it up after winning his first pro game, and Mariucci told friends to wait until their Week Three regular season rematch. San Francisco never trailed, winning 20–10.

When Spurrier was asked why a player wasn't practicing, he often said, "He's not? How come?" That kind of said it all.

After losing the final three games and six of seven in 2003 to fall to 10–22 overall, Spurrier went golfing. He called a few days later to tell Snyder the remaining $10 million on his contract wasn't needed. Snyder wanted Spurrier to stay, but the latter knew he was better off coaching college football. Indeed, Spurrier turned woeful South Carolina into an annually ranked team since 2005.

Joe Gibbs would soon return to Redskins Park, and successor Jim Zorn was so bad that Spurrier's legacy is one of amusement more than agony among fans. Spurrier could be a fun guy, but it's never funny when you're losing.

83 Casserly—Intern to GM

Charley Casserly's story seems too extreme to be true. Yet it is, and he claims others can do so, too.

Casserly rose from unpaid intern to general manager of the Washington Redskins over 23 years, and he has the 1991 Super Bowl championship on his resume as GM and two more titles as assistant GM. Indeed, Casserly stayed until incoming owner Dan Snyder decided to change leadership after buying the team in 1999, a move he later conceded was wrong.

The expansion Houston Texans were next for Casserly from 2000 to 2006 before he was replaced. He now works for the NFL Network and teaches sports management at Georgetown University and George Mason University.

Casserly was a young high school teacher and coach in Massachusetts who dreamed of working in the NFL. He would give anything, and in the end he gave up everything to do so.

It was a gamble. Casserly was 28 years old with $500 in the bank and an old Chevy with 120,000 miles and a door that didn't close. After losing all his possessions in a fire two years earlier, even his furniture was from the Salvation Army. Now he was looking for an unpaid internship?

After writing every team in 1977 for a chance to do anything, Casserly heard from New England and Washington.

"My goal in life is to work for George Allen, so to meet him is thrilling," Casserly said. "I'd already interviewed with three people. I follow him down the hallway, and he starts the interview. We go down the old locker room, and we haven't missed a beat. We go through the coach's locker room. He goes into the john and sits down, and we haven't stopped the interview. I'm shouting over the flush."

Allen told Casserly to write three ways the latter could help the team win. It was something Allen always asked newcomers, to pick their brains.

Allen told Casserly he was looking for someone who would open the office in the morning and close it at night, just like Allen did when he started out 26 years before. Casserly smiled, having read the same quote by Allen years earlier.

Ironically, the Patriots were also interested, so Casserly was hedging to accept Washington's offer if he could remain closer to home.

"George said, 'We'd like you to be part of [our] intern program,' but I wanted to hear from the Patriots," Casserly said. "George said, '[Patriots coach] Chuck Fairbanks, I taught him everything they know. What are they offering? Who do you think you are? You have to think about coming to work for me?'"

After briefly meeting with the Patriots, Casserly accepted Allen's offer.

"Two weeks later, my mattress on the floor after my bed fell apart, I broke out in a cold sweat," Casserly said. "What have I done? I quit my job? I had to be out of my mind."

After spending $8 nightly to stay at a YMCA, Casserly survived on peanut butter. But soon he was receiving free room and board for two months of training camp, then he received expenses for ongoing scouting trips before finally crashing on a couch in a place shared by three Redskins.

Finally, Allen was hired as a scout in January for $17,000 annually. As he rose in the Redskins' hierarchy, Casserly started an internship program for those to follow his path. It is now offered by most NFL teams.

"I was the only intern in 1977. Now you can't count them," he said. "There are a number of guys who started as an intern. It's now grown to a point where guys start at the bottom."

But will today's young prospects be willing to endure Casserly's hardships to reach the NFL front office? He knows they can if they are willing to give everything they have.

"I knew this was the crossroads of my life," Casserly said. "I knew every day I was working for the biggest break of my life. I had already been a high school football coach [and an] athletic director. I had some responsibility in my life and a sense of urgency. Too many young people don't have that."

Which is why very few young people last long enough in the NFL to reach the top.

84 Buy One Piece of Memorabilia

In the Souvenir Nation exhibit, Smithsonian Museum curator William L. Bird said mementos are "a modest little thing that evokes memory [with a] personal connection."

Redskins fans are no different than someone visiting Disney World or the Grand Canyon—everyone wants to bring something back to remind them of a favorite time. It's like taking shells from the ocean beach, pinecones from a lakeside cabin, or rocks from a mountain.

The NFL and the Redskins love their fans as long as the team can see their wallets because it markets nonstop. But if you want to become a memorabilia collector, legendary expert Samu Qureshi says find something with personal meaning, not something sold in the gift shop.

"The value is in things that are real, in some way historic," he said. "Not something that was just manufactured or a card in a pack autographed by RG III. That's a terrible investment because that card won't be worth near anything close to what you paid in 10 years."

Qureshi is considered the foremost Redskins memorabilia collector, and his collection numbers in the tens of thousands of items. Anything from John Riggins' jockstrap and Jack Kent Cooke's fedora to Vince Lombardi's 1969 sideline cleats and Joe Gibbs' headset have been crammed into his museum of 2,000 sq. ft.

Qureshi's collection began with a single card. Here are a few thoughts on what beginners should consider when starting their collection.

For $100 or less, you can still find a personalized item.

"Get something that tells a story," he said. "Buy a game-worn jersey of a player you like, a special teams player you like where you can see the repairs and battle scars on it.

"The programs are manufactured to sell, but they have a purpose. They give you the roster, stories about the players.

"For $100, I'd be inclined to buy a very common player's game-used jersey or a cool program from the 1940s of an important game."

Let's take it up a notch. What would he do with a $1,000 bankroll?

"Get a London Fletcher game-used jersey, maybe a game-used helmet," Qureshi said. "I would also think about getting one of the early championship programs like 1942. It would be a very good condition one but not mint. Or I would go for something unique, maybe artwork. The jerseys and programs are where I would go. You could pick up a team-signed ball from a Super Bowl team like 1991."

Sometimes bargains can be found. Qureshi paid slightly more than the four-figure threshold for the Pocahontas cheerleader uniform from the 1960s. It is now worn by a life-sized mannequin.

"None of these exist because they all got destroyed or thrown away," he said. "The team didn't let the women keep them. There was a room full in RFK Stadium and somebody might have a garage full of cheerleader uniforms or they might have been trashed, but they haven't resurfaced."

If you've hit big money and bankroll isn't a problem, Qureshi has a few suggestions.

Super Bowl rings are always in fashion, but beware salesman sample rings with fake stones that are worthless. "Samples are more widespread than you'd think and can be a costly mistake. But if you want to buy one, spend no more than $2,500.

"A real Super Bowl ring from any of the years they won means you're looking at $20,000. That's not for John Riggins' ring. If he wanted to sell, I'd be surprised if it didn't go for at least $40,000."

Game-worn jerseys of prominent players often cost $2,500. Robert Griffin III's rookie year saw game jerseys cost $8,000 if you could find one, which isn't easy. They're usually sold to corporate sponsors of the team.

Another five-figure investment would be a trophy. Forget team trophies, but hardware from a player sometimes becomes available when the person dies. Look for a Player of the Year trophy from a prominent auction house because you won't find one on eBay.

Usually everything costs more than you'd expect. That's why you should forget items offered in the mail and look for a personal touch. Something that gives you a connection to the team is a memory of a lifetime...and that's priceless.

85 Looney— The Name Says It All

There's something about men with three names that brings fame.

Jack Kent Cooke, George Preston Marshall, and Edward Bennett Williams once ran the Redskins. There were presidential assassins John Wilkes Booth and Lee Harvey Oswald. And there were plenty of presidents whose middle name was at least remembered by an initial, such as John F. Kennedy and Franklin D. Roosevelt.

And so it is with Joe Don Looney, whose last name best described him. His NFL career was a series of off-field incidents with a little on-field production interrupted by a military stint in Vietnam. His post-career included washing elephants' feet before he drove a motorcycle too fast around a bend and crashed into a fence, bringing about his young death.

The *Saturday Evening Post* called Looney "The Marvelous Misfit." NFL Films president Steve Sabol labeled him the most uncoachable player ever. Looney was even seen reading in cemeteries.

Everybody who knew the former Redskins running back would say the same thing—he was crazy.

Oh, not mentally. Then again, Looney did some loony things.

"He was nuts," said Washington linebacker Sam Huff, who was paid $1,000 to room with Looney upon the latter's 1966 arrival. "It was real with him the whole time every day. They put up with him at practice. The coaches ignored him."

Looney was legendary for mostly the wrong reasons. After earning four Fs and one D as a freshman at Texas, he transferred to Texas Christian University where he was soon expelled. Looney earned fame at Cameron Junior College, setting a punting record as the team won the junior college national title. Looney then

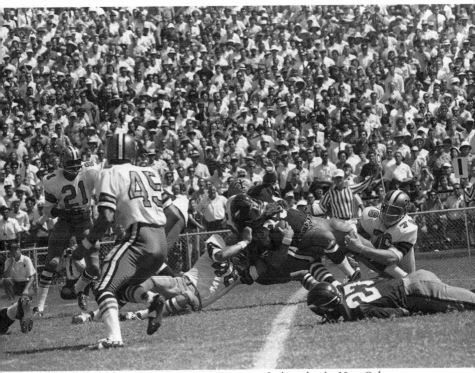

Running back Joe Don Looney (35) gets stretched out by the New Orleans Saints defensive team on a kickoff return in New Orleans on Sunday, September 25, 1967. Laying out the 230-lb. Looney are Saints tackle David Rowe (76) and flanker Dan Abramowicz (46). The Redskins won 30–10.
(AP Photo/JRT)

became an All-American at Oklahoma in 1962 before Coach Bud Wilkinson threw him off the team three games into 1963 for punching a graduate assistant coach.

A first-round selection by the New York Giants in 1964, Looney lasted only 25 days before being traded to the Baltimore Colts after telling Coach Allie Sherman, "If practice makes perfect and perfection is impossible, why practice?"

Looney even ran away from designed plays, saying, "Anyone can run where the blockers are. A good ball carrier makes his own holes."

Baltimore only ran Looney 23 times as a rookie before trading him to the Detroit Lions. Looney managed a fair season with 356 yards on 114 carries in 1965, but he was traded to Washington in 1966 after refusing to carry a play into the huddle, telling Coach Harry Gilmer, "If you want a messenger boy, call Western Union."

Looney didn't do much during his 1966–67 stint in Washington, though he once defended quarterback Sonny Jurgensen from a pass rusher by connecting a right cross to the opponent's jaw.

Looney liked to fight. Indeed, Huff finally refused to room with Looney after they scuffled in practice. Huff was tired of Looney coming in at 2:00 AM, long after bed check. When Looney knocked an unsuspecting Huff into the mud to open practice the next morning, Huff was soon atop Looney, trying to literally knock some sense into the latter.

"We hated each other," Huff said. "I wouldn't sleep at night because he wouldn't let me. He would run around the room. I had to babysit him."

Huff remembered one time having to fool Looney into getting on the team flight.

"Joe Don was up on the patio, yelling at us," Huff said. "I said, 'We can't take off—we have to get Joe Don.' I said, 'Let's just act like we're going to leave him,' and he got on the plane."

Looney's U.S. Army reserve unit was called up in 1968, and he spent a year protecting an oil tank farm in Vietnam. He returned to carry just three times for the New Orleans Saints in 1969 before he quit football.

And then the story gets really weird.

Looney converted to Hinduism and reportedly became a bodyguard for a swami. He washed the feet of elephants and listened at the swami's feet for hours.

By 1974, Looney was convicted of illegal possession of a firearm and sentenced to three years probation. He was later pardoned by President Reagan.

Naturally, this kind of story comes to a premature end. Looney was riding his motorcycle down a rural highway outside of Terlingua, Texas, when he veered off the road, hit a fence, and died.

He was just 45 years old.

86 How Zorn Became Coach

How did Jim Zorn ever become the Washington Redskins head coach? A whole lot of poor preparation by vice president Vinny Cerrato and owner Dan Snyder nearly led to the franchise's collapse.

Anyone who spent time around Coach Joe Gibbs in the waning weeks of the 2007 season knew he was thinking hard about leaving. The murder of safety Sean Taylor combined with Gibbs' grandson undergoing cancer treatments led the coach to often mention that life is short and his heart was in Charlotte with his family.

Ironically, that year was one of Gibbs' best coaching efforts. To hold the team together after a player's murder and win the final four games to make the playoffs left me truly expecting the Redskins to win the Super Bowl. It seemed to be one of those destiny things. Gibbs later admitted to thinking the same thing.

But Washington lost in the first round of the playoffs. Gibbs stood at the podium the next day and dodged a direct retirement question by veteran newsman Jim Ducibella, who himself retired that day.

When Gibbs left the room, the press corps huddled in focus groups to dissect what the coach had just said. That's such a rare thing to happen in a press room. Did Gibbs just tip his hand while wanting to make the retirement announcement at a separate event?

The Worst Coach Ever

No, it wasn't Mike Shanahan, Jim Zorn, or Steve Spurrier, although they came close.

Mike Nixon was worst coach ever at 4–18–2 for a .182 win percentage. An All-American running back at Pittsburgh, Nixon spent 1935 with the Pittsburgh Pirates (as the Steelers were known before 1940) before becoming a coach, though he played briefly in 1942 during the player shortage because of World War II.

Nixon was a Redskins assistant from 1954 to 1958 under Joe Kuharich, who was 26–32–2 when he was fired in 1958. Nixon then coached two years before he was fired. He later was interim head coach with Pittsburgh in 1965 with a 2–12 mark. Nixon then spent 22 years as a Cleveland Brown scout before retiring in 1981.

A blind man could see it, but Snyder and Cerrato didn't. Close team sources said the pair didn't realize Gibbs was leaving until the following day when they watched the retirement announcement on TV.

The downside was that the Redskins were completely unprepared for a coaching search. They could have spent the previous month vetting candidates. Now they would have to compete with other teams, and it was going to be costly.

Cerrato said he had a list of 50 candidates. Well, Zorn must have been No. 51 because the team didn't even talk to him about the job when they hired Zorn as offensive coordinator two weeks earlier. Only when New York Giants defensive coordinator Steve Spagnuolo turned down the Redskins and the search entered the second week of February did the Redskins go to Plan 51.

"I'm very excited about being the Redskins' head football coach," Zorn said. "And that is quite miraculous for me to even say today."

Indeed, Zorn was so surprised he thought Snyder wanted to just talk offense when he was summoned to the owner's mansion in Potomac, Maryland. When Zorn was told that Snyder wanted to interview him for the head coaching position, Zorn left to change into his suit before returning hours later.

"We're proud that our search was diligent, thorough, and resulted in today's announcement," Snyder said. "Jim's track record and reputation as a player, great teacher, and as a coach makes us confident that they will translate to success for the Redskins."

For awhile, Zorn looked like the second coming of Gibbs by opening 6–2. Maybe the former Seattle quarterback was a sleeper waiting for a chance? Nobody saw such a start coming.

And then it all went downhill faster than when Zorn mentioned the "maroon and black" instead of the team's burgundy and gold colors at his introductory press conference. That was one of those "uh-oh" moments that proved true.

Zorn was never even an NFL coordinator before he got the top job. He spent nine years coaching quarterbacks or serving as offensive coordinator at three colleges, plus three years in Seattle as an offensive assistant and quarterbacks coach and two more as Detroit's quarterback coach.

Zorn was a colorful person with offbeat tales, quirky drills, and even "Z Screens" on the sideline to keep the hot summer sun off players. For half a season, he confused defenses that had no film to study of his past play-calling.

But Washington finished 2–6 in 2008, and 4–12 in 2009 was just a sad death march. The media liked Zorn, but the second season was a funeral procession. When Snyder hired retired coach Sherman Lewis—who was calling bingo and delivering meals to the elderly when he was called—as a "consultant," Zorn should have quit then. But three years remained on his deal, so he stayed.

Weeks before the season's end, with fans bringing nasty signs to the stadium that sported large swaths of empty seats, Cerrato was forced out. Hours after the season's end, Zorn was fired.

This time Snyder was ready for a coaching search, which began and ended with Mike Shanahan. At least something was learned during the Zorn Era.

87 Women On the Road

A woman called my name across the hotel lobby. Suddenly she was posing for a photo with me and asking where my room was.

Wait—what?

That brief encounter at a Phoenix hotel on the eve of the Redskins playing the Arizona Cardinals shows just how fast things happen. You're minding your own business and the next thing you know, there's a problem.

The NFL spends much of its three-day rookie symposium on how to deal with situations just like the one that happened to me. Let's be honest—there are women looking for paychecks that prey on pro athletes. A baby is an 18-year annuity. When the press room used to be by the Redskins Park front door, I'd see a Loudoun County sheriff would regularly meet with the team bookkeeper over child support payments.

Young men see these beautiful women, and women see the money. In years past, it was often prostitutes who frequented the players' hotel floor. Tampa Bay was notorious for it. One player said hookers would just knock on their door, asking the players if they wanted to have sex. The player knew not to open the door because he wouldn't be able to say no. Let's just say the women didn't knock without success too often.

Finally, the NFL started putting security by the hotel lobby elevators and on the player floors by the mid-1990s, but players smuggled women through the stairwell. Guards finally figured that out, too, so teams are on lockdown these days. Not that things don't still happen.

Players often have Saturday nights off during training camp. Wives and girlfriends usually showed up when camp was in Carlisle and Frostburg. More than one young lady needed directions to the players' dorm while hauling a suitcase.

One time a florist delivery man showed up at my Frostburg dorm room with a bouquet from a young woman professing gratitude for…. Well, let's just say I had the same room number as the player, who was in the next dorm. I checked the card, sent the delivery man in the right direction, and later asked the player about the young woman just to see his bewildered reaction over how I knew about her.

On the 2002 trip to Osaka for a preseason game, cheerleaders and media were on the Redskins plane—the only time the media traveled on a team flight in recent decades. The press used to stay at the team hotel until owner Dan Snyder no longer wanted the media around when he bought the team in 1999.

Well, it was a 17-hour direct flight each way, so there was plenty of time to, uh, mingle. I happened to sit next to the cheerleaders and finally needed to move because players were crowding me. Things got awfully friendly, though no Mile High Club initiations are known.

Finally, Coach Steve Spurrier came back to glare at the players. He was not happy even though nothing was really happening and there was nothing else to do. Spurrier made the players return to the roomier part of the plane. On the trip back, the plane ran out of beer a couple hours into the flight, which made it seem like the plane took forever to return home after a whirlwind four-day trip.

The Redskins used to stay at a Tampa hotel next to a strip club. Actually, it's pretty hard not to be near a strip club in Tampa. If someone received a court order to remain 100 yards from nude bars, they'd probably have to leave the city.

Well, the Redskins had a few hours off, and I ran into a dozen players in the parking lot, heading in a certain direction. I knew a few were married. They looked at me and winced. "Don't get arrested!" was my advice while minding my own business.

88 Fantasy Ball With Redskins

You love football. You love playing coach and GM, showing friends who's the smartest when it comes to the sport.

So you play fantasy football. And when I say "play," I really mean "obsess."

What could be better than using players from your favorite team, the Redskins?

Some say only a fool mixes business and pleasure. A fan should be most concerned with his favorite team winning and not how the players did on his fantasy squad, so it's better to use other players from around the league.

But what's the fun in that? You're into football because of the Redskins. You believe in Robert Griffin III, Alfred Morris, Pierre Garcon, and Jordan Reed. Why not win with them?

You're better off asking someone else. Oh, I've been around fantasy football since the days of "rotisserie," which now sounds like a chicken dinner. I've been in a few leagues, and I'm amazed how easy it has become to go online and click away.

But you deserve the best advice from the smartest fantasy football expert around—Gene Wang, a *Washington Post* sports reporter

Who's Your Favorite Player?

Ask a fan who their favorite Redskins player is, and the fan's age will always decide the answer.

Backers of quarterback Sammy Baugh have to be at least 70 years old to remember Slingin' Sammy, but he was the team's greatest player ever. At least that's what Sonny Jurgensen says, which is good enough for me.

Jurgensen was the favorite for a generation that watched the 1960s and '70s quarterback no matter how many people slapped "I like Billy" Kilmer stickers on their bumpers.

The 1980s were owned by running back John Riggins, whose Super Bowl XVII touchdown run became an iconic image in many man caves around Washington.

Tight end Chris Cooley was the fan favorite for many years before finishing in 2012. Basically, he was the second coming of Riggins.

Overall, Jurgensen has owned the modern era, but Riggins and Cooley have their fans.

and frequent guest on radio shows nationwide devoted to fantasy football. He's the guy people call and say, "Should I play Calvin Johnson or Dez Bryant this week?" and Gene spits out the right answer in seconds.

Should people use players from their favorite team?

"Depends on your favorite team," he said. "It can be more frustration than joy. For the Redskins in 2014, there are three players I would think about—Morris, Garcon, and Reed. If you're a fan of the Denver Broncos and Peyton Manning, every week is great."

So let's get to what everybody wants to know—what players should be taken and when during their fantasy draft.

First up—Morris. After a team single-season record 1,613 yards as a rookie in 2012, Morris gained 1,275 yards in 2013 on 59 fewer carries, which given a 4.62-yards-per-carry average would have given Morris 1,548 yards on equal carries in 2012. Basically, the Redskins abandoned the run more in 2013 when trailing by large margins early. Offensive coordinator Kyle Shanahan was pass happy, and the team finished with a single-season team record 611 passes. So Morris' second season was really as good as his first.

"[Morris had] big numbers first two years," Gene said. "He doesn't get hurt, which is a huge plus. There's no limit to how good he could be. He could be an NFL rushing champion. He's a late first, second round."

Garcon comes off a Redskins single-season record 113 receptions. Can fans trust him to post a similar number with a new head coach?

"You can trust him again," Gene said. "He was clearly the No. 1 choice. He put up record numbers with RG III and Kirk Cousins. He's going to get looks. Take him in the third round."

Jordan Reed caught 45 passes for 499 yards and three touchdowns as a rookie, but injuries limited him to just nine games. Reed is clearly one of the Redskins top receiving options, but can he stay healthy?

"Injuries worry me," Gene said. "One of my top fantasy categories is availability. If they're not playing, they're not doing me any good. Jordan Reed has potential for top 10 fantasy ends, maybe top six. He has an upside for sure, but I wouldn't take him as one of top six or seven tight ends. He's a sixth, seven-rounder."

Finally, we come to the player that might be the core of the Redskins but maybe not the core of your fantasy team. There are a lot of great quarterbacks to take first. Griffin should be fully healthy for the first time since blowing out his knee in January 2013 and unhindered by a brace—or a coaching staff that reportedly clashed with him.

"You can wait and get him middle to late in the draft," Gene said. "I'd take him as a bye week fill-in and if he gets hot, roll him out there. With the injury and new coach, who knows? He's a sixth rounder."

And the Redskins defense? Okay, that was a joke question.

"Take them and play in my league so I can take your money," Gene said.

89 See Redskins in the Super Bowl

It used to seem so automatic—four trips in nine years made Redskins fans feel like Super Bowl trips were a given.

But 22 years since the last Super Bowl sojourn suddenly has a whole new generation of fans wondering not only what it would be like for the Redskins to reach a Super Bowl but what it would be like to attend the game.

Well, it's expensive, exciting, and eclectic. And it's a trip of a lifetime…as long as the team doesn't lose. Washington deli owner Dave Loeb and his sister, Marlene, attended the Redskins' last Super Bowl when Washington beat Buffalo in January 1992.

"If you're a die-hard fan, you're going to be really excited and thrilled to see your favorite team play in [the Super Bowl]," he said. "To see your team win makes it even better. Our seats weren't that bad. We saw the Redskins win. We had a blast."

One thing every Redskins fan should do is attend a Super Bowl whenever Washington returns to the title game.

Most fans start arriving Thursday with the real throng coming Saturday. For the 2002 Super Bowl in New Orleans, an estimated 250,000 people were in town to party even though only one-fourth of that number would actually see the game.

Sometimes the Super Bowl is just the last part of a fun week, hopefully in a warm-weather city. The NFL used to largely rotate the game between Miami, New Orleans, and Southern California because the owners loved spending the week somewhere warm. Oh, they threw a bone occasionally to a colder venue, but with the Super Bowl now bringing more than $300 million in economic impact to communities, it has become a bargaining chip to get cities to build new stadiums.

Everybody wants to host a Super Bowl, though some cities like Green Bay obviously can't accommodate the crowd. New York hosting the 2014 game without snow problems means any place above the Mason-Dixon Line is now in play.

Teams arrive on Monday, and fans can now watch media day on Tuesday. It's a fascinating pair of one-hour sessions where thousands of reporters ask players about their hopes and dreams. Fans pay $35 to watch. It's a chance to see the teams, so go for it.

Wednesday and Thursday are low-key days. Many fans play golf at local courses, sightsee, and visit amusements. The NFL Experience isn't to be missed—there are lots of interactive events, such as be an NFL official or see Madden Football exhibits.

Everything speeds up on Friday night. Big-name musicians come in for concerts. The Taste of the NFL party has a chef and player from every NFL city creating signature dishes you can try. This event isn't to be missed. There are also NFL legend parties by players and agents where you can meet your favorites.

Saturdays vary per city. Some have parades and fan experiences in the streets. Bourbon Street in New Orleans should not be missed, but go easy on those drinks.

Because of intense security since 9/11, the NFL now uses concerts to lure fans to the game early so there's not a crowd waiting to get inside before kickoff. Arrive three hours beforehand and you'll see terrific pregame concerts. You'll also practice how to use the cards under your seat as part of the halftime show to create an image. Cheesy maybe, but it's also fun.

Hopefully the Redskins win and you'll depart the next morning (reserve airline tickets and hotel rooms the moment the NFC Championship ends) with the memory of a lifetime.

Yes it's expensive, but it's the most fun you'll ever have at a sporting event, and you'll create memories for a lifetime. Just bring me back a souvenir.

90 Lombardi's 5 O'Clock Club

The famed five o'clock club wasn't started by the Hogs drinking in an equipment shed after practice during the Joe Gibbs era. Amazingly, it was Vince Lombardi who brought the tradition to the Redskins.

Yes, the same rigid no-nonsense boss of the legendary Green Bay Packers met with reporters after daily practices during the 1969 training camp—the only one he led before succumbing to cancer the following year.

Lombardi and his assistant coaches would meet with reporters for an informal, off-the-record gathering at 5:00 PM each day. Lombardi would drink Scotch and the press would grab a beer as both sides got to know each other.

"Everything was off the record, so you were never going to violate that because this was a good way to get in touch with someone important with the Redskins," said Steve Guback, who covered the team for *The Evening Star* from 1959 to 1981. "The big value was you could be steered away from something that would embarrass you or find a good story for the next day."

Access to today's NFL coaches is often managed and restricted, but it really depends on the coach. I've covered eight Redskins

247

coaches since Joe Gibbs' first tenure, and each guy had his own style. Norv Turner took reporters to a Carlisle bar once, and he paid for a round of drinks another time in Frostburg. Steve Spurrier drank in the Gingerbread Man in Carlisle briefly during his first camp but decided he couldn't trust NFL reporters because they weren't open supporters like those reporters from his college coaching days.

Most coaches offer one-on-ones and maybe a little more with regular beat writers, but a setting where everyone has a drink and make small talk is probably something lost to societal changes and the Internet's constant need for insider info that coaches don't want to risk. At best, off-season league meetings, scouting combines, and other spots on the road provide the best casual chance to talk with coaches.

Lombardi met with reporters immediately after practice for official comments. The five o'clock club, held at a sorority house on the Dickinson College campus that housed reporters covering camp, was maybe 30 minutes of chitchat.

"You'd talk about other teams, rule changes," Guback said. "It was a good way to familiarize yourself with new trends. It wasn't the kind of thing you were going to write and credit [to] Lombardi because they'd get in hot water. Write it as a column. You were getting background. You'd find out more at the five o'clock club."

Ironically, there was no exact "Lombardi time" for the daily meeting. The coach was known for beginning everything 15 minutes before the announced start, so if you were on time, you were late.

"You have standard time, daylight time, and Lombardi time," Guback said, "and Lombardi time was 15 minutes ahead. [But happy hour] started when Lombardi got there. You'd laugh, talk a little bit, sip beer, and it was over."

Lombardi was new to the Redskins, but he wasn't new to the media. Many reporters also wrote about the playoffs, so they had covered Lombardi press conferences while the Packers won six titles for the coach, including the first two Super Bowls.

"Lombardi and the Packers were always in the playoffs, so I knew him before he came to Washington," Guback said. "I wasn't awestruck by him. I appreciated knowing he was the guy."

And unlike modern coaches afraid to say anything that might give opponents insight before a game, Lombardi was direct when he was on the record—and even more so off the record, but reporters could only use that info for insight. Break that rule and the reporter was cut off. All coaches are like that, not just Lombardi.

"You saw a value anytime you could talk to Lombardi," Guback said. "You'd get a good answer from him."

Guback remembered the last time he saw Lombardi. The coach popped in to talk to rookies before they played Baltimore's rookies. It was the coach's final time with the team after missing the preseason while he was being treated for cancer. He died on September 3, 1970.

"You were very respectful," said Guback, who rode down in the elevator with the coach. "You didn't want to press your luck."

91 Owners Beyond the Grave

Late owners George Preston Marshall and Jack Kent Cooke are still helping Redskins fans.

Marshall has been dead since 1969 while Cooke died in 1997, but both men live on through charitable foundations. Sure, current owner Dan Snyder has also raised millions of dollars for charities and been known to quietly help everyday people in need, but he's still living. Marshall and Cooke are doing it long after their deaths.

The George Preston Marshall Foundation opened in 1972 and is not affiliated with the team. It provides grants to nonprofit groups helping children in Washington, Virginia, and Maryland. Mostly the foundation pays for health services, child welfare, education, and sports and recreation. The group once wrote a $1 million check to a school. A number of private school scholarships are funded by the foundation.

Marshall's will stated funds couldn't be given to groups containing "any purpose which supports the principle of racial integration in any form." Marshall was a known racist who didn't sign black players until forced by the federal government in 1962.

It's not an urban legend. Marshall's will includes the restriction, but granddaughter Jordan Wright told *The City Paper* in 2004 that the language was deemed illegal and the foundation pays no attention to it. Thus, Marshall must be rolling over in his grave now that his money helps people of all colors. The upside is his money is still helping everyone more than four decades later.

The Jack Kent Cooke Foundation was the reason the Redskins were sold rather than passed along to Cooke's son, John Kent Cooke. The Squire decided to fund college educations upon his death, and the team was his main asset despite extensive real estate holdings like the Chrysler Building in New York City plus cable TV systems, communications companies, and even thoroughbred horses.

It was a stunning move in 1997. Cooke never mentioned it, but the scholarship foundation, which is open to those entering graduate schools and recently expanded to undergraduate programs and even high schools, isn't surprising.

Cooke loved the English language and authors. He regularly encouraged young workers to read, saying it was their best chance to advance in life. Donating his money to such a cause seems natural.

The foundation is separate from the team, though some of Cooke's former employees are involved. John Kent Cooke remains on the board as well as former Cooke attorney Stuart B. Haney.

Cooke's foundation received about $600 million after the team's sale, a staggering sum given many people initially expected the team to garner $250 million before eventually being sold to Snyder for $800 million in 1999.

The foundation suddenly possessed so much money that the original intent of just providing college scholarships to community college transfer students and graduate program seekers wasn't enough. The foundation now helps high school students seeking college scholarships. In 2012 alone, the foundation awarded 772 scholarships totaling $12.1 million and 69 grants for $7.9 million.

The foundation has helped many low-income applicants become doctors, filmmakers, artists, musicians, teachers, and administrators around the world. It even led to marriage between two Cooke scholars. Cooke would have called that a "crackerjack" move.

Like Marshall's trust, Cooke's foundation now also provides grants up to $35,000 to community groups in the Washington area that help youth. The Talent Development Award provides a $500,000 grant to educational groups focusing on children from kindergarten to eighth grade.

The amazing part of both foundations is you don't need to know someone or be connected in any way to earn the scholarships or grants. It's a fair process that helps those who simply visit the website to obtain applications.

Cooke loved to quote a ballad about Sir Andrew Barton, a 16th century Scottish admiral who died in battle against the British:

I am hurt, but I am not slain.
I'll lay me down and bleed awhile
Then I'll rise and fight again.

It seems Cooke and Marshall have risen once more to help Redskins fans.

92 Road Trip to Dallas

It felt like being behind German lines in World War II. I felt alone in a hostile land among fans I'd long heard about—and little of what I'd heard was good.

If you're a Redskins fan, you have to go to a Dallas game in Texas. It's pretty much a world turned upside down versus what you see when the rivalry comes to Washington.

My first trip to Dallas was 1995. I was really looking forward to it after a quarter-century of watching the series. All I knew about Dallas was the opening of the TV show *Dallas*, which included a shot looking through the hole in the stadium. You know, the hole that lets God see his favorite team.

And there I was in front of this big old barn and thinking, "This is it?"

The Cowboys have now moved on to AT&T Stadium (where the team never has a good reception when needed), which looks like a spaceship has landed in Arlington, not far from where Washington's baseball team relocated to in 1972. But once you get over the biggest TV screen you'll ever see, it's still the same experience that the old stadium offered.

First, the crowd is of the wine-and-cheese variety. People come to Cowboys games for status—to see and be seen. The women dress up in furs, and few wear game jerseys. It's very different than Washington where women have no problem wearing their favorite player's jersey.

NFC East Rivals

The Dallas Cowboys may be the Redskins' sentimental rival, but the New York Giants have been their rivals the longest while the Philadelphia Eagles offer the most success for the Redskins amongst NFC East teams.

Washington is 81–72–5 against Philadelphia since 1934. The Redskins lost both 2013 encounters after sweeping the 2012 series. The Joe Gibbs era did particularly well against Philadelphia, including 10-of-12 at one point. Sammy Baugh won his first 11 games against the Eagles beginning in 1937. Washington took the first meeting 6–0 in 1934.

The New York series dates to 1932 when the Redskins won 14–6. Two weeks later they played to a 0–0 tie. Gibbs both won and lost six straight to the Giants during his first stint. New York is 95–65–4 over Washington.

Dallas has the upper hand in the rivalry at 64–42–2. Washington also won the first game against this division foe by 26–14 in 1960. The teams then tied two of their next three meetings.

When walking the concourse, you'll be overwhelmed by the large numbers of blue jerseys when you're used to seeing burgundy ones outnumbering the stars. It's like going from king of the playground in middle school to becoming the freshman dork of high school—the power has shifted.

Unlike Philadelphia where visiting fans are in peril, Dallas supporters aren't looking for trouble. Cowboys fans are like Duke basketball fans—they think they're better than the rest of us. Redskins fans amuse Cowboys fans more than they anger them. They'll trade barbs, but it rarely gets heated.

The dome opening is interesting, especially when it rains. You see players get wet, but you're dry in the stands. Actually, that's pretty cool. These days, the stadium roof is usually closed if there's a chance of rain.

You can take a self-guided tour of AT&T Stadium. Only the Cowboys would charge $17.50 to let you wander around the stadium on a tour that naturally begins in the gift shop. The one perk is getting onto the field, but try dancing on the star and the tour probably ends quickly.

It gets crazier. There are tours of the stadium's artwork several times weekly for $24.50. Please—the Smithsonian museums are free in Washington and include the only Leonardo da Vinci in North America.

What else is there to do in Dallas? Well, you can see Southfork, which was supposedly the Ewings' ranch in the classic show. But just like Texas Stadium, you'll say, "That's it?"

There's the infamous hill where sniper Lee Harvey Oswald shot President John F. Kennedy, which some say is one reason why Washingtonians don't like Dallas. The Texas School Book Depository is now called the Dallas County Administration Building on the corner of Elm and North Houston streets. Oswald fired from a sixth-floor window on the southeast corner.

Okay, let's have a little fun. Dallas is a big city that has all the usual attractions. The Zero Gravity Thrill Amusement Park (11131 Malibu Drive) sounds intriguing. It's the world's only theme park with five extreme thrill rides—Bungee Jump, the Nothin' But Net, Texas Blastoff, the Skycoaster, and the Skyscraper. Yee haw!

Washingtonians can always go see former White House resident's George W. Bush Presidential Library and Museum (2943 SMU Boulevard). Since Washington just closed its aquarium after 128 years (bet you didn't know we had one), there's always the Dallas World Aquarium (1801 North Griffin Street).

What about the Eight Track Museum (2630 East Commerce) where you can relive the past? God knows Cowboys fans do.

Finally, dude, you gotta go to a ranch to see the real cowboy way. Check duderanches.com, but one favorite is the Wild Cattle

Ranch (wildcattleranch.com). About 90 miles north of Dallas, it has all the traditional activities from horseback riding to clay shooting.

Just remember to mosey back to the game.

93 Dudley Scored Nine Ways

When announcers say a player can score from anywhere on the field, they're thinking of Bill Dudley.

Dudley once raced 30 yards back to reach a punt, grabbing the ball after it crossed the sideline at the 4-yard line while keeping his feet inbounds. The Redskin then returned it 96 yards for a touchdown against the Pittsburgh Steelers in 1950.

The "Bullet" had done it again.

It was the NFL-record ninth different way Dudley scored in his seventh of nine seasons. The halfback threw and ran for touchdowns while also scoring on a reception plus fumble, interception, punt, and kick returns. Dudley kicked extra points and field goals, too. The only thing he never did was score on a safety.

Slacker.

Dudley played for three different teams while being twice traded and also serving in World War II. The University of Virginia standout, who led the nation in scoring with 134 points in 1941, was the first overall pick in the 1942 draft by Pittsburgh.

"The Pittsburgh Steelers drafted me No. 1. Of course, I knew about the University of Pittsburgh, but I didn't know a thing about the Steelers," he said. "I knew a little bit about the Washington Redskins. We used to go up and see them play."

Bill Dudley, former University of Virginia football star now with the Washington Redskins receives a silver urn from Gov. John S. Battle (right) of his home state during "Dudley Day" ceremonies before the Redskins–Chicago Cardinals game in Washington, D.C., on October 21, 1951. Dudley also received a Ford Station Wagon (background) from his Virginia admirers, many of whom attended the game. Bill's father, James S. Dudley, of Bluefield, Virginia, is at left. (AP Photo/Harvey Georges)

Ironically, Dudley nearly didn't report to Pittsburgh. With many young men entering World War II, Dudley enlisted in the Naval Air Corps. However, his enlistment was nullified because he wasn't 21 years old and didn't have his parents' consent. Dudley instead enlisted in the U.S. Army Air Corps in September but needed to wait six months to report because of heavy enlistments.

Dudley was free to play the season for Pittsburgh. He rushed for a 44-yard touchdown in his first game and scored on a kickoff return the next week. He led the NFL with 696 yards rushing while also throwing two touchdowns.

After attending flight school, Dudley played for Randolph Field of the Army Air Force's 1944 football team, which went 12–0, and Dudley was named the Armed Services' Most Valuable Player. Dudley would later fly two supply missions in the Pacific before the end of the war. He spent the final stint of his service in Hawaii playing three times for Army Air Force's All-Star team.

Dudley returned to Pittsburgh for the final four games in 1945, scoring two touchdowns and kicking two extra points in his first game back. He then became the only person to lead the NFL in rushing, interceptions, punt returns, and lateral passes attempted as the 1946 MVP. Dudley is also the only person to win MVP awards in college, the pros, and the military.

Such a great season ironically earned Dudley a trade to Detroit where he signed a three-year deal and was team captain each season. Dudley led the team in scoring annually, including 11 touchdowns in 1947.

Dudley was traded to the Redskins in 1950, and he roomed with Sammy Baugh. Dudley played two seasons, sat out 1952 with knee problems, and then was mostly a kicker in 1953 before he retired. Dudley led Washington in scoring all three seasons.

All-NFL in six of nine seasons, Dudley rushed for 3,057 yards with 18 touchdowns, caught 123 passes with 18 touchdowns, and returned three punts and one kickoff for scores. He also scored on 2-of-23 career interceptions while kicking 121 extra points and 33 field goals. Dudley led his teams in scoring every year with 478 points overall in 90 games. Not bad for someone whose running style was described as "staggering." Indeed, the Bullet nickname was not for his speed but ability to hit his mark when playing in high school.

Dudley was elected to the College Football Hall of Fame in 1956 and the Pro Football Hall of Fame in 1966 plus the Virginia Hall of Fame in 1972. An insurance salesman in Lynchburg, Virginia, he spent four terms as a state delegate before dying in 2010 at age 88.

"He lived to a high standard," son Jim Dudley told the Associated Press. "He was devoted to service and having a positive effect on those people he associated with, and he did. If that's the measure of greatness, he was a great man."

94 Greatest Nicknames

There was Silverback, Dancing Bear, Squire, and George the Gorgeous plus Hogs and Smurfs. Sometimes they rode a Diesel to the five o'clock club where they met a Fun Bunch, Big Daddy, and Bubba.

A team with a controversial nickname has no shortage of great monikers for its players, coaches, and owners.

Everybody knows the basics—John Riggins was "The Diesel" and "Riggo." Perhaps the team's greatest player was Slingin' Sammy Baugh. There was Dan "Big Daddy" Wilkinson, Chris "Captain Chaos" Cooley, Lorenzo "One Man Gang" Alexander, Ron "The Dancing Bear" McDole, Mike "Cave Man" Sellers, and Stephen "Big Country" Davis.

And perhaps the most popular Redskin ever, at least as a rookie, is Robert Griffin III, known simply as RG III, though teammate Fred Davis created the "Black Jesus" reference.

One of the cooler nicknames in recent years was deep snapper Ethan Albright, whose red hair inspired the "Red Snapper." Trent

Williams is "Silverback" after teammates labeled him a big gorilla. Williams likes the name so much that he has a big gorilla tattoo on his back and buys gorilla art. Santana Moss goes by "Tana."

Sometimes the nicknames could be rough. Receiver Rod Gardner's penchant for dropped balls earned him the nickname "50/50" from teammate Bruce Smith. When a sure Hall of Famer calls you a bad nickname, it sticks hard. Billy Kilmer was known as "Furnace Face" for his reddish face. Coach Mike Shanahan's perpetually sunburned look earned him "The Lobster." Mark Schlereth was "Stinky."

Winning always creates nicknames—some naturally and some for marketing. The Redskins had quite a few during the Joe Gibbs era when they won three Super Bowls.

The Hogs was the most famous nickname, which came from offensive line coach Joe Bugel making his players practice in the dirt as if they were hogs. The 1980s founding core was Joe Jacoby, Jeff Bostic, Russ Grimm, Mark May, and George Starke plus tight ends Rick "Doc" Walker and Donnie Warren. Riggins was later added while quarterback Joe Theismann gained "piglet" status for one block. Jacoby, Bostic, Grimm, and May each earned three Super Bowl rings.

There was a second wave of Hogs in the mid-1980s, including Raleigh McKenzie, Ray Brown, Ed Simmons, Jim Lachey, and Schlereth contributing to two Super Bowl wins. The Redskins tried extending the Hogs by calling a 1990s line "dirtbags," but it never really took.

There are even "Hogettes," a dozen men who wore colorful old lady dresses and pig snouts and sat together at RFK Stadium and FedEx Field for 30 years before officially retiring in 2013. Several of them still appear at charity functions.

Riggins and the Hogs were founders of the modern five o'clock club when they would drink a few beers or more in an equipment shed by the practice field after workouts. Ironically, Coach Vince

The Iranian in the Locker Room

The bet was whether five teammates knew *Pravda* was a Russian newspaper. Guard Shar Pourdanesh thought he had suckered me into buying lunch. I knew the sucker wasn't me.

Pourdanesh was the first and still only Iranian-born player in the NFL that included a stint from 1996 to 1998 with the Redskins. His family fled Iran after the Shah's 1979 fall because Shar's father was a hospital administrator with ties to the deposed ruler. They eventually settled in Los Angeles where Pourdanesh lives today with his three sons.

With a worldly outlook separate from teammates who seldom viewed life outside the goal posts, Pourdanesh knew worldwide publications like *Pravda* and figured his teammates did, too. After all, several of his teammates had attended top academic schools like Stanford.

Pourdanesh figured at least half the team could correctly identify *Pravda*. I bet him that he couldn't find five. After 10 players didn't know, Pourdanesh stopped.

Thanks for lunch, Shar.

Lombardi also had a five o'clock club during the 1969 training camp where he would have a drink with reporters during off-the-record daily sessions.

Those Super Bowl teams also saw three sets of receivers with nicknames. "The Smurfs" were undersized receivers Alvin Garrett, Charlie Brown, and Virgil Seay. The "Fun Bunch" was led by Art Monk and included Brown, Garrett, and Seay plus Walker and Warren. The group jumped together for a high-five after scoring against Detroit in the 1982 playoffs. And don't forget "The Posse" of Gary Clark, Ricky Sanders, and Monk who all reached the Pro Bowl during the 1991 championship.

The 1970s teams under Coach George Allen were known as "The Over-the-Hill Gang" for so many aging vets who reached a Super Bowl. The toughest man on those defenses was Hall of Fame linebacker Chris "The Hangman" Hanburger.

Nicknames extend back to the team's roots. Early nicknames included John "Tree" Adams, Hugh "Bones" Taylor, George "Automatic" Karamatic, Millard Fillmore "Dixie" Howell, Frank "Tiger" Walton, Elzaphan "Zip" Hanna, Charlie "Choo Choo" Justice, Casimir "Slug" Witucki, Herman "Eagle" Day, and "Merlyn the Magician" Condit.

Coaches and staff often earned nicknames, too. During the Gibbs era, assistant coaches included Lavern "Torgy" Torgeson, Richie "Bone" Petitbon, and Joe "Buges" Bugel plus trainer Lamar "Bubba" Tyler, equipment manager "Jay-Bird" Brunetti, and conditioning coach Dan "D-Boy" Riley. Sometimes it felt like nobody used their real name around the facility.

Even owners drew nicknames. Jack Kent Cooke loved being known as "The Squire," though you never said it to his face. It was "Mr. Cooke" to one and all. Founding owner George Preston Marshall was known as George the Gorgeous, G. Presto, Marshall the Magnificent, and Wet Wash, the latter for his laundry business.

As for the Redskins ever changing their name to political pressure, just remember that after losses, some fans call them "The Deadskins."

95 Go to Green Bay

Hopefully, it won't be the frozen tundra when you visit, but Green Bay is a throwback to when America was a different world.

Redskins fans should visit the Wisconsin town whenever Washington plays there. And we mean town, not major city like fellow NFL brethren New York, Chicago, Miami, and Washington. Indeed, Green Bay is barely 100,000 people with paper and meat packing plants as its industries. It's a blue-collar town where a shot and a brat are lunchtime staples.

Lambeau Field is one of those special venues you must see, even if a 2003 renovation partly altered its historic look. It's an old bowl stadium. There are no upper and lower decks—just one continuous stream of 80,750 seats with no blocked sight lines. Think of the University of Maryland's Byrd Stadium.

The Packers finally needed more revenue to keep up in the NFL, so the team built luxury seating atop the bowl in 2003. Gotta have someplace for the rich folks to avoid freezing. Those seats probably aren't for you, though.

As you approach 1265 Lombardi Avenue in late fall, you'll notice not snowmen but Lombardi Trophies built of snow in front of homes. In vacant areas where the snow stretches to the horizon, it seems like there's nothing between you and the North Pole.

And cold? The official Packers color should be orange because many fans in the crowd wear deer hunting gear because late-season games can be brutal—like minus-22 degrees with wind chill during the 1996 NFC Championship. It hurt to be outside for more than a few minutes. Then again, there was also an early October Redskins-Packers game where howling winds cut through you like an Arctic blast.

Translation—bring your heaviest gear. It still won't be enough to keep the chill away.

But it's worth it to see an America that seems more 1960s than today. Where locals sound like the movie *Fargo* and wear cheeseheads. In fact, there's a cheesehead in my den. They're cool. It's okay to buy one.

Visiting Green Bay is about being a pro football fan. Unlike many other cities you might visit for Redskins games, this one lives and breathes football. It's not just another big thing in town that day. It's the only thing in town every day.

"I think it is one of the great atmospheres in all of football," Redskins linebacker London Fletcher said. "It's really like a college atmosphere. I can feel the tradition when I come into the place. The whole city shuts down, and everybody is at the Packers game. There are more people at the Packers game than they have in the city of Green Bay, so that just goes to show how unique a situation it is. It's an awesome atmosphere."

The one problem with attending a game at Green Bay is actually flying into town or staying in the city. It's pretty difficult because there aren't a lot of flights or hotels, and those rare ones are extremely expensive. The best alternative is to fly into and stay in Appleton, Wisconsin, about 40 minutes straight south along the highway. But wait too long to book and you'll end up in Milwaukee, about two hours away. Basically, if you want to go to this game, book the airline and hotel when the schedule comes out in April.

Lambeau Field was named after Curly Lambeau, a founding team player and 29-year coach who also later led the Redskins in 1952–53. Lambeau died in 1965, and residents renamed the stadium, which was built in 1957, after him. It's the NFL's longest continually used venue and third-longest in U.S. pro sports. An expansion of the indoor atrium is expected to be completed by 2015.

Ironically, Green Bay voters approved a 2000 referendum allowing the stadium's name to be sold to a corporation if $100 million could be gained. FedEx paid the Redskins $200 million to rename Jack Kent Cooke Stadium, but surprisingly, no one has offered to take over Lambeau Field, probably because it would be so unpopular. Instead, the naming rights to five entrance gates were sold.

Buying tickets is a little easier after the team added 15,000 seats since 2002, but it's still one of the tougher tickets around the NFL. No-shows have been counted on one hand. Everybody comes to or watches the games in the small town. It literally shuts down. On Sundays after games, eat dinner right away because few restaurants seem to be open after 8:00 PM.

Titletown USA is the best road trip for pure football fans. San Francisco and New York may have more glitz, Miami had gorgeous weather, and Denver and Arizona sport beautiful backdrops, but you'll leave Green Bay as a more seasoned football fan.

96 Buy a Jersey

One day in the future, whether it comes next year or a decade from now, Redskins Nation will have a massive problem—whose jersey to buy when Robert Griffin III is no longer in Washington.

It seems everyone bought Griffin's No. 10 over the past two years. The NFL said he shattered its one-year sales mark in nine months during his 2012 rookie season, though the league won't say how many were sold. Why, that's a state secret, and if the Chinese found out, it would shift the balance of global power.

But everybody wanted RG III's jersey. That runs contrary to standard advice in this era of free agency and short careers. Buying an active player's jersey is risky. Players come and go so quickly that your $200 purchase can suddenly become a relic. And if the player wasn't legendary, you just look like you're wearing white after Labor Day.

Every Redskins fan should own a jersey, preferably burgundy because white shows that cheese dog and those nachos you spilled on it during the game.

But whose jersey should you buy? It's a real question given authentic jerseys—not knockoffs—cost $200 when you add tax

The Best Redskins Quarterback Ever?

Sonny Jurgensen is the team leader in pass rating, but Sammy Baugh led the NFL three times more than Jurgensen.

Jurgensen's 85.0 career passing rating tops those with a minimum of 1,500 passes. Jason Campbell's 82.3 is second, followed by Mark Rypien's 80.2 and Joe Theismann's 77.4.

Baugh led the NFL six times—1937, '40, '43, '45, '47, and '49. Jurgensen was the only other Redskin to do it more than once, in 1967 and '69.

Baugh led the Redskins in passer rating for 14 seasons, while Jurgensen and Theismann led eight seasons each. Theismann led the team a record eight straight years, while Baugh did it seven straight twice and Jurgensen once.

Baugh's 109.9 rating in 1945 was a team record for 150 attempts or more. Robert Griffin III's 102.4 in 2012 was a Redskins rookie record.

and shipping. The worst thing is picking a player who doesn't resonate after he departs.

"It's tough buying a jersey in today's free agency," Levi Swanson said. "Players don't stay on one team their entire careers. At the prices they charge for jerseys now, it's hard pulling the trigger."

So the question I posed to many serious fans who own many jerseys is this—do you choose active or retired players? Active players are more exciting because you're supporting someone out there making plays, but retired is a safer long-term investment. Sonny Jurgensen and John Riggins jerseys remain the most popular jerseys among fans at FedEx Field.

"You can never go wrong getting a retired player's jersey," Miguel Mora said. "I have [Darrell] Green and Riggo in my closet."

Said Chad Woodroof, "I second the retired/legend route. I have a [Sammy] Baugh, Jurgy, Larry Brown, and Darrell Green."

Added Shane Gooseman, "Buy a jersey of a player who is a franchise great or someone you know is not going to be traded."

Next—where do you buy the jersey? Buying from the stadium store or directly from the Redskins means it's an authentic jersey, but that's also the costliest option. Most jerseys are sold during the season, especially before Christmas. Some fans buy off-season specials even if that means waiting months for another season. And there are always knockoffs sold on websites. The jerseys look much the same for a whole lot less money.

"Buy online," Dominic Orsini said. "Knockoffs are very nice and are one-fourth of the price. I would love an 'authentic' one, but I can't drop $200 on one jersey."

Said Bryan Manning, "Don't buy from the team store! They are [priced] higher there than anywhere. And shipping is ridiculous."

But there are die-hards who prefer the real ones no matter the price.

"I like all mine to be official," Woodroof said, "so I'll only buy mine from the Redskins store at the stadium."

The real divide among fans is whether putting your own name on the back is permissible. It is weird when you look at a name and don't remember who that player was because it has the wearer's name, not an old Redskins player.

"I believe having your name on your jersey is a statement of love for your team and shows a desire to be more connected to it," Fikret Markovic said. "Players leave via free agency, trades, retirement. Putting my name on a Redskins jersey was a statement that I am fan of the Redskins, not just the player whose jersey I bought."

Said Shannon Mullins, "I own one and did it for my kids, too. I'm still an okay person, even if I say so myself."

But others say it's too vain.

"It pushes the living-vicariously envelope a little too much," Neeraj Gupta said. "I got a custom one—Monk."

Said Chris Brown, "Leave it blank before going that route."

Added Kevin Dunleavy, "It's fine only if you're 18 or under."

The numbers and names may not always add up, but it's your jersey, your choice.

97 Biggest Draft Bust

First Cal Rossi was too young to be drafted by the Redskins. The second time he was taken, the UCLA running back refused to report.

Washington's biggest draft bust has to be Rossi. After all, two firsts on someone who never showed is pretty hard to beat.

But among those players who did report, who's the worst?

It's a tough choice between Desmond Howard (1992), Heath Shuler (1994), and Andre Johnson (1996). Indeed, Champ Bailey (1999) aside, the decade was pretty miserable for Redskins first-rounders.

Still, it beats the 1970s when Washington didn't draft in the first round once. Indeed, the Redskins only drafted three first-rounders from 1969 to 1990. Fortunately, those selections were Pro Football Hall of Famers Art Monk (1980) and Darrell Green (1983) plus Hogs lineman Mark May (1981).

Anyway, quarterbacks always get too much glory and too much blame, and maybe that's why I'm taking Shuler as the worst pick ever among those reporting.

Coach Norv Turner wanted Shuler, while general manager Charley Casserly preferred Trent Dilfer. The GM needed to let the coach pick the quarterback if Turner's offense, which won two Super Bowls with Dallas, was going to work in Washington. So Shuler became a Redskin while Dilfer later went sixth to Tampa

Bay. Dilfer proved a fair passer who lasted 14 seasons with five teams while winning Super Bowl XXXV with Baltimore.

The Redskins were picking third overall. Cincinnati was taking defensive tackle Dan Wilkinson, while Indianapolis liked running back Marshall Faulk. That left Washington unconcerned about not getting the passer they wanted.

Shuler was the classic mistake NFL teams make by not doing their homework and trying to make a college quarterback fit into the pros. They believed Tennessee coaches who said Shuler possessed enough speed to overcome slow reads. The team later realized that the real goal of those college coaches was to improve their program's reputation by having a quarterback get drafted high.

The problem was that Shuler's athleticism wasn't useful in the pros where everyone is quicker. It worked in college because there are speed mismatches.

Shuler never seemed to learn where the linebackers were. Turner sure tried to help him by screaming at practices after interceptions.

Shuler's biggest problem is that his injuries gave seventh-rounder Gus Frerotte a chance. Washingtonians love nothing more than a backup quarterback who excels, and Frerotte's biggest strength was quickly learning a system before hitting a plateau. It kept him in the league 15 years. Frerotte wrestled the job away from Shuler in their second season.

The Redskins gave Shuler his pick of New Orleans or Green Bay over the 1997 off-season. Shuler chose New Orleans for the better chance of starting rather than be Brett Favre's backup in Green Bay. Washington received a fifth-rounder in 1997 and a third-rounder in 1998, which would become running back Skip Hicks.

Shuler played only 10 games for New Orleans with 14 interceptions and two touchdowns before suffering a severe foot injury. He was released and signed with Oakland in 1998 before retiring after re-injuring the foot.

As a consolation prize, Shuler served three terms as a U.S. Congressman.

Johnson is the second biggest bust. With no first-rounder, the Redskins opted to trade second- and third-round picks to Dallas to take the Penn State offensive tackle. The only problem? Johnson was burned out. He didn't want to play football but couldn't resist the money. Yet it was obvious Johnson was a bust during training camp and didn't play that season before being released.

Johnson passed through Miami in 1997 before landing with Detroit where he played three games in 1998 before getting out of football.

Howard gets No. 3. The Redskins were looking to replenish their aging receivers in 1992 and traded their sixth and 28th overall picks to Cincinnati in 1992 to grab the Heisman Trophy winner with the fourth selection.

Howard seemed smaller than 5'10" with an immature attitude that didn't set well with teammates coming off their third Super Bowl victory in nine years. It just wasn't a good fit. Howard finally started in his third season but managed only 40 catches. He was a standout returner, but that wasn't enough.

Jacksonville became Howard's second of six teams over eight years. He eventually became a two-time All-Pro and was Super Bowl XXXI's Most Valuable Player with Green Bay.

98 The 73–0 Loss

It could have been worse.

A dropped touchdown pass, missed field goal, four failed extra points, and a fumble near the goal line kept the Chicago Bears from beating the Redskins 94–0 in the 1940 championship.

Suddenly 73–0 doesn't seem so bad. At least it didn't press 100 points.

But the worst loss ever in NFL history makes you wonder what in the world happened that day. How could a team that was favored to win, after beating the opponent 7–3 just three weeks earlier, have been so thoroughly crushed?

Well, mistakes were made. Things happened.

Fifty years later, *Washington Post* columnist Shirley Povich recalled the game he covered, saying, "It reminds us of our first breathless visit to the Grand Canyon. All we could say is, 'There she is, and ain't she a beaut.' When they hung up that final score at Griffin Stadium yesterday, all we could utter was, 'There it is and wasn't it awful.'"

It all started with the Redskins surviving the Bears 7–3 on November 17. Washington stopped Chicago on the Redskins 1-yard line to end the game with the Bears claiming pass interference on the final play.

Redskins owner George Preston Marshall called the Bears crybabies, frontrunners, and quitters who couldn't close out games. Well, that didn't sit well with Redskins players, much less the Bears. Washington players thought Marshall poked the bear and they'd get the sharp end of the revenge.

Sure enough, Bears owner and coach George Halas posted Marshall's comments in the locker room.

"Gentlemen, this is what George Preston Marshall thinks of you," said Halas in his pregame speech. "I think you're a great football team, the greatest ever assembled. Go out on the field and prove it."

The Griffith Stadium crowd of 36,034 and announcer Red Barber didn't know the Bears would unveil a new version of the T formation that day. The T wasn't new, dating back to Amos Alonzo Stagg in 1880 at Yale, but Chicago brought some new wrinkles.

Halas met a young local coach, Clark Shaughnessy, a couple years earlier and now paid the Stanford coach $2,000 annually as a consultant. Shaughnessy tinkered with the T with a receiver in motion as well as three running backs behind quarterback Sid Luckman. Shaughnessy later used the new T to coach Stanford to victory in the Rose Bowl over Nebraska three weeks later.

With the Redskins playing a five-man line, the Bears figured out 21 ways to counter linebacker shifts and get outside. Sure enough, on the game's second play the receiver took out a defender on the edge and Bill Osmanski ran 68 yards for the touchdown. It was all Chicago needed that day, but the Bears scored so much the officials asked the Bears not to kick extra points after the final two scores. It seems 11-of-12 game balls were already in the crowd because screens weren't used behind the goal posts then.

Luckman scored on a one-yard run on the Bears second drive, and it was 28–0 at halftime. Marshall said Chicago wasn't a second-half team, but it scored another 45 points despite eventually using their fourth-string quarterback and no starters.

The Bears scored seven rushing touchdowns, an NFL postseason record, plus three touchdowns among their eight interceptions. Chicago gained 519 yards with 381 rushing. Ironically, both teams managed 17 first downs. Chicago's touchdowns included three of 40 yards or more, so they didn't grind out points.

Eleven different Bears scored touchdowns. There was some thought the game might have gone differently if the Redskins' Charlie Malone hadn't dropped a 26-yard pass in the end zone on Washington's first possession, which would have tied the game.

"Sure," Redskins quarterback Sammy Baugh would later say. "The final score would have been 73–7."

It wasn't quite what Marshall had planned when he paid train fare for newspaper reporters within 100 miles of Washington. And the loss didn't set well with the fans who booed when the stadium announcer dared to mention 1941 season tickets were on sale.

Still, the game was a financial success for both teams. The crowd generated a net $102,280. Winning players received $873 and losing players $606. That was a half-season of pay for some players.

The game even included the last person to play without a helmet—Chicago end Dick Plasman. He entered World War II the next season and later returned to find the NFL mandated helmets. Sadly, Plasman endured health problems in his later years and even went blind.

Two years later, Washington avenged the loss by beating Chicago for the championship. Yet no one will forget the 73–0 loss.

99 The Future is Now 2.0

The Washington Warriors playing at Gaylord Stadium?

Will the Washington Redskins eventually change their name and escape "FedUp Field?" Will they ever win another Super Bowl? Will Dan Snyder be the owner for many of our lifetimes?

After writing 98 chapters on the past, let's flash-forward to the future of the team. Since I first watched the Redskins in 1969 as a young Washingtonian and have covered the team off and on since 1983, here are some of my educated guesses on the future.

Will ownership change anytime soon? The owner loves the past, and fans should appreciate that. The team could have been bought by an outsider in 1999, so for better or worse (and it too often seems worse), at least Snyder is a Washingtonian who treats the team as more than an ATM, though it is also the latter.

Top 5 Greatest Games

1. **Super Bowl XVII over Miami.** John Riggins' breakaway 43-yard touchdown put Washington ahead for its first title since 1945. Riggo became a legend, and the Redskins began their greatest era ever.
2. **1972 NFC Championship over Dallas.** It's not just reaching the first Super Bowl and The Over-the-Hill Gang's inspiring play. Beating rival Dallas 26–3 made it extra special and better than two Super Bowl titles.
3. **1982 NFC Championship over Dallas.** Again, beating Dallas is sometimes even better than winning it all. Of course, the Redskins also won Super Bowls after beating the Cowboys twice in conference titles, but still, nothing is more exciting than watching Darryl Grant dance in the end zone.
4. **Super Bowl XXII over Denver.** Scoring a record 35 points in one quarter immortalized the victory. It was simply perfection.
5. **1996 RFK farewell over Dallas.** It was the perfect way to say goodbye to the venue of the team's greatest success. The season-ending victory over the Cowboys saw the stands swaying one last time.

Many fans want Snyder to sell, but he has no desire or financial incentive. Turning 50 years old during the 2014 season means Snyder probably has another two or three decades of ownership. So get over it and move on. Snyder will likely own the team until he dies, just like predecessors Jack Kent Cooke and George Preston Marshall.

Will the team end the use of the Redskins name? Actually, the name and new stadium may be a package deal in 2027 when the FedEx Field lease ends. Yes, the team owns the stadium, but Cooke included a clause that Prince George's County owns it after 30 years. That means the team leaves, and frankly, no one will miss that place.

If the Redskins want to return to a location inside the city's borders, they'll have to change the name to get the RFK site. It's probably the only site left inside Washington, and even then, mass transportation will replace tailgating to make everything fit inside the stadium's old footprint.

If the name is still controversial in 2027, then Snyder might consider surrendering the Redskins name when the team changes stadiums. Make it a franchise-changing moment. By then, many of the old RFK fans who lived through the Super Bowl era will be gone and a younger fan base might be more receptive. If it's no longer a hot issue, then forget it.

This would be the only window for change until Snyder sells the team a decade later. A new owner in the 2030s or 2040s would definitely have the chance to change the name, too. Otherwise, just changing the name in a random year seems unlikely.

What would be the new name? The Warriors might work given its link to Redskins, but anyone pretending to really know the next name is flat-out lying.

My best guess is the new stadium site is the Gaylord complex by the Wilson Bridge. It's still in Maryland with the state paying a sizable chunk for infrastructure, just like it did for the Landover stadium. It's near a plausible metro station given the bridge has a lane for subway tracks. There's probably land available on the edge of the city's border. And the deal could include Gaylord as the stadium's name.

The new stadium will be much smaller—maybe 70,000 max—as high-def TV is already changing how fans watch games. By 2027, they'll probably have 4D TVs that make you part of the game and turn your living room into the field. Teams will forgo traditional venues into something only tech lords envision.

Most importantly, will the Redskins ever return to the glory of the Joe Gibbs era when they reached four and won three Super Bowls from 1982 to 1991?

The NFL is set up for balance, so the team will find a playoff season here and there. But sustained success seems elusive unless one thing happens—Snyder truly backs away. It's probably not happening anytime soon, but maybe in his later years the owner will find the wisdom needed to not interfere with the team.

So look for the 2031 NFC Championship at Gaylord Stadium as Coach Scott (son of Norv) Turner's Washington Warriors face the Dallas Cowboys for the right to reach the Super Bowl.

And history says Washington wins that game.

100 The Last Thing You'll Do

This chapter was saved for last because it really might be the last thing you do before you die.

"Sam" had been to enough Redskins-Eagles games in Philadelphia to know his Maryland license plates would gain interest in the parking lot. This time, he first stopped at a merchandise stand down the street to buy a $5 Eagles cap. It was like purchasing life insurance of sorts.

Sure enough, Sam got out of his car and three big Eagles fans walked toward him. They spotted the cap and said, "You're an Eagles fan?"

"Damn right," Sam said.

"Oh, we thought you were a Redskins fan because of the Maryland plates," one Eagles fan said.

"I know, I have to listen to those [bleeps] every day," said Sam, who safely went on his way.

Redskins fans have long learned that the most dangerous part of the more than two-hour journey to Philadelphia isn't the Delaware toll booths but the Eagles stands. Lincoln Financial Field does have a jail in the basement for fighters, after all.

Wearing Redskins gear is an invitation for a fight. And if Washington wins, Redskins fans sprint to their cars for safety.

One Redskins team doctor didn't know how deep the rivalry was when he drove to Veterans Stadium in his car with Washington, D.C. plates. He returned to find all four tires slashed.

Even Redskins running back Clinton Portis' mom was in a fight during the 2006 Philadelphia game. Rhonnel Hearn punched an Eagles fan who tossed a beer at Portis' family and friends.

"She busted some lady in the nose, but that'll just teach you about messing with her," Portis said. "I think fans take that too serious. If you decide your team is losing and you want to cause trouble, then you're going to get what you're looking for. And whoever that fan was, they got what they were looking for."

Alex Johnson of Bethesda, Maryland, just wanted to see the Redskins for the first time after a 14–1 start when he returned during college break. Several buddies managed to buy tickets from scalpers outside Veterans Stadium only to discover they were in the 500 section.

The 500 section was so notorious it inspired the team to build a jail in the stadium basement to handle the many fights. The group wasn't bothered until they took off their coats. Johnson wore a Darrell Green jersey to quickly draw attention.

"Then the guy sitting in front of us turns around and looks at us in disgust and then instructed us that A) he was not happy we were behind him and that B) if we stand up and cheer, we would face repercussions," Johnson said. "He explains, 'If you stand and cheer, people behind us will throw hot dogs and beer at you, and anything that misses you is going to hit me. When they miss you and hit me, then I'm going to turn around and hit you...so stay in your seat.'

"We complied and survived the game. We did see many other fights in the upper level and did our best to keep our head down."

It didn't hurt Johnson that the Redskins lost 24–22 to end the season 14–2. Washington soon won its third Super Bowl, while Philadelphia missed the playoffs despite finishing 10–6.

So what do you say—do you have guts like Alex Johnson? This book was all about things to know and do before you die, and wearing a Redskins jersey inside Lincoln Financial Field might be a one-way trip to the great beyond.

Just kidding. Eagles fans are tough—probably second only to Raiders fans, who are even scarier.

Eagles fans won't appreciate your Redskins jersey. They might spill beer on you or rub their knuckles across your noggin.

But die? Well, maybe that's in the next book.

Bibliography

Books:

Smith, Thomas. *Showdown: JFK and the Integration of the Washington Redskins.* Boston: Beacon Press, 2012.

Keim, John, Rick Snider and David Elfin. *Hail to RFK: 35 Seasons of Redskins Memories.* 21st Century Online Publishing, 1996.

Spagnola, Mickey, John Keim, David Elfin, and Rick Snider. *America's Rivalry: The 20 Greatest Redskins-Cowboys Games.* 21st Century Online Publishing, 1997.

Daly, Dan. *The National Forgotten League.* University of Nebraska Press, 2012.

Shrake, Bud. *Land of the Permanent Wave: An Edwin "Bud" Shrake Reader.* University of Texas Press, 2009.

Patroski, Joe. *The Dallas Cowboys: The Outrageous History of the Biggest, Loudest, Most Hated, Best Loved Football Team in America.* Back Bay Books, 2013.

Loverro, Thom. *Hail Victory: An Oral History of the Washington Redskins.* Wiley, 2007.

Wolfe, Jane. *The Murchisons—The Rise and Fall of a Texas Dynasty.* St. Martin's Press, 1989.

Nash, Bruce and Allen Zullo. *Football Hall of Shame (Book 2).* Pocket, 1990.

Benjey, Tom. *Keep A-Goin': The Life of Lone Star Dietz.* Tuxedo Press, 2006.

Shesol, Jeff. *Mutual Contempt: Lyndon Johnson, Robert Kennedy, and the Feud that Defined a Decade.* W.W. Norton & Co., 1998.

Newspapers:
Washington Post, December 9, 1940.
Reading (PA) Eagle, December 11, 1942.
Toledo Blade, August 24, 1952.
Dallas Morning News, December 12, 1958.
Herald-Journal, December 18, 1979.
Washington Post, August 21, 1988.
Syracuse Post Standard, April 23, 1994.
Washington Times, January 8, 2000.
Washington Times, September 6, 2001.
City Paper, May 7, 2004.

Websites:
americanindianathletichalloffame.com
answers.com
articles.latimes.com
bleacherreport.com
blog.redskins.com
books.google.com
cmgww.com
espn.go.com
foreshock.wordpress.com
gnfafootball.org
helmethut.com
jewsinsports.org
mmqb.si.com
NFL.com
nfluniforms.blogspot.com
nytimes.com
ProFootballHOF.com
pro-football-reference.com
redskins.clubs.nfl.com
redskins.trufan.com

sports.yahoo.com
sportsillustrated.cnn.com
tombenjey.com
washingtonpost.com
washingtontimes.com
wikipedia.org

Television:

Booknotes with Brian Lamb, C-SPAN, November 30, 1997.